THE BEST

OF

Word THE FOR TODAY

VOLUME III

BOB AND DEBBY GASS
WITH RUTH GASS HALLIDAY

Synergy Publishers
Gainesville, Florida

Index of Abbreviations

NIV	New International Version
TM	The Message
NAS	New American Standard
NCV	New Century Version
NKJV	New King James Version
KJV	King James Version
CEV	Contemporary English Version
AMP	Amplified Bible
NLT	New Living Translation
TLB	The Living Bible

Old Testament

Listed Alphabetically

Amos	AM	Judges	Jg
1 Chronicles	1 Ch	1 Kings	1 K
2 Chronicles	2 Ch	2 Kings	2 K
Daniel	Dn	Lamentations	Lm
Deuteronomy	Dt	Leviticus	Lv
Ecclesiastes	Ec	Malichi	Ml
Esther	Es	Micah	Mic
Exodus	Ex	Nahum	Nh
Ezekiel	Ez	Nehemiah	Ne
Ezra	Ezra	Numbers	Nu
Genesis	Gn	Obadiah	Ob
Habakkuk	Hb	Proverbs	Pr
Haggai	Hg	Psalms	Ps
Hosea	Ho	Ruth	Ru
Isaiah	Is	1 Samuel	1 S
Jeremiah	Jr	2 Samuel	2 S
Job	Job	Song of Songs	Sgs
Joel	Jl	Zechariah	Zec
Jonah	Jon	Zephaniah	Zep
Joshua	Js		

New Testament

Listed Alphabetically

Acts	Ac	Mark	Mk
Colossians	Col	Matthew	Mt
1 Corinthians	1 Co	1 Peter	1 P
2 Corinthians	2 Co	2 Peter	2 P
ephesians	Eph	Philemon	Phm
Galatians	Ga	Philippians	Phil
Hebrews	He	Revelation	Rev
James	Jas	Romans	Ro
John	Jn	1 Thessalonians	1 Th
1 John	1 Jn	2 Thessalonians	2 Th
2 John	2 Jn	1 Timothy	1 Ti
3 John	3 Jn	2 Timothy	2 Ti
Jude	Jd	Titus	Titus
Luke	Lk		

FACING THE NEW YEAR (1)

Launch out into the deep.

Luke 5:4

*A*fter fishing all night, without so much as a mackerel to show for it, Jesus tells His disciples to, "Launch out into the deep." Why? Because when you want what you don't have, you've got to risk doing what you haven't done yet!

A visit to The World Trade Center will help get your priorities back in order. Many who survived the attacks changed careers immediately afterwards. What a wake up call! Initially they'd taken the job for a lucrative paycheck. But when the world's tallest buildings fell, some of the world's best paid workers realized how fleeting it all can be. So they went home, wept, hugged their families, re-evaluated their lives and realized that you can have *half* as much, yet be 10 times better off in every other way. Sad, isn't it, that it takes tragedy to get us there?

Know what's even sadder? To be given chance after chance and *still* not get it. Don't wait until the bottom falls out before you count the cost of what you're really living for. The Bible says, "Make every minute count . . . find out what the Lord wants you to do" (Eph 5:16-17 CEV). Did you get that? Make sure that what *you* want, is what *God* wants for you! Once stretched by a God-given vision, you never snap back into your original shape again.

As you face this New Year, stop and take inventory; check the price tag on God's will for your life, against what you're *already* spending. Then *compare* the rewards of both. Once you see beyond where you are—you'll never look back.

FACING THE NEW YEAR (2)

Launch out into the deep.
Luke 5:4

*M*ediocrity is just the best of the worst, and the worst of the best. Is that what *you* want? No? Then be willing to forfeit the safety of being where you are, in order to go where God wants you to be. Helen Keller said, "Security is a myth. The reason we don't experience it is because it doesn't exist. Avoiding danger or failure is no safer in the long run than outright risk. Life is either a daring adventure or nothing at all." Smart lady, eh? She also said, "The only thing that's worse than being blind, is having sight but no vision."

The danger in not wanting much, is that you usually get it. So ask yourself, "What do I want this year, that's worth risking *everything* for? Like 30 minutes less sleep in the morning in order to pray, read my Bible and work on my relationship with God? To pursue my degree, or business opportunity? To work on my marriage? To break this destructive habit?"

"Launching out" means: (1) setting goals, establishing a plan to reach them, and becoming accountable; (2) staying tuned to God's "leadings;" (3) confronting old fears and discovering the incredible rewards on the other side of them; (4) looking in the mirror and respecting what you're becoming; (5) devoting your life to something greater than yourself, and being blessed in doing it; (6) having a "Thou art with me" attitude, and attempting even greater things for God. So, are you ready to "launch out" this year?

STOP STRUGGLING!

Flesh gives birth to flesh, but . . . spirit gives birth to spirit.
John 3:6 NIV

*I*f you want to see God's promise fulfilled in your life this year, don't rush things—or you might give birth to an Ishmael! Ishmael was born because Sarah tried to orchestrate events and bail God out. And the world's been living with the consequences ever since. Be sure that your plans are born of God's Spirit. Don't try to salvage anything that's flesh-based. God said, "My covenant will I establish with Isaac" (Ge 17:21), because Isaac was the result of God's will, done God's way, in God's time.

Jesus said, "Flesh gives birth to flesh, but . . . Spirit gives birth to spirit." Everything that's conceived in you comes from one of two sources: the flesh or the Spirit. Be careful; people will try to involve you in all kinds of schemes to rescue and promote yourself. God doesn't need help to bless you; He can do it all by Himself. That's why, whenever Satan attacks you need to be able to point him to your spiritual birthplace and remind him that you didn't *begin* this project, therefore, you don't have to *finish* it. What God ordains, He sustains!

If God's dealing with carnality, pride or any other obstacle in your path, don't get in His way. Like rescuing a drowning man who's frantically trying to save himself, until you stop flailing around God can't do anything for you. Give it up! Try less and trust more! The Bible says, "He who began a good work in you will carry it on to completion" (Php 1:6 NIV). So relax and stop struggling!

FOLLOW THE LEADER

*For as many as are led by the spirit of God,
they are the sons of God.*

Romans 8:14

*T*he Greek word for "led" is *"ago,"* it depicts a horse being led by a rein. It means that we should be so surrendered to God, that *wherever* He tells us to go and *whatever* He tells us to do, we obey willingly and without resistance.

But this word "ago" is also the root of the Greek word "agon," from which we get agony. Agon pictures "an intense conflict, such as a struggle of the human will." It's in our nature to want our own way! So when we choose to walk with God and let Him direct our lives, His leadership creates a struggle between our old nature and our new one.

How many times as a child did you rebel against your parents' authority because you neither understood nor agreed with them? So this verse could be translated: "Following the leadership of the Holy Spirit is one great benefit of being a child of God, although, learning to submit to Him can be an agonizing process."

If you want to live this way, God will give you the grace day by day to do it! Just pray: "Lord, this year I want to learn to follow You, not just in *some* things but in *all* things. Help me to understand Your leading and to respond to Your 'nudge' in my heart. In Jesus' name, Amen." Once you've prayed that prayer, fall in step and—follow the leader!

REAL FORGIVENESS (1)

Forgive, if ye have ought against any.
Mark 11:25

*B*efore discussing what forgiveness is, here's what it's not:

(1) Approval! Jesus forgave the woman caught in adultery, but He didn't approve of her sin. Listen: "Go, and sin no more" (Jn 8:11). *(2) Excusing!* Why do we do that? To make it easier for us to forgive! *(3) Pardoning!* This is a legal term meaning, "to release from consequences." While you can't impose your consequences on the offender, you can't shield them from God's dealings. *(4) Reconciliation!* Reconciliation requires two people to agree. What if one of them won't? *(5) Denying!* Only when we fully acknowledge and come to terms with what was done to us, can we truly forgive. *(6) Forgetting!* It's impossible to forget any significant event. We choose not to remember!

In *Total Forgiveness,* R.T. Kendall writes: "It's no spiritual victory to think we are forgiving, when we are only avoiding facing up to their wrong behavior. We are saying 'I want to forgive them, but I don't think I could if they actually did what it seems they did.' So we postpone recognizing the true offense to keep from experiencing the pain. Total forgiveness is painful. It hurts when we kiss revenge goodbye. It hurts to think the person is getting away with what they did and that nobody else will ever find out. But when we know fully what they did, and accept in our hearts that they'll be blessed without any consequences [imposed by us], we cross over into the spiritual realm. We begin to be a little more like Jesus, to change into the image of Christ."

REAL FORGIVENESS (2)

Have everyone leave my presence.
Genesis 45: 1 NIV

*T*wenty-two years after betraying him and selling him into slavery, Joseph's brothers stand before him. And now he's Prime Minister of Egypt! How would he deal with them? What would you have done? For the next few days let's observe the life of Joseph and discover 7 ways to know you're walking in real forgiveness.

You won't tell! Why did Joseph make everyone leave the room except his brothers? To make sure no one would ever know what they'd done! Joseph didn't tell—and God doesn't tell either. Listen: "Thou wilt cast all their sins into the depths of the sea" (Mic 7:19). God has enough on each of us to bury us, but He won't tell. So why do we? To punish! Listen: "Perfect love drives out fear, because fear has to do with punishment" (1Jn 4:18 NIV). What are we afraid of? That they'll get away with it. We want them punished, so we tell what was done to us. And when we do, 2 things happen: *(1) We step into God's territory!* God says, "Vengeance is mine; I will repay" (Ro 12:19). Only God knows the weakness that caused them to do it, if they've truly repented, and the degree to which they've changed. *(2) We set the standard for our own judgment!* Listen: "You will be judged in the same way that you judge others" (Mt 7:2 NCV). Can you live with that? If not, then carefully read these words: "Be kind and loving to each other, and forgive each other just as God forgave you in Christ" (Eph 4:32 NCV).

REAL FORGIVENESS (3)

They were very afraid of him.
So Joseph said to them, "Come close to me."
Genesis 45:3–4 NCV

You won't intimidate! Why? Because the Bible says, "There is no fear in love" (1Jn 4:18). Even though he holds their lives in his hands, Joseph approaches his brothers in tears of compassion. Notice, he didn't do 6 things we usually do when someone hurts us: (1) Keep them at a distance. (2) Remind them of his dream and their disbelief. (3) Enjoy watching them freeze in his presence. (4) Gloat as they twist in the wind. (5) Demand that they acknowledge his success. (6) Say "I told you so!" That's because Joseph wanted to be loved, not feared. He wanted restoration, not revenge. He understood that the long-term benefits of healing far outweigh the short-term satisfaction of revenge. Bottom line: Joseph understood that by releasing them, he was setting himself free to be blessed!

And isn't this how God deals with us? Listen: "For you did not receive a spirit . . . of fear, but you received the Spirit of son-ship. And by him we cry, 'Abba, Father'" (Ro 8:15 NIV). The word Abba simply means, "Daddy." How wonderful! God doesn't bring up our past. He doesn't keep us at arm's length because of our imperfections. No, He wants us to know that we can come to Him at any time, crawl up into His lap, feel secure in His everlasting arms and call Him "Daddy." And *that's* the kind of love and forgiveness God wants us to show to others— a love that does not want them to feel afraid in our presence!

REAL FORGIVENESS (4)

Be not angry with yourselves for selling me.
Genesis 45:5 NIV

You won't guilt-trip! Imagine their guilt as Joseph's brothers stood before him! But Joseph said: "Be not . . . angry with yourselves . . . for God did send me before you to preserve life" (Ge 45:5). Why do we guilt-trip others? Because we've forgotten the grace we ourselves received when we didn't have a leg to stand on.

Our forgiveness is worthless unless it makes it possible for others to forgive themselves. Self-forgiveness was Paul's hurdle! Listen: "I wasted the church" (Gal 1:13). After imprisoning and beheading Christians he now preaches to them. And who's in the audience? The widows! The orphans!

The ancient Persians punished murderers by strapping the victim to their back. It dragged them down, identified them with their past, the smell of it drove others away and eventually it robbed them of their very life. Was this what Paul had in mind when he said: "Who will rescue me from this body of death?" (Ro 7:24 NIV). Nothing's heavier than guilt. It will: (1) drag you down and turn living into merely existing; (2) cause you to leave a bad taste wherever you go. Even your friends will become exhausted and say, "Get over it;" (3) destroy every new relationship you've got. Who wants a person having an affair with a corpse? You'd only be using the new to numb the pain of the old; (4) shorten your life because you aren't built to carry it. Cut it loose! Cry if you need to, but when the grieving is over bury it and move on. And *that* is what real forgiveness does for others!

REAL FORGIVENESS (5)

It was not you that sent me hither, but God.

Genesis 45:8

You'll let them save face! Joseph's brothers listen in amazement as he says, "It was not you that sent me hither, but God." Is he serious? "God did it?" This takes forgiveness to a new level! Saving face—that's what God lets us do! With full knowledge of our sinful past and our present struggles, He covers us with grace. And He expects us to do the *same* for others. You can make a friend for life by allowing someone to save face.

Reading the genealogy of Jesus in Matthew, Chapter 1, you might think the sin of adultery between David and Bathsheba was part of the divine strategy all along. Of course it wasn't, and David paid a high price. Yet Matthew records these events as though they were supposed to have happened in just that way.

For the one who really forgives from the heart, there's no place for self-righteousness. We're able to forgive because: (a) we remember what we ourselves have been forgiven of; (b) we acknowledge what we're capable of; (c) we see God's hand at work in the bigger picture; (d) when we come through it we're wiser, stronger and more Christ-like. So Joseph wasn't being condescending or patronizing; nor was he thinking, "I'll be admired for being so gracious." No. During his years in prison God had operated on his heart and changed his attitude. So when he said, "You meant evil against me, but God meant it for good" (Ge 50:20 NASB), Joseph *did* mean it. And *that* is real forgiveness!

REAL FORGIVENESS (6)

Go up to my father, and say unto him,
"Thus saith thy son Joseph."

Genesis 45:9

You'll protect them from their greatest fear! Not only did Joseph forgive his brothers, he anticipated their worst nightmare—having to go back to tell their father what they had done to him 22 years before. But Joseph is a step ahead of them; he tells them what to say—and what not to say! *Joseph knew that practicing real forgiveness doesn't mean destroying others in the process!* "I think they should have been forced to confess what they'd done to their father," you say. Really? Wouldn't that have given the old man an even greater problem—struggling with regret over his lost years with Joseph, not to mention having to fight bitterness toward his other sons? Joseph was wise. And it made his brothers respect him all the more.

There's a difference between confessing and "dumping!" Hearts have been broken and lives irreparably damaged because someone sought relief by dumping the details of their guilt on somebody who couldn't handle them! Sometimes confessing is the proper route—but only after talking with an experienced counselor or spiritual adviser. Note: after David had sinned with Bathsheba he wrote: "Against you [God], you only, have I sinned and done what is evil in your sight" (Ps 51:4 NIV). When you consider that God knows all about your sin yet promises to keep it a closely guarded secret, it should: (a) increase your gratitude exponentially; (b) cause you to keep your mouth shut; (c) make you refuse to hold anybody else's sins or shortcomings over their head.

REAL FORGIVENESS (7)

And he reassured them.

Genesis 50:21 NIV

You must make it a life-long commitment. Seventeen years after reuniting with his long-lost son Joseph, Jacob dies, and Joseph's brothers suddenly panic! Listen: "When Joseph's brothers saw that their father was dead they said, 'What if Joseph holds a grudge against us and pays us back for all the wrongs we did to him?'" (Ge 50:15 NIV). So they concocted a story and sent word to Joseph saying: "Your father left these instructions before he died . . . forgive your brothers the sins and wrongs they committed in treating you badly" (Ge 50:16-17 NIV). Now if their father had really said this he wouldn't have told Joseph's brothers, he'd have told Joseph himself before he died. He wouldn't have gone to his grave with the fear that Joseph would exact revenge. When Joseph heard that his brothers doubted his forgiveness, he wept and told them: "Don't be afraid. I will provide for you and your children. And he reassured them and spoke kindly to them" (Ge 50:19-21 NIV). Notice the words " he reassured them."

Real forgiveness is a life-long commitment! You must practice it every day until you die. No one ever said it would be easy. If Jesus had waited until His enemies repented, He'd never have prayed, "Father, forgive them, for they know not what they do" (Lk 23:34 NKJV). Sure it's easier to forgive when others acknowledge their offense, but if *that's* the prerequisite you may *never* experience victory! And what you don't forgive, you relive! So for your own sake, forgive, take back your life and begin walking in the blessings of the Lord!

REAL FORGIVENESS (8)

Bless those who curse you, pray for those who mistreat you.
Luke 6:28 NIV

You must pray for them to be blessed! Are you serious? Absolutely! Real forgiveness is difficult because: (a) it goes against our strongest impulses; (b) nobody else will ever know that we forgave the offense; (c) our hearts could break as God blesses the offender in answer to our prayers, and as if they'd never sinned against us.

Praying like this, to quote John Calvin: "Is exceedingly difficult." Chrysostom called it "the highest summit of self-control." Job's suffering didn't end until he prayed for those "friends" who had become his thorn in the flesh (See Job 42:10). When we're able to pray this way we're becoming more like our Heavenly Father. Listen: "Love your enemies, bless them that curse you, do good to them that hate you, and pray for them which despitefully use you, and persecute you; that you may be the children of your Father which is in heaven" (Mt 5:44-45).

If you're saying: "How can anybody live that way?" look at the life—and death—of Stephen. While his enemies were stoning him he prayed, "Lord, do not hold this sin against them" (Acts 7:60 NIV). Therein lay one of the secrets of his great effectiveness. So if you're asking, "How can I know I'm walking in *real forgiveness?*" The answer is: (1) you won't tell; (2) you won't intimidate; (3) you won't guilt-trip; (4) you'll let them save face; (5) you'll protect them from their greatest fear; (6) you'll do it for life; (7) you'll pray for them to be blessed.

WHEN IT COMES TO MONEY

Out of Your own [hand] we have given You.
1 Chronicles 29:14 AMP

*W*hen it comes to money, always keep 3 things in mind:

(1) God owns everything! Your name may be on the account, but don't get any mistaken ideas. Listen: "All things come from You, and out of Your own [hand] we have given You" (1Ch 29:14 AMP). So when God tells you to give a certain amount or to a particular cause, don't say: "I'll think about it," for beyond every act of obedience there's a blessing waiting. God said, "Oh, that their hearts would be inclined to . . . keep all my commands always, so that it might go well with them" (Dt 5:29 NIV). Want things to go well for you? Then do what God says!

(2) God is your source! Remember, every good thing you have came from Him! It's okay to enjoy your money, just don't trust in it. Paul says, "Trust [only] in God who giveth us richly all things to enjoy" (1Ti 6:17).

(3) Every spending decision is a spiritual decision! Your checkbook reflects your values and priorities. So, what does yours say? When it came to giving, the Macedonian Christians were a class act. Listen: "They gave not only what they could afford, but far more . . . their first action was to dedicate themselves to the Lord and . . . whatever direction God might give them through us" (2Co 8:3-5 TLB). When God has access to your heart He'll have access to your finances. True financial freedom comes when giving no longer threatens your security, because you *know* that God's the supplier of your every need!

WORRIED ABOUT YOUR KIDS?

All your children will be taught by the Lord,
and they will have much peace.
Isaiah 54:13 NCV

*E*ighty-five percent of all children raised by praying parents develop a strong personal faith—before age 13. *"But my kids are already grown."* God's name is "Redeemer"—He can give you another chance. Repent and commit your life to Christ; that's how generational cycles of failure are broken. *"But I'm concerned about bringing a child into this evil world!"* It's children of light who push back the darkness. God's promise to you is, "My Spirit and my words that I give you will never leave you or your children or your grandchildren, now and forever" (Is 59:21 NCV). *"But how can I compete with the negative influences around me?"* Every study confirms that a parent has by far the greatest influence—greater than friends, school or media—in determining the character and direction of a child.

Think of it as a relay race! Success isn't based on how well you run as an individual, but on how well you pass the baton. Only when the story of future generations is told will you know whether you won or lost. David says, "You have taught me from my youth . . . now also when I am old . . . do not forsake me, until I declare Your strength to this generation, Your power to everyone who is to come" (Ps 71:17-18 NKJV). Don't drop the baton! Make it your goal to raise children who'll pick up your legacy of faith and take it further than you did. When you commit to doing that, God will work with you!

BETROTHED (1)

For I promised you as a pure bride to one husband, Christ.
2 Corinthians 11:2 NLT

*A*s believers we're betrothed to Jesus, and Him alone. In Biblical times betrothal wasn't just an engagement, it was part of the marriage ritual. From the moment of betrothal the two were considered one. However, the marriage wasn't consummated for a year or more. During that period the groom would build a home for the couple, continue courting his bride, getting to know her, allowing her to know him as much as possible. And the bride would prepare herself, learning all she could about him so that she could please him in all respects. Finally when the groom brought his bride to their new home and they began to live as husband and wife, all controversies were laid to rest.

As the bride of Christ we should each long for the time when our union with Him will be consummated and we'll partake of the Marriage Supper of the Lamb. Until then, Jesus is fulfilling His part of the betrothal: preparing a place for us; praying and interceding for us; continuing to woo us, to lavish His love upon us and to bring us into "the knowledge of Him." And what's our part? Remember the parable of the 10 Virgins? We're to keep our lamps lit with the fire of the Holy Spirit, renew our minds with God's Word, pray without ceasing, rejoice at all times, and love one another as He loves us. Most of all, we're to be continuously aware that we are His bride, a reflection of His name, nature and glory in the earth.

BETROTHED (2)

For I promised you as a pure bride to one husband, Christ.
2 Corinthians 11:2 NLT

*W*hy is it so critical that we faithfully follow and imitate Jesus? Because everything we do *reflects* on Him. We're His betrothed! He gets the credit each time we restrain ourselves from saying and doing things we shouldn't say and do. He receives honor when we humble ourselves and reckon our flesh dead. We present a particularly compelling witness of His goodness when we love our enemies and those who hate us, persecute us or reject us. Unfortunately He also gets a bad name when we act like the world and walk according to the tendencies of our lower nature.

A single person only has his or her own reputation to worry about—what they say and do reflects only on themselves. But a married person's conversation, conduct and words, reflect on their spouse. No man wants his wife running around town writing bad checks, engaging in lewd conversation, getting drunk and obnoxious in public, or flirting with other men. He wants her to refrain from those behaviors because he loves her and wants her reputation to be good. He also wants his wife to be a godly reflection on him and their family.

We are eternally blessed with a Bridegroom that's perfect. His reputation is stellar in all respects, His character unblemished, His strength and courage unmatched, His love for us beyond imagination. So, our betrothal to Him demands that we no longer live for ourselves—but for Him! Why? Because how we live each day, reflects on Him!

A GOOD DOSE OF SELF-WORTH!

Absolutely nothing can get between us and God's love.
Romans 8:39 TM

*F*eel like you don't measure up? Listen: "With God on our side like this, how can we lose? If God didn't hesitate to put everything on the line for us . . . is there anything else He wouldn't gladly . . . do for us? And who would dare tangle with God by messing with one of God's chosen? Who would dare even to point a finger? The one who died for us—who was raised to life for us—is in the presence of God at this very moment sticking up for us. Do you think anyone is going to be able to drive a wedge between us and Christ's love for us? There is no way! Not trouble, not hard times, not hatred, not hunger. Not homelessness, not bullying threats, not back-stabbing, not even the worst sins listed in Scripture . . . none of this fazes us because Jesus loves us. I'm absolutely convinced that nothing—nothing living or dead, angelic or demonic, today or tomorrow, high or low, thinkable or unthinkable— absolutely nothing can get between us and God's love" (Ro 8:31-39 TM).

Imagine being loved like that—by God! No matter how unworthy you feel, you cannot shut off or in any way diminish the flow of His love toward you. Nothing can change the way He feels about you. Nothing can alter the fact that He's going to continue to love you no matter what you do or say. *Never lose sight of that because God's love will heal your emotions, raise your self-esteem and put a foundation of self-worth and dignity under you.*

HELLO, PEOPLE PLEASER!

Our only goal is to please God.
2 Corinthians 5:9 NCV

*B*efore an airliner takes off the attendant tells you that if the plane gets into trouble, secure your own oxygen mask before attempting to help others with theirs. That's wise! Unless *you* get enough oxygen, how can you help anybody else?

Are your spiritual and emotional needs being met? If not, it's time you stopped taking care of others and started taking care of yourself before you burn out. You can't travel quietly through life hoping others will see when your plate's full. Speak up, or they'll just keep pouring on more problems and responsibilities! Personal empowerment begins by taking control of your life. Overloaded people fail; they always have and they always will. They fail at marriage, ministry and management. They fail at parenting, partnership and professional endeavors.

You're like an airplane; if you carry too much baggage you won't get off the ground. Motivated by the need to please or impress, you'll take on too much and in the end fail to reach the heights God planned for you, or crash because you ignored your limitations.

Every situation that arises does *not* warrant your attention! Jesus left the crowd to be alone with the Father. Did He evoke criticism from the crowd? Yes! Did He enjoy communion with the Father? Yes! And you'll have to make that same choice too! People who don't recognize your needs and respect your goals will drain you, divert you and keep you grounded. What's the answer? Give what you can, learn when to say "enough," then let go and fly!

PASTOR, REORDER YOUR PRIORITIES (1)

A . . . priest . . . likewise, a Levite . . .
passed by on the other side.

Luke 10:31–32 NKJV

*W*hen a mugging victim was left for dead on the Jericho Road, a priest and a Levite both "passed by on the other side." But what if they overlooked the man not because they lacked compassion, but because they were late for a Bible study or a prayer meeting? Would they have been justified?

One pastor said, "This parable didn't register until I'd been in ministry for years. I'd walked past so many people who could've used my help, but because I was too distracted by church programs, broken lives by the roadside rarely fit into my agenda. Love isn't *efficient;* it can't be *scheduled.* This hurting man couldn't have waited 3 weeks for an appointment, or for the Samaritan to launch a ministry to care for similar victims." Life's most rewarding experiences rarely come in neat little packages. They're found in unexpected encounters, and at critical times in the lives of your congregation. In fact, chances are some people who can't remember your last sermon, can tell you *in detail* what you said to them in the hospital or over coffee last year—it touched them personally. Nothing's more seductive than thinking your work on behalf of the multitudes justifies ignoring those who can only be reached individually. Jesus said, "If a shepherd has one hundred sheep, and one . . . is lost . . . won't he go . . . search for the lost one?" (Mt 18:12 NLT). When Peter said, "Lord . . . I love you!" Jesus replied, "Then take care of my sheep" (Jn 21:16 NIV)? Pastor, He's saying the same thing to you!

___

PASTOR, REORDER YOUR PRIORITIES (2)

The good shepherd puts the sheep before himself.
John 10:11 TM

*O*ne pastor says, "I'll never forget my guidance counselor's face when she heard I was going into the ministry. 'But you don't even like people!' she exclaimed. I remember thinking, 'So what? Ministry's about preaching and leading a congregation to greater heights. I don't have to worry about individuals.' But that's a myth. We dare not become so program-focused that we flee from the next person God sends our way. I'm amazed how far bureaucracies will go to make *systemic* change rather than making an exception that would easily fix the problem. Personal needs are too significant to commit to the rigidity of any program. Some of us think the problem with handling needs personally is, they can multiply like rabbits. Plus, programs exist to *prevent you* from becoming overwhelmed, right? Wrong! The 'ministry myth' that says, 'What you do for one you must do for all,' is a recipe for burnout!" Jesus' life was spent helping individuals. He said, "The good shepherd puts the sheep before himself." But in order to do that you must: (a) make room in your life for the unexpected; (b) learn to say no graciously.

Too many pastors hide behind busy schedules (and secretaries) just to avoid saying no. Jesus knew when to get involved and when not to. You'll never be able to respond effectively, if you feel obligated to meet every need all the time. And God's not asking you to. He only expects you to respond to what *He* sends your way—and encourage others to do the same.

___

PASTOR, REORDER YOUR PRIORITIES (3)

Jesus said, "Let's get away . . . for a while and rest."
Mark 6:31 NLT

*W*ayne Muller said, "Because we don't rest, we lose our way. Poisoned by the belief that good things come only through unceasing determination and tireless effort . . . for want of rest our lives are in danger." There are two kinds of "tired." The dissimilarity is like the difference between puffy spring rain clouds and those that precede a tornado. One's temporary and normal. It comes from a job well done and after a period of rest you bounce back. The other's a chronic inner fatigue that accumulates over months and doesn't always manifest itself in physical exhaustion. In fact, it's masked by frenetic activity and compulsive behavior: (a) You can't relax over a meal or coffee. (b) You keep checking and rechecking your messages and emails. (c) Your nightstand's piled high with periodicals designed to keep you "ahead of the game." (d) Taking a day off seems impossible. (e) You don't take breaks or vacations and work every holiday. (f) You can't sleep. (g) Any free time you have is spent in "escapist behavior" like eating, drinking, spending or watching TV.

But while you're busy working hard and looking important you can lose your ability to hear the voice of the One who called you to the position initially. Sure God expects you to work hard, but not by endangering your health, your family or your time with Him. If that's where you're at today Jesus is saying, "Let's get away . . . for a while and rest." So stop what you're doing, take a break and spend some time with Him.

PASTOR, REORDER YOUR PRIORITIES (4)

In returning and rest shall ye be saved.
Isaiah 30:15

*W*hen you're emotionally and spiritually drained, out of control, tossed and turned by other people's expectations, it's easy to become numb to the full range of human emotions. And while it can seem like a relief to be free from negative emotions, the *positive* ones also become elusive because you don't feel much of anything—good or bad. When that happens you're very likely to end up being directed by impulses such as: (1) over-scheduling; (2) poor time management; (3) performance anxiety; (4) having few boundaries; (5) tolerating toxic relationships; (6) unresolved grief or pain; (7) wrong goals.

So what's the answer? God said, "In returning and rest shall ye be saved." In other words, for fast acting relief—slow down! Instead of pushing on and struggling to keep going, stop and talk to God about what's happening. Rather than feeling isolated and weighed down by the impossibility of your situation, invite Him into the equation by praying: "Lord, help me keep my mind stayed on You. During this time of busyness and stress help me to reorder my priorities according to *Your* will, to think *Your* thoughts and to let the mind of Christ have its rightful authority in my life. Your Word says You've ordained peace for me. Because You're my Fortress and my Deliverer I will not allow myself to be troubled or afraid. Thank You for keeping my heart and mind at rest through Christ Jesus."

DOING YOUR BEST!

To win . . . you must deny yourselves . . . things that . . .
keep you from doing your best.
1 Corinthians 9:25 TLB

*A*n agency once created an ad for a Rolls Royce that said: "At 60 m.p.h. the loudest noise in the new Rolls Royce is the electric clock." When they ran the ad by a company executive he smiled and said, "I guess we've got to do something about that clock!" Never stop trying to do it better!

The moment you start believing you're successful enough or smart enough to rest on your laurels you're in trouble. You've set a ceiling on your potential! The Bible says: "Do you know a hardworking man? He shall be successful and stand before kings [get the boss's attention]" (Pr 22:29 TLB). Success belongs to the one who'll show up early, stay late, go the extra mile and keep asking, "Is there a better way?"

A young man once asked Henry Ford, "How can I make a name for myself and be successful?" Ford replied, "Decide what you want then stick with it. Never deviate from your course no matter how long it takes or how rough the road, until you've accomplished your purpose." Everybody wants what successful people have, they just don't want to do what successful people do to get it! Successful people don't quit! No matter how many times they fall, they get back up and start over. Paul J. Meyer says, "Ninety-nine percent of those who fail are not actually defeated. They simply quit." So, refuse to quit. Oh, and one more thing: "Commit your work to the Lord and then your plans will succeed" (Pr 16:3 NLT).

THE IMPACT OF OVERCOMING FAITH!

Paul and Silas . . . were praying and singing . . .
and the other prisoners heard them.
Acts 16:25 NIV

*B*eing locked up in a Roman prison was no cakewalk. Offenders were stripped, flogged and placed in leg irons. Their blood-soaked clothing wasn't even changed in the dead of winter! And the "inner cells" (v.24) where Paul and Silas were imprisoned were the worst. Lack of water, cramped conditions, and the stench of toilets (if that's what you could call them), made sleep impossible and waking miserable. Prisoners there routinely begged for death while some even committed suicide.

But after Paul and Silas were "beaten, and . . . thrown into prison . . . [they] were praying and singing . . . and the other prisoners were listening." *The Message* says, "The other prisoners couldn't believe their ears." Talk about impact! Paul's attitude impressed them before his religious beliefs did. Anybody can sing in church, including hypocrites. But praise in prison—now that's something else! How did they do it? Perspective! It's not what you've *lost* but what you've *left* that counts! Paul didn't just sing in prison, he wrote some of his best stuff. Listen: "Everything happening to me in this jail only serves to make Christ more accurately known, regardless of whether I live or die. They didn't shut me up; they gave me a pulpit! Alive, I'm Christ's messenger, dead I'm his bounty. Life versus even more life! I can't lose" (Php 1:20-21 TM). Wow! What are you going to do with a man like this? He's beyond your threats! His strength comes from within and is not diminished by things without. *Overcoming faith—it'll impact them every time!*

STAY CONNECTED TO YOUR SOURCE!

Anyone who wants . . . come and drink of the water of life.
Revelation 22:17 NLT

*H*ow long can you hold out? That's what the Babylonians were asking as they encircled Jerusalem. Nebuchadnezzar had cut off their food and other essential supplies. So how long *could* they survive? A month passed, then two, then an entire year, still they held out.

The secret of the city's survival lay in a hidden water supply which came from a spring outside the city walls. King Hezekiah had cut a 1,777-foot tunnel through solid rock. From there, water passed under the city walls to a reservoir inside called the Pool of Siloam. Without it God's people would've gone down in defeat.

There's a lesson here for you. To live victoriously you must: (a) be able to identify your life's true source; (b) draw daily from it; (c) protect it. If your security, your strength, your self-worth or your strategy for living comes from any source other than God, you're vulnerable! *Everything* you need comes from God, so protect that relationship, nurture it for it'll always be the focal point of Satan's attack. A day without God's Word isn't a slip, it's set up for failure! Prayerless-ness isn't carelessness, it's craziness or arrogance! "Well, I'm doing okay and I don't pray much." Maybe you haven't reached your hour of testing yet. When it comes, and it will, what will you draw on? Answer this: if you can do it *without* God, is it even *of* God? If it's not, it'll go up in smoke (See 1Co 3:13). So, stay connected to your source!

THE "ANGER TEST"

Don't sin by letting anger . . . control . . . you.
Ephesians 4:26 NLT

*U*ncontrolled anger is like jumping into a Ferrari, gunning the engine, then discovering the brakes don't work. The Bible says, "Don't sin by letting anger . . . control . . . you . . . [it] gives a . . . foothold to the Devil." Did you get that? Uncontrolled anger opens the door to Satan. Then it's all down hill from there! So before you say something you'll regret or can't take back, ask yourself:

(1) Is my anger appropriate? Some anger is. You can't love roses and not hate weeds. But it's easy to let small stuff like thoughtless comments and cranky kids make you overreact. For anger to have a healthy result it needs to be measured and constructive. This is a control issue! Listen: "The mind controlled by the Spirit is life and peace" (Ro 8:6 NIV). A controlled response and a gracious response is a Christ-like response. It always wins!

(2) Is it really worth dragging other people into? Anger invariably affects those around you because it's only human to take sides, even if you've "no dog in the fight." Dragging others in is usually a way to feed our own ego and justify our bad behavior.

(3) Is the relief I'll get from venting, worth the aftermath? The Bible says, "A gentle answer turns away wrath . . . harsh words stir up . . . anger" (Pr 15:1 NLT). By sounding off, you usually end up making the finest speech you'll ever regret! By its very nature anger encourages exaggeration. It makes you say things you can't take back. Long after you've moved on, its words maintain their power to wound and divide.

KEEPING THE FAITH

I have kept the faith.

2 Timothy 4:7 NASB

*J*esus said, "In this world you will have trouble" (Jn 16:33 NCV). And sure enough life keeps handing us fresh challenges that test our faith. How do you know how much weight a bridge will handle? Put some weight on it!

Daniel was the victim of a major sting operation. Knowing he prayed regularly, his enemies persuaded King Darius that all prayers should be made to him. What ego! Nevertheless Daniel kept praying each day—in front of an open window, no less! When the king heard, he threw Daniel into a lions' den. But next morning Daniel came out, his enemies went in, and the king announced, "Daniel's God is the living God" (Da 6:26).

Shadrach, Meshach and Abednego refused to worship the king's idols. Even when warned to bow or burn they said, "Our God . . . is able to deliver us . . . but if not . . . we will not serve thy gods" (Da 3:17-18). And because they "kept the faith" God delivered them—and promoted them!

David faced down Goliath and refused to wear the king's armor. Why? Listen: "I cannot go with these; for I have not proved them" (1Sa 17:39). So what did he go with? Listen: "I come to thee in the name of the Lord" (1Sa 17:45) and the rest is history! Now, chances are you'll never find yourself in a lions' den, a fiery furnace, or facing a giant—although some days it'll feel like it! But when you're under attack: (a) pray and claim God's power; (b) keep the faith; (c) go "in the name of the Lord."

DATING

Seek His will . . . and He will direct your paths.
Proverbs 3:6 NLT

*T*here's nothing like a few "dud dates" to make you more selective. Now, while being selective limits your options, it does improve the quality of your relationships. Unfortunately there's no definitive test to predict how a date will ultimately work out, but here are 5 questions you should ask:

(1) What's my first impression? For example, who does your date hang out with? What kind of parties do they enjoy? Do they drink? Smoke? Swear? Do drugs? This kind of information can save you untold heartache. And, not to judge a book by its cover, until you really get to know somebody, what else can you go by? *(2) How well do I know them?* Isn't it wiser to date somebody you've known for a while, instead of a stranger? *(3) Are they courteous/respectful of others?* Nothing's worse than a man who brags about his previous conquests or a woman who constantly criticizes her ex? Would you trust them with your reputation—or your heart? *(4) Are our values in sync?* Opposites may attract, but that's not a good rule when it comes to values. You need to know that your date's a committed Christian who lives by their convictions. What kind of standards do they have about things like money, morals and movies? *(5) Do they keep their promises?* In previous relationships did they flirt, cheat or remain loyal? A promise-breaker usually becomes a heartbreaker! God says, When you "seek His will . . . He will direct your paths," so pray about these 5 things before you date.

THE BLESSING OF TITHING!

Bring all the tithes into the storehouse . . . Try it!
Malachi 3:10 NLT

A pastor received the following letter from a couple in his church: "We were behind with our rent and car payments. We had $40,000 in debt, no food in the fridge and we'd just started a construction business. So when you challenged us to tithe as part of our Christian commitment we thought, 'How can we give what we don't have?' Nevertheless we decided to go ahead and honor God by giving Him the first tenth of our income.

"The very first week we met a contractor who asked us to build a house, with more to follow. Now we no longer questioned how we'd fulfill our commitment to God; in fact, we increased our giving! And if the story ended there it would still be a good one. But you can't out-give God! Through a series of divinely orchestrated events we went from being renters to homeowners. Today we're enjoying financial blessing. And even though this story's all about trusting God, on reflection we're still trying to answer one question: *"What exactly was it we sacrificed?"*

Beware of developing "a sense of entitlement" where you think your money is something you earned all by yourself. Anytime you struggle to give God what's rightfully His, it's because you've become more attached to the gift than the Giver. God said, "Bring all the tithes into the storehouse . . . I will open the windows of heaven [and] pour out a blessing . . . you won't have . . . room to take it in. Try it! Let me prove it to you." Ready to take Him up on that challenge today?

PASSING THE TORCH

Make disciples of all . . . nations . . . teaching them
to observe all . . . I commanded you.
Matthew 28:19–20 NASB

*P*ick up any newspaper and you'll realize that big corporations rise and fall on one thing—leadership. But leadership is also crucial in other areas of life like marriage, ministry, education and career. Each of these areas requires *strategy, discipline,* and *initiative.* Those who don't demonstrate these qualities usually end up helping others fulfill *their* dreams.

If Jesus' only goal on earth was to die for sin, why didn't He go directly from His baptism in the Jordan to the cross? Because for the next 3-1/2 years His intention was to plant the seeds of leadership in the lives of those who'd ultimately carry His message to the world. Because of the principles Jesus taught, His disciples were fruitful long after He'd departed. The Gospels are His training manuals; intense preparation for those who spent every day talking, sleeping, eating and traveling with Him, so they didn't miss an opportunity to learn about their mission and the methods needed to fulfill it.

Jesus said, "Make disciples of all . . . nations . . . teaching them to observe all . . . I commanded you." And do you know what? He wants *you* to use the gifts He's given you! Not just to shake up your kids' and grandkids' generations—but your *own!* Your best contribution to future generations is the inspiration of watching you slay *your* giants and move *your* mountains. That way when it's *their* turn they can pray with confidence, "God, you've done impossible things in the past and You can still do them today." What a legacy! Don't mess it up.

GOD'S "A & B TEAMS"

The Spirit . . . decides which gifts to give . . . each of us.
1 Corinthians 12:11 CEV

*T*here's a commonly held misconception that the church is supposed to be a democracy. But that's not how God sees it. No question, every person deserves equal treatment in terms of kindness, love and respect. But we don't all have the same abilities or assignments because God "is the one who gave these gifts to the church" (Eph 4:11 NLT). The Bible says, "He verified the message by . . . giving gifts . . . whenever *he* chose to" (He 2:4 NLT).

You love your kids, but they don't all have the same talents and abilities, right? Plus, they don't all look good in the same clothes or the same hairstyle. Likewise, God doesn't show us all the same thing or give us all the same gifts. His Word says, "The Spirit . . . decides which gifts to give to each of us." And God never makes mistakes!

Even among his own disciples Jesus had "A" and "B" teams; and He used both. One team He took with Him up the Mount of Transfiguration, the other He sent into the city to work. When Peter, James and John went up the mountain with Jesus they may have experienced things the others couldn't have handled. But that's what they needed to fulfill the assignment God was calling them to.

Notice something important: Jesus didn't try to take *everybody* up the mountain so that nobody would feel slighted. As a leader you've got to move beyond other people's opinions. When you know something's right, you have to do it and let the chips fall where they may.

RECOGNIZED BY GOD

Man looks on the outward appearance,
but the Lord looks at the heart.

1 Samuel 16:7 NIV

*O*thers may not recognize your potential or think you're important, but God does. Remember David? When others saw a shepherd boy, God saw a king! But before David could become king he had to overcome 2 obstacles. *(1) His own family's failure to recognize him!* When Samuel came looking for a king amongst Jessie's sons, David was excluded! Why? Because he was the youngest? Because his other brothers seemed more qualified? Because his father decided to put his best foot forward? *(2) Samuel the prophet's failure to recognize him!* When Samuel saw the oldest brother, Eliab, a general in King Saul's army, he thought: "Surely the Lord's anointed stands here" (1Sa 16:6 NIV). But God set Samuel straight: "Man looks at the outward appearance, but the Lord looks at the heart."

David's dilemma's a common one: many of us don't believe in ourselves because we weren't recognized or encouraged by our parents. You may be a great musician, but because nobody cared enough to give you music lessons when you were a child, you've given up on yourself. Or you've a real entrepreneurial gift, but you've always been put down for your "foolish ideas" about how to do business. Maybe you've compromised your character and given up the dreams of your youth. If so, it's time to: (a) reclaim who you are; (b) pray that God will open your eyes and put someone in your life who'll confirm what God's placed within you.

DON'T GRIEVE THE HOLY SPIRIT

And grieve not the Holy Spirit.
Ephesians 4:30

 $\mathcal{T}$ he word "grieve" comes from the Greek word *lupete.* It denotes pain experienced between 2 people who are deeply in love. It pictures a husband or a wife who's just discovered that their mate has been unfaithful to them.

Your relationship with the Holy Spirit is so important! If you don't believe it, try living a day without Him. Just as someone in love constantly thinks about and longs to be with the one they love, so the Holy Spirit comforts us, protects us, guides us, strengthens us, desires to be close to us and wants to reveal Himself to us. But when we act like the world, talk like the world and respond like the world, we cause the Holy Spirit to experience the pain of betrayal.

We need to realize how precious the Holy Spirit is in our lives and honor Him by making sure we walk in integrity and live lives of commitment. If our behavior's been wrong we should confess our sin and receive cleansing through the blood of Jesus so that we can be restored to fellowship. So, before you rush out into another hectic day, stop and pray, "Holy Spirit, is there *anything* in my life which causes you grief? If there is, reveal it to me so that I can deal with it. Forgive me for allowing my attitudes and actions to dishonor You. Starting today, I want to live every moment with the intent to please You and never cause You grief again. In Jesus' name—Amen."

TRAPPED BY OUR FEAR

I was afraid and . . . hid your talent.
Matthew 25:25 NKJV

$\mathcal{J}$esus told the story of 3 men who received talents. Two invested theirs wisely and doubled them; the third was afraid to take a risk so he buried his. When the master came looking for a return on his investment this timid soul said, "I was afraid, and . . . hid your talent in the ground." His master wasn't pleased. Listen: "You wicked and lazy servant . . . you ought to have deposited my money . . . and I would have received back . . . with interest . . . take the talent from him, and give it to him that has ten talents. For to everyone who has, more will be given, and he will have abundance; but from him who does not have, even what he has will be taken away" (Mt 25:25-29 NKJV).

God expects a return on His investment in you! Part of fulfilling your calling means taking appropriate risks to maximize the opportunities you've been entrusted with. Playing at faith is *not* commendable, avoiding risk is *not* to be rewarded, living out of the fear of what others will think should *not* be what motivates us.

Why does Jesus come down so hard on this issue? Because *our* loss isn't the only one suffered. Our loved ones also lose out when we don't pursue our dreams. There's a domino effect; others get cheated out of the greatness lying dormant within us.

But it's not too late. Like Lazarus being called out of the grave, Jesus calls each of us today to step over our fear, take risks in obedience to faith, and experience the fullness of who God made us to be.

"NIGHT FAITH" (1)

God said, "Let there be light" . . . and it was so.
Genesis 1:14–15 NIV

*A*nytime God blesses you, get ready for the complainers who think He should have blessed them instead (or at least as much)! When a dispute arose about which tribe should lead the Israelites, God told Moses to have each tribal leader write his name on his walking stick and place it overnight in the tabernacle. Then God said, "The man I have chosen . . . buds will grow on his rod! Then this complaining will stop" (Num 17:5 TLB). Imagine, an old stick with no roots or sap, blossoming in the dark! Understand this: faith can't grow without hardship. It must incubate in the darkness of adversity.

There's a stage at which you don't even know you've been chosen; only *God* knows. He told Jeremiah "Before I shaped you in the womb, I knew all about you" (Jer 1:5 TM). Before you were a bleep on a monitor, God had plans for you. You didn't die on the operating table or in that car accident because His hand was on you. And He didn't choose you because you're such a wonderful person! No, He chooses, "What the world thinks is unimportant . . . so . . . no one can brag" (1 Co 1:28-29 NCV).

When God created the heavens and earth the Bible says, "Darkness covered the face of the deep" (Ge 1:2 NRS). But as soon as God said, "Let there be light" . . . it was so. And today God can *still* bring light out of your darkness and hope out of your despair. He's not intimidated by the darkness—it's where He does some of His best work!

"NIGHT FAITH" (2)

God called . . . the evening and the morning . . . day.

Genesis 1:19

*N*otice: during the creation process God counts days based on the previous nights. He doesn't say, "The morning and the evening were the first day." No, the Bible says, "God called . . . the evening and the morning . . . day." *God specializes in bringing light out of darkness; you just have to get through one to get to the other!* In the Old Testament God told Moses that the Angel of Death would strike during the night. But wherever God saw "the blood upon the lintel" (Ex 12:23), that household was saved. The Bible says in Exodus that God, "Sent a . . . wind that blew all night until there was dry land . . . and the Israelites walked through" (Ex 14:21-22 CEV). How wonderful, God worked in the darkness!

David said, "Weeping may endure for a night, but joy comes in the morning" (Ps 30:5). The dawn is always more brilliant because of the preceding darkness, just as your progress is all the more remarkable when painted against a backdrop of pain, challenge and breakthrough. Great mornings come from rough nights! Look at somebody who's having a great day and chances are, you're seeing somebody who's been through a dark night. Whenever they finally shout the victory it's because they've spent the night weeping before God.

Paul says, "Let us hold fast . . . hope without wavering . . . He who promised is faithful" (Heb 10:23 NKJV). Trusting God is more than just wishful thinking; it's knowing that if He said it—He'll do it; that He doesn't just control creation, He also controls your circumstances—so "hold fast!"

"NIGHT FAITH" (3)

You turn darkness to light.

2 Samuel 22:29 CEV

*S*ince the world is continually revolving, it means whenever the sun's shining in one hemisphere it's dark in another. While one person's experiencing midnight, another's rejoicing because daybreak has finally arrived. Same time— just different locations. So when you're having a nighttime experience, if you can just hold on a little longer things will change. That's a guarantee! The same way you rotated into the darkness you'll rotate out of it again. God, the night watchman, will "turn your darkness into light" if only you'll keep trusting Him.

In Genesis, while Adam was sleeping God reached in, performed surgery and made Eve. At midnight, while the other prisoners slept Paul and Silas prayed and sang praises to God in their jail cell and He delivered them. When Peter was locked in the inner prison, at midnight God sent an angel to liberate him. When Jesus was crucified the earth was plunged into darkness. But on Easter morning the light came on—forever!

Paul says, "We walk by faith, not by sight," (2Cor 5:7). *You've got to expect some nighttime experiences. The "dark room" is where He develops you into the image of Christ. Enduring just gives you the credentials to walk out into the daylight—having earned the right to be there!*

Night faith is tenacious, radical and relentless. When it's backed into a corner it stands its ground and declares, "I've lost my job, my mortgage is overdue, my symptoms don't look good, but I believe God." *That's* the kind of faith that gets results!

5 KEYS TO GOOD RELATIONSHIPS

Don't think only about your own affairs . . .
be interested in others.

Philippians 2:4 NLT

*I*t's too easy to "think only about your own affairs." But God says, "Be interested in others." Here are 5 ways to do that:

(1) Give them a push! Barnabas became known as a great encourager because he "encouraged the believers" (Acts 11:23 NLT). Ever notice what happens when you push kids on a swing? Eventually they start pumping and doing it themselves; they just need a little help to get going. Even a smile can work wonders. Job said, "When they were discouraged, I smiled... My look of approval was precious to them" (Job 29:24 NLT).

(2) Honor your word! The Bible says, "In the last days . . . men shall be . . . truce-breakers" (2Ti 3:1-3). But you don't have to fulfill that prophecy! If you say you'll do it, do it! Character is measured by action not words, so be someone whose word has meaning.

(3) Hold your tongue! Always say less than you think. Remember, "A fool uttereth all his mind . . . a wise man keepeth it in" (Pr 29:11). And since how you speak is as important as what you say, always be kind and courteous.

(4) Be cheerful! Solomon said, "A cheerful heart brings a smile . . . a sad heart makes it hard to get through the day" (Pr 15:13 TM). Don't dump your problems and disappointments on others, take them to God in prayer.

(5) Show genuine interest! The Bible says, "Laugh . . . when they're happy; share tears when they're down" (Ro 12:15-16 TM). But you can only do that by taking the time to find out what's going on in their world.

TOUGH LOVE

Discipline isn't much fun.

Hebrews 12:11 TM

*A*s parents we need to teach our kids how to handle financial responsibility. But what do you do when they're young adults and already awash in a sea of debt? Well, here are 3 ways you can help them without jeopardizing your own nest egg:

(1) Pay only specific bills. Throwing money at their problems is never a long-term solution. For "survival" expenses like rent, food, utilities, and medical, you can write a check to the specific company. However, when their major problem is credit card debt—do nothing. Your kids need to learn that credit cards are luxuries, not necessities.

(2) Establish ground rules. When your adult children move back home you need to establish: (a) how much they'll be contributing towards household expenses; (b) how long this living arrangement will be necessary; (c) if they're unemployed, ways they can pull their weight around the house while they look for work.

(3) Think twice before co-signing a note. As the parent you may not necessarily see the monthly bill. That means if your child falls behind you can end up with a black mark against you. And 2 more suggestions: (a) Have them refinance the note in 6-12 months in their own name. (b) Have the bill sent directly to you. That way you can make sure the account's current, then pass the bill on to them for payment. God says, "Discipline isn't much fun . . . [but] later it pays off." While holding kids accountable can seem hard, in the long run, you both end up winning. *To do less, is not love!*

BUILDING A BETTER MARRIAGE (1)

Use your head . . . so . . . your love is sincere
and intelligent, not sentimental gush.

Philippians 1:9–10 TM

A woman awoke one night to find her husband wasn't in the bed. She found him in the kitchen looking very serious so she asked, "What's going on?" He replied, "Remember in high school when your dad caught us kissing and said if I didn't marry you immediately he'd make sure I was jailed for 20 years? Well, I'm sitting here thinking—I'd have gotten out of jail today!" Seriously, a strong marriage means falling in love over and over again—with the same person! The Bible says make sure "your love is . . . not sentimental gush." You do that by working through the challenges. Here are some thoughts to help you:

(1) Recharge your batteries regularly. It's impossible to escape marital stress but you can control it by taking breaks from the daily grind. Take a walk together, throw a Frisbee, go for coffee, do whatever "reconnects" you. And tell your children you're taking a time-out!

(2) Keep talking. Even though something seems obvious to you, don't assume your mate can read your mind. And never resort to "the silent treatment." Tell them what's bothering you, even if it means working through a disagreement. It's when you don't care enough to disagree, that you need to worry!

(3) Be open to counsel. The Bible says, "Pride . . . breeds quarrels, but wisdom is found in those who take advice" (Pr 13:10 NIV). When you reach a stalemate get input from a trusted friend or counselor, before it becomes a crisis.

BUILDING A BETTER MARRIAGE (2)

Live in . . . harmony.

Romans 15:5 NLT

*J*ean Kerr says, "Getting married is like buying something you've admired for ages in a shop window. You love it, but when you get it home it doesn't always go with everything!" Paul says, "Live in . . . harmony." Here are 3 suggestions:

(1) Stay teachable. Solomon says, "Answering before listening is . . . stupid and rude" (Pr 18:13 TM). Keep an open mind. Don't form your response while your mate's still talking. The Bible says, "Do not merely look out for your own . . . interests, but also for the interests of others" (Php 2:4 NASB). Never become so entrenched in your position that you don't consider your mate's viewpoint. Listening is about connecting and acknowledging where the other person's coming from.

(2) Keep humor alive. God says, "A cheerful heart brings a smile . . . a sad heart makes it hard to get through the day" (Pr 15:13 TM). When you're experiencing money woes, family problems, illness or plain old exhaustion, humor eases the tension and restores perspective.

(3) Eliminate the "D" word. Although God permits divorce under certain circumstances it's never His ideal. One couple, who worked through their marriage troubles said, "We're glad we didn't give up during the difficult years. We hung in long enough to realize that it really can get better with time." By committing to work on the relationship, no matter how things ultimately end up, you'll never regret your efforts.

BUILDING A BETTER MARRIAGE (3)

Be willing to listen.

James 1:19 NCV

*H*ave you seen the t-shirt that says, "I'm talking and I can't shut up!" Whenever you're dating you can talk for hours. But when you're married, unless you work at it, conversation sometimes becomes superficial and leads to disagreements. God says, "Be willing to listen and slow to speak," because there's an art to communicating:

(1) Let your mate lead. When they're talking about things outside your field of interest, remember, God said, "submit to one another" (Eph 5:21 NIV). Sometimes that means asking your partner, "What do you want to talk about?"

(2) Shorter can be better. "Honey, can we talk for a few minutes" is less threatening than the ominous "We need to talk" announcement! Some people can only stand so much "soul-baring;" pressuring them just gets the wrong result. If your spouse is unresponsive on an issue, discuss it with a trusted friend; then give your spouse the condensed, less emotional version.

(3) Be a friend, not a mentor. Don't try to change your mate by nagging. Asking, "Why can't you?" or "Why do you always?" sounds more like parenting than partnering. Tell them once what's bothering you, not 1,000 times! Ask yourself, "Would I say this to a valued friend?" If not, don't say it.

(4) Be affirming. It takes 12 compliments to neutralize one criticism. Your partner won't know how wonderful they are unless you tell them!

KEEPERS OF THE FLAME

I will give you shepherds after my own heart,
who will lead you with knowledge and understanding.
Jeremiah 3:15 NIV

*P*icture this: Joshua's soldiers are down in the valley fighting the Amalekites. Above him, on a hilltop, sits Moses with his hands raised toward heaven. As long as he does, the battle goes their way. But if you've ever tried to hold your hands up for long, you quickly grow weary and lower them. The moment Moses did that, the battle went against Israel. So Aaron and Hur moved to his side, held up his arms, and the tide turned again in their favor. Notice, it wasn't Joshua's ability to fight, it was Moses' ability to hold up his arms that won the day. Two men kept one man from fainting, so that an entire nation could be saved.

If your pastor's arms drop from exhaustion, God will judge you, not him, because you weren't there to strengthen him. Take a moment and let that sink in!

If God's given you a pastor who leads you and feeds you —support him! In the Old Testament tabernacle, the candlesticks had to be kept burning day and night because their light represented God's presence amongst His people. If a candle so much as flickered, designated servants moved in immediately to refuel it and restore it to its original glow.

It's *your* responsibility to make sure that the light doesn't flicker in your church, or the fire go out in your pulpit. So, pray for your pastor every day and be sure to encourage him every chance you get! Over one half of those who enter the ministry leave it within 10 years—because of discouragement! What a challenge to the keepers of the flame!

"POST-DATED!"

Moses my servant is dead. Now then . . . get ready.

Joshua 1:22 NIV

*J*oshua had already tasted the joys of the Promised Land, but now he had to go back and wait. Why? Because his assignment was post-dated. Certain things had to happen first: *(1) Moses had to die!* Moses represented the old system. It was good for then, but not for now! When you align yourself with what *was,* instead of what *is,* you're not ready yet. You're still looking for approval. There are still too many folk you need to impress. You're so tied up with systems and philosophies that when God says it's time to move, you have to consult somebody else. In order to reach your destiny, God will give you new instructions, new insights and a new plan for your life. The interesting thing is, the children of Israel mourned Moses' passing, yet they didn't see him die. They had to "reckon" him dead before they could move forward. Are you getting the idea?

(2) Every doubter had to be buried. There were lots of voices around Joshua telling him it couldn't be done, and he had to wait until everyone of them died in the wilderness. And every voice of doubt that's holding you back has got to die and be buried too; including the voice of your low self-esteem, your childhood fears, your anxieties, yes, even your critics! Gather them up and put them in a box, bury it, stand on top of it and say, "Ashes to ashes and dust to dust!" Only when you've taken those 2 steps are you ready to enter your Promised Land. Think about it!

DO YOU KNOW WHAT'S IN YOU?

According to His power that is at work within us.

Ephesians 3:20 NIV

*T*here are words in your Bible that have so much *life* and *power* in them, they're stronger than any therapy. God can give you a word that goes back into your past and heals your yesterday, secures your today, and anchors your tomorrow. That's why Satan clutters your life with so much junk that you don't have time for God's Word. He knows it'll unmask him and reveal the "God" potential that's lying dormant within you.

Before Jeremiah rose to prominence as a prophet God told him: (a) "Before I formed you in the womb I knew you" (Jer 1:5 NIV). Your parents didn't get the first look at you, God did. Nothing about you surprises Him. In spite of what you've been through, He hasn't changed His mind about who you *are* or what you're destined to *become*. (b) "Before you were born I set you apart" (Jer 1:5 NIV). Stop looking for acceptance in places where you don't belong! You're on a mission from God. That's why the enemy has tried so hard to take you out. Once you understand that, your struggles will begin to make sense.

Only as you read God's Word, will you begin to sense the awesome, mind-renewing, thirst-quenching, life-changing potential that was deposited within you from before the foundations of the world. Listen: "Now to him who is able to do immeasurably more than all we ask or imagine, according to his power that is at work within us" (Eph 3:20 NIV). *So, start tapping into that power today!*

PURPOSE AND PERSISTENCE

Do not be weary in well doing.

Galatians 6:9

*M*ost *of us underestimate the time it takes to achieve anything of lasting value.* You've got to be willing to pay your dues. James Watt spent 20 years laboring to perfect the steam engine. William Harvey worked day and night for 8 years to demonstrate how blood circulated in the human body. Then it took him another 25 years to convince the medical establishment he was right.

Cutting corners is a sign of impatience and poor self-discipline. The way to any breakthrough is to follow through! Albert Grey says, "The common denominator of all success lies in forming the habit of doing things that failures don't like to do." If you find yourself continually giving in to your moods and impulses, you need to change your *approach* to doing things. The best method is to set standards for yourself that require accountability. Suffering a consequence for not following through will keep you on track like nothing else. Once your new standards are in place, work according to them, not your moods; that'll get you going in the right direction.

Self-discipline is a quality that's only won through practice. Successful people have learned to do what does not come naturally. They're willing to confront discomfort, distractions, fear, and act in spite of them. R. H. Macy, founder of Macy's Department Stores, failed at 5 different professions—whaler, retailer, gold-miner, stockbroker, real estate broker—before he finally succeeded. What sustained him through failure after failure? Two things: purpose and persistence! *That's what separates those who achieve, from those who merely dream!*

BE KIND!

Charity suffereth long, and is kind.
1 Corinthians 13:4

*M*ost conflicts aren't caused by differences of opinion, but by lack of understanding. So why aren't we more understanding?

(1) Fear. William Penn said, "Never despise what you don't understand." Yet most of us do. Either we open our minds to a new idea and grow, or reject it and stay the same size. We compare what we don't understand, with what we think we do —like the all-wise folks who told Columbus the earth was flat and that he'd fall off the end. Harry Truman said, "When we understand the other fellow's viewpoint and what he's trying to do, 9 times out of 10 he's just trying to do right."

(2) Self-centeredness. Somebody quipped: "There are two sides to every question—as long as it doesn't concern us personally." We grow up learning to put ourselves first. Ever play with a 2-year-old? They choose the best toys for themselves and always insist on having their own way. When we grow up, our toys just cost more!

(3) Failure to appreciate differences. It takes more than one color to make a rainbow. When you learn to appreciate the difference in people, you'll discover we all share the same hopes and fears. Two common problems are "gift-envy" and "gift-projection." One happens when we compare our gifts with others and feel "less than." The other happens when we expect everybody else to feel equally passionate about what we're called to do. Listen: "There are different kinds of service . . . but it is the same Lord we are serving" (1Co 12:5 NLT).

YOU COULDN'T AFFORD IT!

What must I do to inherit eternal life?
Luke 18:18 NIV

$\mathcal{T}$he rich young ruler was educated and respected. He'd already achieved the 3 P's of success: power, prosperity, and posterity. He was a bottom-line guy who cut to the chase and asked, "What must I do to inherit eternal life?" Even the way he worded the question suggests that he thought he could get eternal life the way he'd gotten everything else in life—by self-effort. So when Jesus replied, "Sell all that you possess . . . he became very sad, for he was extremely rich" (Lk 18:22-23 NAS). He'd mistakenly assumed that heaven was just a payment away. But it's not!

Paul says, "What the law was powerless to do . . . God did by sending his own Son" (Ro 8:3 NIV). Only a cold-hearted God would sell salvation to those who can afford it! That's a hard concept to grasp, since we've always been rewarded for our *performance.* But just as you wouldn't impress the space-shuttle crew with your paper airplane, or you wouldn't display your crayon sketches before Picasso, so your character and good works don't qualify you for heaven. Eternal life costs more than you can afford. That's why you don't need a resume —you need a Redeemer!

Money wasn't this man's problem, self-sufficiency was. It wasn't his big income, it was his big ego! And it's not just the wealthy who've difficulty grasping this; so do the educated, the strong, the good-looking, the popular, even the religious.

To receive salvation you must first declare that you're spiritually bankrupt; that your cupboard is bare, your reputation worthless, and your options gone. You can't approach God demanding justice—you can only come pleading mercy. So come to Him today!

STAY CONNECTED

I am the vine; you are the branches.
John 15:5 NIV

*J*esus takes His disciples aside to prepare them for His departure, and the problems they'll face after He's gone. Listen: "I am the vine; you are the branches . . . apart from me you can do nothing . . . I chose you . . . to go and bear fruit— fruit that will last" (Jn 15: 5&16 NIV). Notice:

(1) You only understand who you are, in relationship to Christ! He tells them: "Apart from me you can do nothing." When you forget that, you end up trying to do things only God can do; like solving your problems your own way, or promoting yourself through clever strategies. You're not blessed in any endeavor because of your performance, you're blessed because of your connection to the vine. Unless you understand that, you'll waste your time chasing people who have no more power than you do. Your strength and success are in the vine! Just stay connected!

(2) Before you get the fruit that remains, you have to lose the fruit that's temporary! Listen: "Every branch that does bear fruit he prunes" (Jn 15:2 NIV). You can be a good branch connected to a good vine bearing good fruit, and suddenly God starts cutting back certain things in your life. Things you thought would always be there are taken away. Now it feels like you're going backwards. It takes *faith* to believe that God would permit you to lose what you're proud of, what you draw your security from, in order to give you something better— fruit that remains; enduring success. So the word for you today is, "Let it go. God has something much better in store for you."

BE RELENTLESS!

Woman, you have great faith! Your request is granted.
Matthew 15:28 NIV

$\mathcal{L}$isten: "A Canaanite woman . . . came to him . . . 'Lord . . . My daughter is suffering terribly' . . . He answered, 'I was sent only to . . . Israel . . . It is not right to take the children's bread and toss it to their dogs.' 'Yes, Lord,' she said, 'but even the dogs eat the crumbs that fall from their master's table.' Then Jesus answered, 'Woman, you have great faith! Your request is granted'" (Mt 15:22-28 NIV).

This woman was an outsider, yet she pushed through and got what comfortable insiders often miss because they're complacent. Talk about hurdles! First, Jesus refused to answer her. Next, He said, "What I have is only for the Jews." Finally, He said, "It wouldn't be right to give the children's bread to dogs." But she refused to be shut down, put off, or discouraged. Listen to her: "Have mercy on me." She's not asking for what she *deserves,* she's crying out for what she *needs.* As a result Jesus broke every precedent, removed every obstacle and answered her prayer. And if you'll persist, He'll do the same for you too!

In reality, this woman told Jesus: "Let the children have the bread, all I need are the crumbs." Church folks neglect the bread (of life), waste the bread, complain about the bread, don't even show up for the bread—but desperate people pick up the crumbs and find life! They know that if there's power in the loaf there's power in the crumb, and when a crumb from God is all you can get, a crumb is all you need. So, what do you need from Jesus today? How badly do you want it? Be relentless!

FORGIVE IT AND DROP IT!

If you have anything against anyone,
forgive him and let it drop.

Mark 11:25 AMP

*S*atan will try to convince you that if your *feelings* haven't changed toward the person who wronged you, you haven't truly forgiven them. That's a lie! You can make the *right* decision and still have the *wrong* feelings! This is when you need faith to carry you through. You've done your part, now you're waiting on God to do His part, which is heal your emotions and make you *feel* well and whole. Only God has the power to change your feelings toward the one who hurt you, and He will.

Another misconception is, that all we have to do is make a decision to forgive, then our job is finished. No, listen: "Invoke blessings upon and pray for the happiness of those who curse you, implore God's blessings [favor] upon those who abuse you" (Lk 6:28 AMP). Bless them? Yeah! And that word *bless,* actually means "to speak well of." Ouch! You're extending mercy to those who don't deserve it! But isn't that what God does for you?

The truth is, you cannot truly forgive without the Holy Spirit's help. None of us can. So today why don't you pray, "Holy Spirit, breathe on me and give me strength. I forgive _____ [name] for what they did. I loose them from this debt and ask You to bless them. I turn the situation over to You. I trust You for my total restoration. Help me, Lord. Heal me of my wounds. In Jesus' name, Amen." *Now, by faith, leave it all in your Father's hands!*

WOULD YOU DIE FOR JESUS?

I saw . . . those who had been slain because of the
Word of God . . . and the testimony they had maintained.
Revelation 6:9 NIV

*W*hat kind of people are these anyway? People who've given their lives for the word of God, and the testimony they've maintained before a hostile world. Try measuring yourself by that standard! "Are you trying to make me feel bad?" you say. No, just:

(1) More grateful. "Grateful for what?" you ask. That your faith and your testimony are so threatening to the enemy, that you're on his hit-list. He doesn't attack low-impact Christians, he serenades them.

(2) More prayerful. Listen: "Remember those in prison as if you were their fellow prisoners, and those who are mistreated as if you yourselves were suffering" (Heb 13:3 NIV). "But what does that verse mean to me?" you ask. Next time you bang your thumb with a hammer and your whole body aches, remember those words; then begin immediately to pray for the great big world-wide body of believers, many of whom are still being persecuted, imprisoned, tortured, and killed in Christ's name.

(3) More faithful. Richard Wurmbarnd, who wrote *Tortured For Christ,* said: "What a person really believes, is not what he says in his creeds, but what he's willing to die for." Now, the odds are you'll never be called upon to die for Jesus. But the real issue is, if you're not willing to *die* for Him, what are the chances that you'll actually *live* for Him? Before you answer, ask yourself, "How much of my time, my treasures and my talents, am I investing in Christ's kingdom?"

INTERCESSORS NEEDED!

He said He would destroy them—had not Moses . . .
stood in the breach before Him.

Psalm 106:23 NIV

*P*rayer isn't just about you, it's about *others.*
Behind every great spiritual awakening, the kind that radically changes people and shakes up communities, there's an unseen, unstoppable force known as "intercessors." Many of the victories we celebrate in the open, were first won in the secret place of prayer by these intercessors! It's their specialized ministry. And God could be calling you to be one of them!

It's a two-fold calling; first you minister to the Lord through worship, then you minister to the lost through witness. Even though your feeble limbs can't carry you beyond your own front door, through *prayer* you can limit Satan's movements and defeat his best-laid strategies. "How?" you ask. By calling the forces of heaven into any situation, anywhere, anytime, for anybody. No wonder the enemy will do "whatever it takes" to keep you from praying!

Check out these 2 Scriptures: (a) "Ask of me, and I shall give thee the heathen for thine inheritance, and the uttermost parts of the earth for thy possession" (Ps 2:8). It's time to move beyond your "bless me" prayers, and begin to touch nations! What you prayerfully declare on earth, (as long as it lines up with His word), God will authorize in heaven. (b) "The harvest is plentiful but the workers are few. Ask the Lord of the harvest, therefore, to send out workers into his harvest field" (Mt 9:37-38 NIV). It works like this: your prayers move God. God moves people. People move nations. Nations are changed. The whole thing begins with one praying person—today let that person be *you.*

VEXED

She vexed [him] unto death.

Judges 16:16

*W*hen you're vexed you're vulnerable. Before Delilah destroyed Samson she, "vexed [him] unto death." When you're vexed long enough you'll make bad decisions—potentially harmful ones. You can attend church regularly and read your Bible from cover to cover, but it'll do you little good if you're running around vexed. It's hard to live with a vexed person and almost impossible to help them. You can't bless anybody with a vexed spirit because their mind is in the grips of a negative force.

Samson should have been more discerning. Joseph ran from Potiphar's wife and won; Samson stayed with Delilah and lost. There are some things you ought to run from, and we're not just talking about sin. No, we're talking about *anything* that drains you, diverts you, or causes you to lose your vision. And the older you get the more important this becomes, because now you have less time.

"What should I do when I'm vexed?" *First, check the company you keep!* How do they influence you? *Next, worship!* Worship enables you to get back your spiritual equilibrium. As you focus on God He floods your soul with peace and gives you back your stability. It's the ultimate therapy. Only when you've worshipped, are you ready to experience the healing effects of God's Word.

Today, if you're sick of being vexed, lift up your heart and say, "Father, I worship You. I'm tired of this. I don't like what I'm becoming. Create in me a clean heart, and renew in me a right spirit." Go ahead, try it and see what happens!

LIVING EXPECTANTLY!

Let us hold firmly to . . . hope . . .
because we can trust God to do what He promised.
Hebrews 10:23 NCV

*L*ook around you: so many of the people you know live without hope. They smile but their eyes are dead; they talk but the music has left their voice. They're like mannequins, all dressed up and going nowhere—they feel hopeless!

Our hope isn't luck, like winning the lottery. No, it's *expectancy;* it's *confidence* that God will do what He's promised! Listen: "Let's keep a firm grip on the promises that keep us going. He always keeps his word" (Heb 10:23 TM). What keeps us going? "God's promises!" Nobody knew this better than David; he'd every reason to lose hope. After God anointed him to be King, he waited 7 more years while a paranoid leader occupied the throne. He had to flee for his life and hide in caves surrounded by enemies. He saw Israel devastated by war, his friends killed and his family taken captive. Listen: "My foes taunt me, saying . . . 'Where is your God?'" (Ps 42:10 NIV). Faced with circumstances that would wipe most of us out, David *still* said, "You are my hope" (Ps 71:5 NKJV); "I hope in Your word" (Ps 119:147 NKJV). You can't lose with an attitude like that! David became Israel's greatest king because he never lost his confidence in God: it kept him focused; it kept him on top of the circumstances; it kept him going!

So, "Let us hold firmly to . . . hope" (He 10:23 NCV). Why? Because God will keep every promise He's made to you!

YOUR PLACE

There is a place by Me.

Exodus 33:21

*C*an you imagine taking your child to an unknown destination and laying him on an altar as a sacrifice? That's what was happening in Abraham's life when we read, "On the third day Abraham looked up and saw the place in the distance" (Ge 22:4 NIV). It's the last place your flesh wants to go because: (a) it's the place where God exposes your true motives and values. God didn't want to kill Isaac, He just wanted to know, "Abraham is there anything you value *more* than me?" (b) it's also the place where you discover the supply for your every need. Listen: "Abraham looked up and there in a thicket he saw a ram caught by its horns" (Ge 22:13 NIV). Notice the word "caught." When you get to where God wants you to be, you'll find that your provision is *already in place*. You can't lose it and nobody can take it from you!

Now, if you think *getting* to this place is tough, try *living* there! When Paul writes, "Neither give place to the devil" (Eph 4:27), he's talking about the same place. When he tells the Ephesian Christians to put on the whole armor of God, he ends by saying, "Having done all, to stand [in your place]" (Eph 6:13). You won't have to go out and fight the devil each day; he'll bring the battle to you. Why? To get you out of your place!

God told Moses, "There is a place by me. Come and stand in it, and I'll cause all my goodness to pass before you" (See Ex 33:22). If you're serious about enjoying God's goodness, get to your place—and stay there!

WHAT WILL YOUR LEGACY BE?

A good man . . . leaves an inheritance.

Proverbs 13:22 NIV

*E*ach life touches other lives in seen and unseen ways. You don't necessarily have to *know* somebody in order to experience the blessings of their legacy. Like walking into an empty room and catching a whiff of somebody's perfume, your influence can continue to be felt long after you're gone.

Usually we don't like to think about this because: (1) we associate legacies with dying, and we don't particularly enjoy thinking about that topic; (2) we assume that since our legacy won't be revealed for years, we don't need to start investing now; (3) we feel like we've little or no control over what we leave behind anyhow.

The Bible says, "A good man . . . leaves an inheritance." So what will yours be? More important—what's it going to cost? If you just want to leave material things, that's easy. Work hard, invest wisely and build your net worth. But since the best gifts aren't always handed down in your will, why not leave something more meaningful—something that points to who you *were?*

It's one thing to measure your success by the money in your bank account, the size of your estate holdings, or the value of your stock portfolio. It's entirely another to measure it by intangibles like being a faithful, loving spouse, raising godly children, being a spiritual mentor, and leaving the lights on when you go!

All great legacies come with a price tag. To move beyond mediocrity, you must invest *every day* in the invisible accounts of those who follow you!

WHAT'S YOUR DREAM?

Depend on it: God keeps his word.

Romans 3:4 TM

*P*aul writes: "What advantage then hath the Jew? . . . Much every way . . . unto them were committed the oracles of God" (Ro 3:1-2). God has spoken certain things concerning you. Those things are His *will* and His *purpose* for your life. Your job is to recognize them, believe them, carry them within you and speak them often, because they give you a tremendous advantage.

Then Paul adds: "For what if some did not believe? Shall their unbelief make the faith of God without effect? God forbid" (Ro 3:3-4). Get over the idea that the majority has to agree with you, or believe what God said about you. Your dream must be independent of outside support. This is a difficult concept, especially in a democracy where others vote and the majority rules. The kingdom of God is a theocracy where only one vote counts—God's!

Refuse to put your dream on hold, waiting for everybody to get on the same page with you. Not only do they not have to support you, they don't even have to *believe* what God has told you. You can't wait until others become comfortable with your dream before you pursue it. They can misunderstand you, talk about you, laugh at you, spit on you, ostracize you, alienate you, not invite you over, refuse to support you, and you can *still* get there without them! Why? Because your God is a covenant making, covenant keeping God, and what He has spoken over your life, He will surely bring to pass: "Depend on it: God keeps his word" (Ro 3:4 TM).

THE SOURCE OF YOUR DREAM

Flesh gives birth to flesh, but the spirit gives birth to spirit.
John 3:6 NIV

*Y*ou'd be surprised at the number of people who are tormented by a dream God never gave them—who waste their lives trying to do things He neither called nor equipped them to do.

What's the source of your dream? Did the most influential people in your life impose their dreams on you? "So-and-so always thought you'd make a wonderful doctor or lawyer." Stop and ask yourself, "Is it me? Others? The enemy? God?" It's not too late. If your dream's not of God, go back and seek Him and He'll give you one that is.

Look deep within; who are you trying to impress? Are you trying to prove to your ex-husband or wife that you can make it without them, or show your parents you're just as talented as your brother or sister, or demonstrate to the world that you can overcome your beginnings and pull yourself up by your own bootstraps? Your dream cannot be born out of your unresolved issues. That only breeds a need for control and recognition, and dooms you to fail.

Furthermore, if your dream is from God, you mustn't be impatient like Abraham and try to "make it happen." God's promises can never be fulfilled through fleshly effort. If only Abraham had waited, he could've had Isaac who represents "The blessing of the Lord which maketh rich—and adds no sorrow" (See Pr 10:22). No matter how long it takes, wait for God's timing, prepare yourself thoroughly, and go only when He says "Go!"

WHAT'S THE RESOURCE FOR YOUR DREAM?

It is God which worketh in you.

Philippians 2:13

*I*f God's the *source* of your dream, He'll also become the *resource* for it. Don't try to "get in" with certain people thinking they'll open the right door for you, only to become resentful when it doesn't happen and develop a "You owe me" complex. Listen: "These are the words of him who . . . holds the key . . . What he opens no one can shut" (Rev 3:7 NIV). God holds the key to your future, not others!

Once you understand that, God will challenge you to look *within* yourself. Why? Because you always have enough to create what you need! You may not recognize it yet, but it's there just waiting to be tapped. Stop saying, "I don't have what it takes." God's given you *everything* you need to get you where you ought to be!

Start looking in the mirror! Go ahead, hug yourself and announce, "I'm full of untapped potential." Until you pull out what God's placed within you, you'll live like a spectator envying the success of others.

It's not who *has* the most who wins, but who knows how to *use* it. With all due respect to some of the world's greatest singers, there are folk washing dishes who could sing them under the table. The "biggies" only *got* big, by identifying what they had, and making the most of it!

So get rid of your false piety. Stop talking about what you *don't* have and begin using what you *do*. Listen: "It is God which worketh in you." Today pull out the "God element" that's within you, and put it to work!

THOUGHTS FOR DREAMERS

For ye see your calling, brethren.

1 Corinthians 1:26

You don't have to have a dream that others consider *great, for it to be important in God's eyes.* If your dream's to be a great parent, that doesn't mean you don't have great faith, it just means you understand your calling. All Moses' mother did was to give birth—but oh what a baby! God protected her son when she couldn't do a thing to help him. Then He brought her to Pharaoh's house and *paid* her to raise him. And when you discover your purpose, God will provide for you too! If you want to see the resources come, get the mission straight!

No matter how big your dream is, don't let it intimidate you! As a child Joseph dreamed of being a great leader—which first landed him in a pit, then a prison. "Where's your dream now, Joseph?" Understand this: your dream won't always look like it's coming together. Sometimes it'll seem to die before it springs to life. The Bible says that Abraham ignored the fact that his body was almost dead, believed God and fathered Isaac, even though biologically speaking, it seemed like a lost cause.

Paul dreamed of taking on the world for Christ and folks around him called him a fool. Did that derail him? Not one bit. Listen: "We are fools for Christ" (1Co 4:10 NIV). God uses *radical* people who don't care what they look like, people who've survived difficult pasts, defied the odds, held on to their dream and declared, "My God is able!" And you can be one of those people!

THE HIGH COST OF BITTERNESS!

Forgive anyone who does you wrong.
Colossians 3:13 CEV

*T*he woman who wrote this letter, thought revenge would bring closure. She was wrong:

"I found my husband with another woman. Although he begged me for forgiveness I wanted my pound of flesh, so I filed for divorce, even though our kids asked me not to. Two years later my husband was still trying to get me back, but I wanted none of it. He'd hurt me and I wanted revenge. Finally, he gave up, married a young widow with 2 children and rebuilt his life without me. They're all so happy, and I'm just a lonely, miserable woman who let bitterness ruin her life."

Now, there's no question, infidelity is wrong. But without forgiveness, bitterness is all that's left! There comes a point at which anger is no longer just an emotion—it's a driving force. Like cocaine, you need larger and more frequent doses. Once that happens, you move even further from forgiveness, because without your anger you've no source of energy at all. It's what drives hate groups like the KKK and the Skinheads. Without bitterness they've no reason to exist! If you take bigotry from the racist, revenge from the zealot, chauvinism from the sexist, what's left?

God says, "Forgive anyone who does you wrong . . . as Christ has forgiven you," because bitterness is fatal. It kills your soul. So how do you stop yourself from becoming bitter when you've been hurt? *By looking into the face of the one who hurt you, and instead, seeing the face of the One who showed you mercy when nobody else would've given you another chance!*

"THE SIFTER."

Satan hath desired to . . . sift you as wheat.

Luke 22:31

*J*esus told Peter, "Satan wants to sift you as wheat." Just as wheat is separated from chaff, so Satan wants to separate you from God. One way he accomplishes this is through temptation, so here are some things to watch for:

(1) When you fall, refuse to stay down. Don't accept the lie that says, "If you were really a Christian you wouldn't fall." Birth and growth are separate processes. When Jesus saves you, your spirit is immediately changed, but until your emotions, appetites and desires come under His lordship, you'll always be vulnerable. This has nothing to do with your salvation and everything to do with becoming mature. Salvation is instant; becoming mature is the work of a lifetime.

(2) Be quick to confess your sins. David said, "The Lord is near to the brokenhearted, and saves the crushed in spirit" (Ps 34:18 NRSV). God always responds to a repentant heart. He'll meet you at your lowest point and walk with you through the valley where even your closest friends can't go.

(3) Once you're free, stay free. When you uproot a plant it may look good for a while, but unless it's replanted in healthy soil and properly tended, it'll die. When God delivers you from something harmful, it's to attach you to something healthy. He takes you out of a bad situation in order to place you into a good one; otherwise, you'll seek out your old connections. So, look out for "the sifter!" You'll only win over temptation if you *want* to, and *prepare* to!

ARE YOU TOO BUSY?

A . . . Samaritan . . . came where he was.
And when he saw him, he had compassion.
Luke 10:33 NKJV

*A*re you too busy to care about the needs of others? Are you so preoccupied *being* good instead of *doing* good, that you're missing opportunities right under your nose? Remember, nobody was busier than Jesus, yet He always responded to those in need.

In Luke 10, Jesus tells of a Jewish traveler who was mugged by a gang and left to die on the road. First a Levite and then a priest passed by. They were religious leaders; surely they'd have compassion on this wounded man. But no, they both had important appointments to keep and didn't stop. Then a Samaritan came along. Of all people, he'd the most reason to look the other way, because the Jews and the Samaritans were long-standing enemies. But the Bible says, "He . . . came where he was. And when he saw him, he had compassion." Compassion will rearrange your priorities! The Good Samaritan decided that where he was going, wasn't as important as where he was at that particular moment.

What would you have done that day? Do you think you'd have acted like this Samaritan? How about when God tries to interrupt your inflexible, tightly organized, written-in-concrete schedule and asks you to take time for someone who's hurting? Are you willing to shelve your personal agenda and do what He wants? If you're too busy to reach out to those who are hurting, you're just too busy! Today ask God to help you begin thinking and acting like Christ, and don't miss another opportunity to serve.

FIVE TRAPS LEADERS FALL INTO

I set you apart for a special work.

Jeremiah 1:5 NCV

*I*f you're a leader, consider these 5 traps:

(1) The need to be well-rounded! Great achievers are usually not well-rounded. They're focused! Striving to be well-rounded only sounds good. It actually forces you to invest time and energy into areas where you'll never excel.

(2) Authority without competence! Every leader has authority over areas in which he has little or no competence. When he tries to exercise authority there, he often hinders everything and everyone under his watch. To put it bluntly, there are things you're responsible for, that you should keep your nose out of.

(3) The success intoxicant! Success is an intoxicant, and intoxicated people seldom have a firm grip on reality. Leaders often assume that their core competencies are broader than they actually are. This trait is easy to see in others, but next to impossible to see in ourselves. Admitting weakness doesn't make you less effective, it just expresses what everybody around you has known for a long time.

(4) Guilt! We feel guilty about delegating our weaknesses. We assume that everybody hates to do what we hate to do. Wrong! Delegation allows somebody else to shine. Your weakness is their opportunity.

(5) Unwillingness to develop others! Sure it's easier to do things yourself. But leadership isn't just about getting things done right, it's about getting things done through others. If you can't find somebody to hand things off to, look in the mirror. Your people are exactly where you've led them. If you've nobody to delegate things to, guess who needs to change?

DON'T BE A PRODIGAL (1)

A certain man had two sons.

Luke 15:11

*T*he Prodigal Son made the following mistakes—
be sure you don't make them too!

(1) He wanted to control his own future! The first step into
trouble is always the one that takes us away from God. Like the
Prodigal we leave home saying, "Give me." And if we're
fortunate enough to survive our own best thinking, we come
back saying, "Forgive me."

*(2) He didn't get into trouble until he left his father's
house!* Satan will do whatever it takes to get you out from
under God's influence and protection. He'll put "a restless
spirit" on you so that nothing keeps you happy, and you run
around like a rolling stone singing, "I can't get no satisfaction."
The 2 "blessed places" he'll particularly try to get you out of
are: *(a) your marriage:* that's why you need to constantly work
on it. The only reason there are weeds in your garden instead of
roses, is because you don't spend enough time working there.
Hello! Your marriage is not just a covenant before God, it's a
shelter for your passions and dysfunctions; *(b) your church:*
who's feeding you? Who's monitoring your spiritual growth?
Would you let your kids stay home from school because they
didn't like the teacher or want to learn? There are things God
will say to you in His house that He won't say to you anywhere
else. Jeremiah said that God's Word was like "a hammer that
breaks the rock in pieces" (See Jer 23:29). You need to be sure
that when that hammer falls on Sunday morning—you're
under it!

DON'T BE A PRODIGAL (2)

A certain man had two sons.

Luke 15:11

The Prodigal Son wanted it before he was ready for it! To know if something's good for you, you need to understand where the desire for it came from. Loving parents don't give their kids things because they cry for them; they reward them for acting responsibly. They know what's age-appropriate. And God's a loving parent! We all know of good, well-intentioned people whose gifts elevated them, only to watch them devastated because of some undisciplined area in their lives. So, listen to your Heavenly Father and don't leave home until He says you're ready!

The enemy's after your substance! Listen: "[He] wasted his substance with riotous living" (Lk 15:13). Notice the word "substance." The enemy's after more than your possessions, he's after your integrity, your self-esteem, your staying power, your purpose. Prodigal, if you don't make a U-turn, you can actually lose your desire for life itself! Like a slow leak in a tire, you can be going places, yet be only a few steps from the hog pen. "How will I know when I'm there?" you ask. Listen: "He . . . joined himself to a citizen of that country; and he sent him into his fields to feed swine" (Lk 15:15). Notice the word "joined." If you want to know where you are spiritually, look beside you. Who do you call? Who calls you most? Who are you joined to?

But there's hope; when the Prodigal returned, his father was waiting for him—and yours is too! Just don't stay away too long!

DON'T BE A PRODIGAL (3)

And when he came to himself.
Luke 15:17

$\mathcal{M}$ark Twain said that when he was 14, his dad was so ignorant he could hardly stand him. But by the time he was 21, he was amazed how much the old man had learned in 7 years. God knows better than you. David said, "Goodness and mercy shall follow me all the days of my life" (Ps 23:6). The more you see lives ruined by wrong choices, the more you'll say, "It was only God's goodness and mercy that kept me from that."

Look at the Prodigal: from one of the best families in town, penniless, friendless, eating pig swill—trying to satisfy a legitimate hunger in an illegitimate way! *That's* why we get into extra-marital affairs, go on benders, rip off other people, or work ourselves to death, sacrificing our families in the process. Get this: there's a God-shaped blank in you—that nothing but God can fill!

Finally the penny dropped: "He came to himself." If you'll let Him, God will stop you in the nick of time. He'll remind you of *who* you are and *where* you belong. You'll start seeing the mud you're wallowing in, the false friends, the empty achievements, the people around you who are no happier than you are. If that's where you are right now, come home. Your Father is waiting to wipe your slate clean. He still loves you. The table is spread and your seat's reserved. You haven't gone too far—yet! Tell the devil, "I've changed my mind," and come back while you still can!

THE SACRED SUMMIT

When Jesus saw the crowds, He went up . . . a mountain.
Matthew 5:1 CEV

*I*n this particular verse the Bible doesn't say that when Jesus saw the crowds He sat down in the middle of them, or that He healed them or taught them. There were occasions when He did all those things. But this time before going to the masses, He went to the mountain. Before ministering to the crowd, He drew strength from the Father. Have *you* learned to do that yet?

Before getting caught up in the daily rat race, make time for a "sacred summit." "What's that?" you ask. It's a place of stability in a shallow world—where the view is unobstructed and the frantic pace of everyday life is left behind. There you gain a perspective that only comes from being in God's presence. There Jesus reminds you that there's *nothing* you'll face today, that He hasn't already handled.

It's easy to recognize those who've been to the summit. Their struggles are no different from yours. Indeed their problems may be more challenging. But they've an inner peace that can't be derailed by family problems, health concerns, or budgetary shortfalls.

You can endure the hard times with grace when you know the summit is just a prayer away. Jesus said, "Are you tired? Worn out? Burned out? . . . Get away with me and you'll recover . . . I'll show you how to take a real rest" (Mt 11:28 TM). Call "time out" today. Leave it all aside for a while and follow Him up the winding path to the summit. *If you do, you'll come back different!*

THE UNBREAKABLE LINK

He will reward each according to his works.
Matthew 16:27 NKJV

*H*ow you live now, determines what will happen to you after you die. Bruce Wilkinson calls this, "The Law Of The Unbreakable Link." Like the law of gravity, it's always working. The choices you make in your life each day don't come to nothing when you die. They matter! And they'll continue to matter throughout eternity.

Your eternal destination is the result of what you *believe.* Your eternal reward is the result of how you *behave.* Do you agree with that? Really? If you do, it will radically affect: (a) how you think about your life; (b) how you think about God; (c) what you choose to do one minute from now. God wants you to know that the positive consequences of your actions today, can change your eternal prospects in astounding and wonderful ways—and He doesn't want you to waste another minute.

You don't have to worry about what awaits you on the other side of your last heartbeat. Others don't decide that. Even God doesn't—you do! When the truth of this dawns on you, you'll say, "I can't believe I've prepared for my children's future or my old age, but not given a thought to my *real* future!" Or as one man said, "I've always thought about finishing well, but now it turns out that death is just the starting gate."

You can't do anything about your past, but *starting right now* you can change your future—one choice and one act at a time.

GOD RECORDS AND REWARDS

You shall be repaid at the resurrection.
Luke 14:14 NKJV

*W*hen Jesus was invited to the home of a prominent religious leader, He offered this unsolicited advice. "When you give a dinner or a supper, do not ask your friends, your brothers, your relatives, nor your rich neighbors, lest they also invite you back, and you be repaid . . . When you give a feast, invite the poor, the maimed, the lame, the blind. And you will be blessed, because they cannot repay you; for you shall be repaid at the resurrection" (Lk 14:12-14 NKJV). Notice the words, "you will be repaid at the resurrection." God will repay you for some things *after* you're dead. This contradicts what many of us believe—that God rewards us only on earth. No, these words show that when you do a worthy deed for someone who cannot repay you: (a) you will be repaid; (b) much of your reward will come in the next life.

If you fail to understand this you'll find yourself saying: "I serve God faithfully, so why am I struggling? Doesn't God notice or care?" Friend, God notices and God cares! But He doesn't promise that work for Him now, will always result in gain from Him now. Many of the rewards God has for us are so great, it'll take *eternity* to appreciate and enjoy them!

Jesus said, "Whoever gives you a cup of water to drink in My name . . . will by no means lose his reward" (Mk 9:41 NKJV). No deed for God will be overlooked or go unrewarded —not even a cup of cold water, or a prayer in the middle of the night.

THREE TESTS

The fire will test each one's work.
1 Corinthians 3:13 NKJV

*H*ow will God evaluate and reward what we did for Him during our lifetime? By 3 tests:

(1) The test of intimacy! The life God rewards is not a life of performance apart from relationship with Him. Jesus said unless we abide in Him and obey His commands, we will not bear fruit for Him (See Jn 15:5). He commended one church for their good works, then turned around and condemned them because they hadn't kept their love for Him alive. Listen: "I know your works, your labor, your patience . . . Nevertheless I have this against you, that you have left your first love" (Rev 2:2-4 NKJV).

(2) The test of motive! Listen: "Take heed that you do not do your charitable deeds before men, to be seen by them. Otherwise you have no reward . . . in heaven" (Mt 6:1 NKJV). What should our motive be? To serve God and bring Him glory. Even ordinary actions like eating and drinking can bring God glory (See 1Co 10:31). On the other hand, our most religious actions are worthless, if our motive is to enhance our own ego and reputation.

(3) The test of love! Listen: "Love your enemies, do good, and lend, hoping for nothing in return; and your reward will be great" (Lk 6:35 NKJV). When it comes to good works, *why* is always more important to God than *what!* The Bible warns: "Look to yourselves, that we do not lose those things we worked for, but that we may receive a full reward" (2Jn 8 NKJV). You should constantly pray, "Lord, keep my heart right and my motives pure."

HOW GOD PROVIDES (1)

My God shall supply all your needs.
Philippians 4:19

$\mathcal{G}$od will use different people at different times to meet different needs in your life. He used Pharaoh to feed the Israelites. Imagine that! When famine hit, He led His people down to Egypt and made Pharaoh feed them for 400 years. Get this: when you ask God for something, don't dictate to Him *who* He'll use to meet your need. Notice the words of Jesus: "Shall men give into your bosom" (Lk 6:38). *When God wants to bless you, sometimes He'll send a person!* But if you're too proud to accept their help, you won't get it. Or if you limit Him to working through people you know and like, you'll miss the boat again. God used Pharaoh because he's not the kind of guy you're apt to fall in love with. God doesn't want you getting hooked on anybody but Him. He can bless you through your boss, the tax man, the car dealer, the mortgage lender, or even those who mean you no good! It was betrayal by his brothers that eventually caused Joseph to become Prime Minister of Egypt. People will enter your life and people will leave it. Praise God when they come and praise Him when they go, and remind yourself: "If He blessed me before, He'll do it again"— and keep truckin'.

Egypt only became a problem when God's people stayed there too long! Don't lean on the arm of the flesh too long, or the instrument of your blessing can become an idol (or a source of control). And that's a problem, for God said: "Thou shalt have no other gods before me."

HOW GOD PROVIDES (2)

What is it?

Exodus 16:15 NIV

*G*od will wean you from dependence on any hand but His. He'll allow the Pharaoh who fed you last year to abuse you this year. Then He'll bring you into the wilderness and teach you to trust in Him alone. Notice:

(1) At first, you may not recognize your provision. The word manna means "What is it?" They'd never seen anything like it. It required faith to receive it. Don't be afraid of something because it doesn't come prepackaged the way you like it. Instead say, "Lord, if it's according to Your Word I'm going to receive it, thank You for it, enjoy it and start living off it."

(2) It had to be gathered first thing each morning. Why? Because by noon the sun had melted it. Before you do anything else, go get your manna. Feed yourself on God's Word before the enemy gets a chance to hit you. Once you've done that, you can handle whatever the day brings.

(3) You receive according to your need, not your neighbor's. God won't bless you so that you can keep up with the guy in the next tent; if he's got more kids to feed, he gets more manna. Stop measuring your blessing by what somebody else has. Your blessing is predicated on 2 things: (a) The amount needed to fulfill your God-given assignment. (b) The degree to which God can trust you with it. So quit comparing and complaining about what God gave your neighbor, and start being grateful for the "What is it?" that He's placed at the door of your tent.

HOW GOD PROVIDES (3)

And the manna ceased.
Joshua 5:12

*L*isten: "That very day, they ate . . . the produce of the land: unleavened bread and roasted grain" (Jos 5:11 NIV). How do you get bread and grain? Produce them! God was saying: "I can provide through men or deliver it from heaven, but now I'm planning to bless the work of your hands."

Some of us fall apart when the manna ceases. "Lord, what's wrong? Nobody's helping me anymore!" Nothing's wrong. It's time to grow up and start believing God to bless you so that you can *become* a blessing to others, instead of constantly asking Him to bless others so they can take care of you! It's time to discover your gifts and start making a difference. You don't need God or anybody else, to do for you what you can do for yourself!

You don't require a lot of talent in the wilderness, just faith for your next meal. In essence, God told His people, "When you enter this land, I want you to live in such a way that the rest of the world will sit up, take notice and start asking, 'What have they got that we don't?'" Instead of us going to the world for advice, they should be coming to us for it! Jesus said, "You are the light of the world" (See Mt 5:14 NIV). That means you should be the brightest student, employee, parent or leader around. God told His people, "All the nations will call you blessed" (Mal 3:12 NIV). Who's He referring to? Those who unlock their talents, put them to work, and honor God in all they do!

HOW GOD PROVIDES (4)

They are bread for us.

Numbers 14:9

*L*isten: "Joshua and Caleb stood before the Israelites and said, 'Neither fear ye the people of the land; for they are bread for us.'" There's food in the fight! There are blessings in the battle! You can reach a place of maturity where you begin to *feed* off the very stuff the enemy throws at you. God's promises are "to him that overcometh" (Rev 3:21).

But Israel didn't want to fight. Actually, they wanted to stone the guys who forced them out of their comfort zone. As a result God said, "Not one of them will ever see the land I promised" (Nu 14:23 NIV). God's greatest pain is to be doubted. With a track record like His, could you blame Him? But are we so different? Before you answer, understand clearly that there are 3 things you'll always have to deal with.

(1) Wanting to stay where you are, because where God wants you to go means confronting your family-of-origin fears and conquering old habits the enemy has placed between you and your destiny.

(2) Instead of being confident because of what God has *already* done for you, you walk around talking like He's running on 1 or 2 cylinders.

(3) Even though you know the enemy is squatting on your property and defying you to do anything about it, you've no stomach for the fight. Tomorrow we'll talk about the enemies *inside the land,* but right now you need to look *within* yourself, and start dealing with those that have the ability to stop you from entering and enjoying what God has for you.

HOW GOD PROVIDES (5)

Because my servant Caleb has a different spirit and follows me
wholeheartedly, I will bring him into the land.

Numbers 14:24 NIV

*C*aleb had "a different spirit," one that dared to defy
the enemy and say: "We will swallow you up; you're just bread
for us." (See Nu 14:9 NIV). Instead of intimidating you, the
enemy's threats should nourish you and make you say, "Bring
it on: when the dust settles I'm coming out of this stronger than
I was when I went in."

Have you ever seen jet fighters being refueled in mid-
flight? Our God does that too! Just when you're thinking, "I
don't know how much longer I can take this," the Holy Spirit
comes along side, hooks you up, refills you and makes you an
even *bigger* threat to the enemy. It's time you understood how
much the enemy fears you and stop backing down, hiding out,
or trying to negotiate a truce with him.

Before Joshua's armies conquered Jericho, Rahab told his
spies, "We've heard how the Lord turned the Red Sea into a red
carpet and drowned the entire Egyptian army before your eyes"
(See Jos 2:10). Your reputation precedes you! The enemy
knows you're marked for blessing. He fears your every move.
That's what the battle is all about! Just keep fighting. When
God's on your side, obstacles become growth opportunities!
Listen: (a) "God . . . will soon crush Satan under your feet"
(Rom 16:20 NIV). (b) "I give . . . you power . . . over all the
power of the enemy" (Lk 10:19). (c) Greater is he that is in you,
than he that is in the world" (1Jn 4:4). And there are a whole lot
more promises where those came from!

HOW GOD PROVIDES (6)

The Lord is with us: fear them not.

Numbers 14:9

*M*odern Israel is *still* fighting over the place God gave them 4,000 years ago—a place of permanent provision, of covenant blessings, of such influence that they stay on the front page of every newspaper. And what was a physical place in the Old Testament, is now a *spiritual* place where every redeemed child of God has been called to dwell. But it's still a fight!

"The devil isn't bothering me," you say. Maybe that's because you're no threat to him! The moment you get serious about God, you're in for a fight! Did you think the devil was going to send you a congratulatory telegram? No, listen: "As servants of God we commend ourselves in every way: in great endurance; in troubles, hardships and distresses; in beatings, imprisonments and riots; in hard work, sleepless nights and hunger; in purity, understanding, patience and kindness; in the Holy Spirit and in sincere love; in truthful speech and in the power of God; with weapons of righteousness in the right hand and in the left; through glory and dishonor, bad report and good report; genuine, yet regarded as imposters; known, yet regarded as unknown; dying, and yet we live on; beaten, and yet not killed; sorrowful, yet always rejoicing; poor, yet making many rich; having nothing, and yet possessing everything" (2Co 6:4-10 NIV).

Go back and re-read those words several times. Why? *Because they're "basic requirements" for every citizen who wants to enjoy the benefits of God's kingdom.*

ARE YOU AN "URGENCY ADDICT?"

There is a time for everything.
Ecclesiastes 3:1 NLT

*U*ntil you value yourself you won't value your time. And until you value your time you won't use it wisely. Urgency is addictive. If you find yourself habitually reacting to outside demands, you may be "hooked." Like other addictions, urgency: (a) temporarily meets a need to feel needed; (b) creates a sense of "getting things done;" (c) falsely enhances your self-esteem; (d) often makes the problem worse because "haste makes waste." If you're an urgency addict consider this:
   (1) In our society busyness equals status; people *expect* you to be in demand. Now, while constantly abandoning your goals to help others accomplish theirs may make you feel more appreciated, it sidetracks you from your God-ordained purpose and creates a false sense of significance.
   (2) Sometimes it's hard to say no, because as a Christian you feel "obligated." But not every problem is a call for you to jump in and solve it. Your decision to get involved in anything should come from God. Before you react, pray! Listen: "In all thy ways acknowledge him, and he shall direct thy paths" (Pr 3:6). If you're a "fixer" by nature, you probably get fulfillment out of solving problems, meeting needs and expectations, influencing behavior and outcomes. "So what can I do?" you ask. Recognize that you're vulnerable to urgent pleas and have a hard time saying "No." *Identifying your response pattern can stop you from getting "hooked in," and help you to stay focused on what God's already called you to do.*

LEARN TO WAIT!

Having patiently waited, he obtained the promise.

Hebrews 6:15 NASB

*W*aiting is difficult, but it serves a vital purpose. Over 40 times in the Old Testament God says, "Wait." At 75, God promised to make Abraham the father of many nations. But he had to wait for 24 more years before he "obtained the promise." God promised to free Israel from Egyptian slavery, but it took 400 years, including 40 in the wilderness, before it even began to come to pass. Please notice 2 things:

First, what waiting accomplishes. Waiting isn't just something you have to do in order to get what you want. No, waiting produces patience, understanding, maturity, and character. What God accomplishes in you while you're waiting, is often more important than the thing you're waiting for. It also forces any potential weakness to the surface. The truth is, time spent waiting is time spent learning and growing!

Second, what waiting isn't. Waiting is not an excuse for dodging reality, shirking responsibility or not doing the right thing. For example, if you're in a financial mess because of overspending, don't sit around waiting for pennies from heaven. They're not coming! Instead discipline yourself and make it a priority to learn sound financial principles like budgeting, tithing, and not purchasing things until you can pay for them.

Above all else, waiting means making a *daily* decision to trust and obey God, even when things aren't going the way you planned. It's saying, "Lord, I'm counting on You—and I don't have a back-up plan!"

"A NEW COMMANDMENT" (1)

I give you a new commandment . . . love one another.
John 13:34 NRSV

$\mathcal{T}$his "new commandment" Jesus gave is truly amazing when you consider its historical background:

First, there was the law of revenge. Before Moses, the law of the land was the law of the jungle. It said, "If you hurt me I'll hurt you—and then some!" Enemies actively sought ways to settle old scores because revenge wasn't just acceptable—it was encouraged.

Next, there was the law of retribution. In Moses' time revenge was replaced with retribution which allowed, "An eye for eye, and a tooth for tooth," but no more. (See Ex 20:25). You could do to your enemies only what they'd done to you. Nowadays that sounds harsh, but back then it was major progress!

Now, there's the law of love. When Jesus said, "I give you a new commandment . . . love one another," it was a radically different approach. It meant you didn't have to get even, you could choose to forgive instead. This new commandment demonstrates the unconditional, sacrificial love God shows to us—then calls us to live the same way!

Here's how one class of high-school students demonstrated this law of love! When their buddy was undergoing chemotherapy and losing his hair, they showed their love and support by shaving their heads so he wouldn't be embarrassed about returning to class. A local newspaper photographed them with their bald heads, under a headline which read, "Everything We Do, We Do Together." *That's* the kind of love Jesus was talking about when He said, "Everyone will know that you are my disciples, if you . . . love . . . one another" (John 13:35 NRSV).

"A NEW COMMANDMENT" (2)

I give you a new commandment . . . love one another.
John 13:34 NRSV

*S*ome years ago General Omar Bradley made a business trip on a commercial airline, wearing a regular suit instead of his military uniform. When he reached his seat he started doing some paperwork. As it turned out, the man seated next to him was a young Army private who didn't recognize Bradley. So after take-off he turned to the General and said, "Since we're going to be together for a while, it would be nice if we got to know each other. My guess is that you're a banker." Not wishing to seem rude but needing to finish his work, Bradley replied, "No, I'm General Omar Bradley, a five-star general in the U.S. Army. I head up the Joint Chiefs of Staff at the Pentagon in Washington, D.C." Without missing a beat the young private replied, "Well, sir, that's a very important job. I sure hope you don't blow it!"

Your job is to love—don't blow it! God's love is the most powerful force the world's ever seen, and it's up to us to carry the torch and keep it burning! The Bible says, "Clothe yourselves with tenderhearted mercy, kindness, humility, gentleness, and patience . . . [But] the most important . . . clothing you must wear is love. [It] . . . binds us all together in perfect harmony" (Co 3:12-14 NLT). It's nice to quote scriptures, pray long articulate prayers, study theology and attend church, but only when people see your love, will they be impacted by your life. *Love, not words, is the real test of your discipleship!*

IT'S A PROCESS

Unwrap him and let him go.

John 11:44 NLT

*W*henever you accept Christ, He changes you from the inside out. But certain experiences in your past can slow you down, keep you bound, and determine how you see yourself. While the Holy Spirit does the initial work, transformation is a process. It doesn't happen overnight; it takes time.

When Jesus stood at His friend's grave and called, "Lazarus, come forth" His friend who'd been dead for 4 days shuffled out, *still* bound from head to toe like a mummy. Notice, his old grave clothes which were a major hindrance to him, didn't just *fall off* the minute Jesus called him. No, Jesus told his friends "Unwrap him and let him go," and with their help Lazarus was freed to pursue a new life.

The Bible says, "Anyone . . . in Christ . . . is a new creation; the old has gone, the new has come" (See 2Co 5:17 NIV). When Jesus saves you, you emerge from the tomb wrapped in the grave clothes of your past. What past? (a) Negative influences and thought patterns. (b) Low self-esteem. (c) Old addictions and habits. (d) Destructive relationships. That's why God sends people to love you, unwrap you and release you into your potential.

It's important that you *identify* these relationships and *build* your life around them. It's also why you need to develop an intimate relationship with God through prayer and Bible reading. Through His Word you get an accurate picture of how He sees you. Through prayer you get to know His heart and start seeing yourself through His eyes. When that happens, you'll never see yourself the same way again!

CAREFUL OR FEARFUL?

The Lord . . . will deliver me.

1 Samuel 17:37 NIV

*F*earful people often excuse their fear as just being careful! They say, "I'm not afraid, I'm just being careful. You can't rush these things, you know." Doubtless King Saul wouldn't have admitted he was afraid to face Goliath, yet behind all his talk of "calculated risks" and discussions about "what was best for the nation," he was just plain *scared*. As you evaluate your response to the risks you face right now, ask yourself: "Am I careful or fearful?" You must wrestle that question to the ground!

You see: (1) Careful is thoughtful; fearful is emotional. (2) Careful is fueled by information; fearful is fueled by imagination. (3) Careful calculates risk; fearful avoids risk. (4) Careful wants to achieve success; fearful wants to avoid failure. (5) Careful is concerned about progress; fearful is concerned about protection.

Saul was fearful; he did nothing. David was careful; he moved forward and killed the giant. And in that moment something significant happened. The Israelites suddenly got the courage to fight. The Philistines, who moments before had been beating their chests, suddenly ran for cover. One act of bravery, just one, gave everybody else what they lacked—courage. And *that's* the heart of leadership! Leaders instill courage in the hearts of those who follow—not just by their words, but by their actions.

So if you want to be a leader, you have to go first! In stepping out, you'll give the gift of *courage* to those who are watching. And depending on your situation, your one act of courage may change everything around you for the better!

FINDING BALANCE

He who abides in me . . . bears much fruit.

John 15:5 NAS

*I*n John 15, Jesus said that those who abide in Him bear fruit, more fruit, and much fruit. But first you have to find balance between 2 popular extremes:

(1) Those who say the Christian life is only a bed of roses —that you'll never be sick, broke, or have problems; that unless you live in a mansion and drive a Mercedes you don't have faith. No, real faith is proven in affliction. It's when you've nothing, that you need faith to believe God's your provider. It's when you're sick, that you need faith to believe He's your Healer. Listen: "He who abides . . . bears much *fruit.*" The blessing comes from abiding—you get the fruit on the other side. Getting people excited about fruit before they even have seed means they end up serving God for what He does, instead of who He is. And one more thought: don't use your faith to belittle others. Just because you've graduated, don't burn down the school! The God who brought you through will bring them through too!

(2) Those who think the Christian life is only a battlefield —they love to talk about how the enemy's always attacking them and how difficult life is. Check your Bible: Satan attacks those who are in line for promotion!

The truth lies in the middle. To be mature you need balance. Sure you'll be pruned and cut back for greater fruitfulness, but that's when it's even *more* important to abide. Don't give up and don't collapse—beyond this test you'll have a testimony!

SUCCESS IN THE PLACE OF FAILURE

We have toiled all night and caught nothing; nevertheless at Your word I will let down the net.

Luke 5:5 NKJV

$\mathcal{G}$od has a wonderful way of restoring us when we've failed. He doesn't: (a) criticize or belittle us; we do that to ourselves; (b) simply overlook our shortcomings; (c) tell us to try harder next time. *No, He brings victory from defeat by taking us back to the place of failure and producing something good from it.*

We assume that because we weren't successful at something, it wasn't God's will. But the truth usually is, we failed because we relied on our *own* strength instead of His! After Peter had fished all night and caught nothing, Jesus didn't say, "Don't worry, you won't be doing this much longer anyway." No, He said, "Row . . . into the deep water and let your nets down" (Lk 5:4 CEV). When Peter obeyed, "they caught so many fish that their nets began ripping" (Lk 5:6 CEV).

God has a way of getting our attention through failure! That rocky marriage, that child you're about to give up on, that assignment that seems too hard, God won't just let you abandon them. No, He wants you to learn from them, to discover the difference He can make in your situation. Even though Peter wanted to give up, he replied, "Nevertheless at Your Word I will let down the net." One word from Jesus, just one, can change everything and put success within your reach again. And where do you find such a word? In His presence— and in His book.

"SHOUTIN' TIME!"

Give a loud shout; then the wall . . . will collapse.

Joshua 6:5 NIV

*A*re you fighting a battle you're afraid you won't win? You won't, if you're depending on yourself. Today God is saying to you: "Do not be afraid . . . for the battle is not yours but God's" (2Ch 20:15 NIV). And God's never lost one yet!

Listen to what God told Joshua, "I have delivered Jericho into your hands, along with its king and its fighting men" (Jo 6:2 NIV). Note, God didn't say, "I *will* deliver" or "I *might* deliver." No, He said, "I *have* delivered Jericho into your hands!" Israel already had the victory. Now they were being called to *act* on it and take possession. But the question remained, how?

Joshua told the Israelites, "When you hear . . . the trumpets . . . give a loud shout; then the wall of the city will collapse and [you] will go . . . straight in" (Jo 6:5 NIV). Nobody in his right mind would expect a shout, no matter how loud, to bring down the walls of a city. But this was no ordinary shout—it was a *shout of faith* based on a *guarantee* God had made to them. Even though victory looked impossible at this point, when Israel shouted, God responded by bringing down the walls and opening the door to the Promised Land.

When you're facing overwhelming odds the last thing you feel like doing is shouting, right? But here's why you need to do it regardless: (1) The shout of praise always precedes victory. (2) It puts your faith "on the record." (3) It confuses the enemy. (4) Obedience, even when you don't understand, always brings results. *So shout today—for the victory is yours!*

FAVOR

She won his favor.

Esther 2:17 NIV

"*N*ow the king was attracted to Esther more than any of the other women, and she won his favor" (Es 2:17 NIV). One moment of God's favor can change everything! If you want God's favor in your life, study the life of Esther.

(1) She prepared herself. Listen: "Before a girl's turn came to go in to King Xerxes, she had to complete twelve months of beauty treatments" (Es 2:12 NIV). Study. Preparation. Discipline. Those who pay the price to succeed aren't lucky, they're rewarded!

(2) She sought only the king's approval. Esther probably turned a lot of heads, but she sought only the approval of one— the king. Why do you want God's anointing? To please Him, or others? The higher God takes you, the more frequently you'll have to answer that question.

(3) She discovered her assignment and fulfilled it. Haman planned to annihilate every Jew. Only someone greater could save them, like the king's wife. That's when Mordecai told Esther, "You have come to the kingdom for such a time as this" (Es 4:14 NKJV). You were born with a set of instructions; you'll discover them in the presence of the One who made you. God told Jeremiah, "Before you were born, I set you apart" (Jer 1:5 NIV). That's why you don't fit in anywhere else.

(4) She gave her all. To approach the king uninvited meant death, but Esther recognized a cause greater than herself, "If I perish, I perish" (Es 4:16). And the result? The nation was saved and Haman was hanged on his own gallows. God's favor —it's an awesome thing!

DON'T LOSE HOPE!

You will have courage because you will have hope.
Job 11:18 NLT

*T*here's a mental condition that's essential to the life God wants you to live. It's the fuel your heart runs on. It's the single biggest difference between those who persevere and those who give up. It's called—*hope.* It's a powerful force that arouses your mind to explore every possibility and overcome every obstacle.

Hope is what makes couples say "I do," without any guarantees, and later after all the broken promises, makes them pick up the pieces and try again. It's why composers agonize over a score and artists over a canvas, believing some glimmer of beauty will emerge from the struggle.

As an old man, the painter Henri Matisse was crippled with agonizing arthritis. When asked why he continued to wrap his swollen fingers around a paint brush every day he replied, "The pain goes away; the beauty endures." *That's hope!* Laboring to paint the ceiling of the Sistine Chapel, Michelangelo grew so discouraged that he wanted to quit, but every morning hope pushed him up the ladder to fulfill his magnificent vision. Hope made Abraham leave home without knowing where God was taking him. It's what made Paul defy the system. It's what fueled the Old Testament prophets to keep taking on city hall! David said, "For you have been my hope . . . my confidence since my youth" (Ps 71:5 NIV).

Don't lose hope! You can survive many losses, but lost hope paralyzes your spirit. Listen: "You will have courage because you will have hope" (Job 11:18 NLT). So regardless of your circumstances, keep your hope alive today by—staying focused on God!

SPIRITUAL VOYEURISM

The people remained at a distance,
while Moses approached . . . where God was.

Exodus 20:21 NIV

*N*o doubt the Israelites wondered, "What does God's presence *feel* like? What does His voice *sound* like? What does His glory *look* like?" Only Moses knew. And it seems that most folks were happy to let it stay that way. Listen: "The people remained at a distance, while Moses approached . . . where God was." Sound familiar? Like S.M.O. Christians? (Sunday morning only!) They told Moses: *"You* tell us what God says . . . but don't let God speak directly to us." Why? Were they afraid God might tell them something they didn't particularly want to hear? When you haven't carried out His last set of instructions, it's hard to be enthused about the next set.

John writes: "How can we be sure that we belong to him? By obeying his commandments . . . those who obey God's Word really do love him" (See 1Jn 2:3-5 NLT). So, how about it? Are you only interested in being a 'spiritual voyeur'—an onlooker who gets a vicarious thrill out of watching God move in the lives of others, instead of accepting the discipline required to have a personal relationship with Him yourself? Do you want His gifts and His favor, but not the commitment that goes along with them?

God doesn't want you to be infatuated with the Bible, or the church, or even His blessings. No, He wants you to fall in love with *Him!* He's looking for a bride, not a girlfriend, somebody who'll stick with Him when the going gets tough. So, are you ready to put on the ring of commitment today?

SLIGHTLY IRREGULAR

Make allowance for each other's faults.

Colossians 3:13 NLT

*M*ost department stores have a section with merchandise labeled, "as is," or "slightly irregular." There's a stain that won't come out, a missing handle, a wobbly leg. Now, they don't tell you where the flaw is, you have to look for it. And once you buy it there's no return, no refund and no exchange. Stop and look around you! You're living in this department. Think about those you know and love. Aren't they "slightly irregular?" A flaw here, a streak of deception there, a hot temper, a passive/aggressive attitude? If you've been looking for perfection, you've walked down the wrong aisle! The only way to have a relationship with anybody is to love and accept them "as is."

Don't buy into the myth that most folks are normal (whatever that means) except the people in your life. Based on that misconception relationships become an endless quest to *fix* others, *control* them, or *pretend* they are what they're not. Thomas Merton says, "Love is letting those we love be perfectly themselves, and not twisting them to fit our own image. Otherwise we love only the reflection of ourselves we see in them." One hallmark of maturity is acknowledging that nobody's perfect, and loving them despite their shortcomings. Paul says "Make allowance for each other's faults," so that when you discover them, and you will, you're not disillusioned. But there's another lesson here. It means acknowledging something you probably don't like to admit. "And what's that?" you ask. *That you belong in the "slightly irregular" department too!*

THE COURAGE TO FACE CURRENT REALITY

Anoint thine eyes with eyesalve, that thou mayest see.
Revelation 3:18

*P*rofessor Howard Henricks was once asked to assess the declining membership at a certain church. After attending service for several weeks he met with the board and made this recommendation. "Put a fence around it and charge admission so that people can come and see how church was done in the 1950's." In other words, you're hopelessly behind!

Because our ego is on the line we've a tendency to put a positive spin on things, while ignoring all evidence to the contrary. The danger is, that over time we lose sight of what is *actually* happening around us. Good leaders refuse to do that; they're relentless in their quest to know the score. They root out misinformation and refuse to reward those who deliver it. In so doing, they create a culture that's transparent concerning what *is,* and what *isn't* taking place.

To ensure that you live this way, obey these 7 commandments: (1) Thou shalt not pretend. (2) Thou shalt not turn a blind eye. (3) Thou shalt not exaggerate. (4) Thou shalt not shoot the bearer of bad news. (5) Thou shalt not hide behind the numbers. (6) Thou shalt not ignore constructive criticism. (7) Thou shalt not isolate thyself.

Attempting to make progress while turning a blind eye to reality is like treading water: it can only go on for so long. Eventually you sink. You must be willing to face the truth regardless of how painful it might be. And if you don't like what you see—change it!

"CLASSES FOR HUSBANDS!"

Be good husbands to your wives.
Honor them, delight in them. . . . Treat [them] as equals.

1 Peter 3:7 TM

*S*ome wag composed this ad entitled, "Classes for Husbands:" Sir, maybe you'll see something you need to sign up for!

How to fill ice cube trays. Toilet rolls: do they grow on the holder? Fundamental differences between the laundry basket and the floor. Dishes: can they levitate and fly into the sink or dishwasher? Loss of identity (or) losing the remote control to your wife! Finding things by looking in the right place instead of screaming and ransacking the house. Health watch: bringing your wife flowers isn't harmful to your health. Real men ask for directions: (survivor testimonials). Basic differences between your mother and your wife! Becoming the ideal shopping companion: (relaxation & breathing techniques). Fight "Cerebral Atrophy" by remembering birthdays & anniversaries: (shock therapy & lobotomies available).

Now, on a more serious note, if you want to know what God has to say to husbands, listen up: (a) "Go all out in your love for your wives . . . as Christ did for the church—a love marked by giving, not getting" (Eph 5:25 TM). (b) "Be good . . . to your wives. Honor them, delight in them. . . . Treat [them] as equals." (c) "Live happily with the woman you love . . . the wife God gives you is your best reward" (Ecc 9:9 TLB). So the next time your wife gets under your skin, instead of complaining, remember the qualities that first attracted you to her, and the blessings she brings to your marriage: like caring, nurturing, trust, satisfaction, fulfillment, helpfulness, and happiness. *And if you love her—tell her often!*

UNMET EXPECTATIONS

Are you really the Messiah . . . or should we keep looking?

Matthew 11:3 NLT

*J*ohn didn't deserve imprisonment in a filthy dungeon. After all, he was the forerunner of the Messiah and the voice of repentance in the community; plus, he was Jesus' cousin! So, he sent a message to Jesus asking, "Are you really the Messiah . . . or should we keep looking?"

Paraphrased: "When are you going to get me out of here?" It was a human question motivated by unmet expectations.

Have you ever been there? Have you ever wondered, "Where's God when I'm hurting?" And it feels even worse when you're *working* for Him! Writing about her daughter's death, Meg Woodson says: "I'll never forget those shrill, piercing screams; that the God who could have helped, looked down on this young woman who was devoted to Him . . . and decided to sit on His hands and let her death top the horror charts." Talk about unmet expectations!

The Jesus who walked on water, cast out demons and raised the dead could easily have saved John. But He didn't. Instead He sent back word, which, in essence, said, "Don't worry, everything's on target. The Kingdom is being built; you fulfilled your assignment well" (See Mt 11:4-5). It probably wasn't the answer John hoped for or expected. He was looking for solutions to temporal problems, while Jesus was busy establishing an eternal kingdom.

So, next time God doesn't seem to meet your expectations or time frames, it's not that He doesn't care, it's that He sees the big picture, and is handling issues you can't begin to comprehend. So trust Him!

CHURCH BUILDERS AND CHRIST SEEKERS

Having a form of godliness but denying its power.
2 Timothy 3:5 NKJV

*W*hen the ancient Emperor Shah Jahan's favorite wife died, he decided to honor her by building an elaborate temple for her tomb. So he placed her wooden coffin in the middle of a field and the builders began to build around it. No expense was spared: her final resting place would be spectacular. However, as the years passed the building project itself consumed them, crowding out everything else. Then one day while he was working on the site, the Shah noticed an old, dust-covered wooden box and ordered it to be thrown out. The one he'd originally planned to honor was discarded—but the temple was erected anyhow.

If you think that's hard to believe, next time you're in church just look around! Those who truly find Jesus never forget Him. They stand impressed before His empty tomb and occupied throne like servants before a king, while those who see just the edifice, doze and yawn. Their eyes wander. Their feet shuffle. They're bored. Oh, they love the building, know the programs inside out and even praise the pastor. But the Bible describes them as, "Having a form of godliness but denying its power." Why? Because the One they originally came to worship, is missing from among them. Church builders and Christ seekers in the same church, on the same day, at the same time. One sees the building with all its activities and says, "What a church!" The other sees the Lord and says, "What a Christ!" Which one are you?

"PROMISE-PRAYERS" FOR YOUR CHILDREN

I will pour out my spirit and my blessings on your children.
Isaiah 44:3 TLB

*I*n the Old Testament, parents laid hands on their children, passing the blessing of God from generation to generation. You can do the same! You can pray, claiming God's promises over your family, declaring that His will be done in their lives. Are such prayers effective? Absolutely! God says, "The words I speak. They will not return to me empty. They make the things happen that I want to happen, and they succeed in doing what I send them to do" (Is 55:11 NCV). Here are some "promise-prayers" you can pray on behalf of your children.

(1) "I will pour out my Spirit and my blessings on your children . . . 'I am the Lord's,' they'll proudly say" (Is 44:3-5 TLB). (2) "My Spirit and my words that I give you will never leave you or your children or your grandchildren, now and forever" (Is 59:21 NCV). (3) "Do not weep any longer, for I will reward you. Your children will come back to you from the distant land of the enemy. There is hope for your future says the Lord" (Jer 31:16-17 NLT). (4) "You can also be very sure that God will rescue the children of the godly" (Pr 11:21 TLB). (5) "Blessed is the man who fears the Lord, who finds great delight in his commands. His children will be mighty in the land; the generation of the upright will be blessed. Wealth and riches are in his house, and his righteousness endures forever" (Ps 112:1-3 NIV).

(3) *Clarity.* Uncertain times require clear directions. The vision may come at once, but the steps are revealed over time. Don't allow your lack of answers to leave you paralyzed. Be clear about your goal, even though you're not certain as to the details.

(4) *Coaching.* You may be better than most, but without a coach you will never be as good as you could be. Elisha needed Elijah. Timothy needed Paul. If you're hoping to learn everything from personal experience, good luck—you'll have to outlive Methuselah.

(5) *Character.* You can lead without character, but you can't be a leader worth following. Character provides the moral authority necessary to bring together the people and resources needed to fulfill God's plan for your life. Your talent has the potential to take you places where your character can't sustain you. That thought ought to humble you—and keep you on your knees.

STAYING ON THE CUTTING EDGE (1)

For this reason was I born.

John 18:37 NIV

*P*astor, here are 3 principles you need to live by:
*(1) Don't go to your Bible for something to preach, go for
something to eat.* Those who listen to you, know when you're
saying things that aren't a reality in your own life.
(2) Love the people, but only fall in love with the Lord.
They're God's people, not yours! Your assignment to them is
for a reason and a season. When it's complete, release them into
God's care. Then get a life—and center it around Christ.
(3) Your message is timeless, your methods are temporary.
What brought you to where you are, won't necessarily get you
to where you need to be. Everything God calls, moves. To be
"called" means you'll always be moving *from* something,
toward something, otherwise you're not called at all! If what
you're doing isn't working, do something different. If it's not
productive, cut it off, and go back to God for fresh instructions.
If your goal is to fit comfortably into the framework of where
you started, you'll never enjoy what God has for you up the
road. You can't pray for growth and defy change. Do you know
why Jesus didn't heal all blind people the same way? So we'd
never be able to claim, *"This* is the way God works."
"That's heavy stuff," you say. Sure, it's the stuff that keeps
you sharp, keeps you fresh, keeps you growing, keeps you on
your knees, and keeps you effective in the service of God.

STAYING ON THE CUTTING EDGE (2)

And the Lord said unto Moses, "Go on before the people."
Exodus 17:5

*T*here are 2 stages you must go through as a leader:
Stage 1. Spending time with your people! For 400 years
Israel had been leaderless. They'd no identity. They'd a slave
mentality. So Moses walked amongst them, because sheep gain
confidence by smelling the shepherd and rubbing up against
him. Pastor, if you're afraid to get close to your people, maybe
you've too much to hide. When people feel loved, they listen
better because they feel like a family.
Stage 2. Getting out ahead of your people! How do you
know when it's time to move to this stage? Listen: "The people
murmured against Moses" (Ex 17:3). Why? Because there was
no water and thirsty sheep always complain. When the
murmuring starts you've probably spent too long socializing.
It's time to transition! Listen: "The Lord said unto Moses, 'Go
on before the people . . . smite the rock, and there shall come
water out of it'" (Ex 17:5-6). When you stop trying to fit in and
get out ahead of them, God will give you supernatural
resources equal to the challenge. No vision is ever stopped by
lack of finances, only by a lack of faith, courage, and a
willingness to get out on the cutting edge and discover that God
can "supply all your needs according to his riches in glory"
(Php 4:19). According to what? His riches! And they're waiting
for the one who's willing to get out of their comfort zone and
claim them. Is there a message here for you?

ARE YOU ENVIOUS?

Saul was David's enemy from that time forward.
1 Samuel 18:29 NRS

*D*r. Seuss wrote hundreds of children's stories. But one of his most famous was about *The Grinch,* a cartoon character who got so jealous of others, he would bite himself! Envy does that; it makes you target others, but ends up consuming you.

In the Old Testament God blessed King Saul and elevated him to the highest position in Israel. But when David's great military accomplishments were recognized by the people, Saul became insecure and threatened. Instead of *rejoicing* that God had sent David to help him fight the enemy, Saul grew *resentful* and became "David's enemy from that time forward."

Envy is so destructive; it poisons your life by making you: (a) compare yourself unfavorably with others; (b) forfeit your joy and contentment; (c) become ungrateful and self-centered; (d) assume that God's resources aren't sufficient for Him to bless others and still bless you. Go back, re-examine those 4 things and ask, "Are they working in my life?" Saul's envy so preoccupied him that he neglected what was really important, brought pain and suffering all around, and eventually destroyed his own family and future.

When you're unable to rejoice in the success of others, you're on dangerous ground! Don't let envy infect your attitude; repent before it robs you of your destiny. Remember, God made *all* of us His children when *none* of us deserved it! So whenever you feel resentful toward some ask God to remind you of the many ways He's blessed you—when you didn't deserve it!

ASK THE LORD ABOUT IT!

The children struggled . . . within her; and she said,
"If all is well, why am I like this?"

Genesis 25:22 NKJV

*T*hroughout her pregnancy, Rebekah sensed the conflict that already existed between the twin boys she was carrying. They even competed for attention and favor in utero! Sometimes you'll experience that same tension when you're trying to birth your dreams. They can appear to be in conflict with each other, with one seeming to cancel out another. But immediately this kind of inner conflict arose, the Bible says Rebekah "asked the Lord about it" (Ge 25:22 TLB). That's always a wise move!

Rebekah said, "If all is well, why am I like this?" Can't you relate? How many times have you experienced fear or foreboding in the middle of your success and wondered, "What's wrong with me? Things are going well, so why am I so anxious?" You've finally achieved your business goals and your family is starting to come together after a long hard struggle. But now instead of feeling happy, you're disappointed that you're not experiencing the joy and fulfillment you expected; you're actually worrying about how your choices will impact your future. At times like this, bring your turmoil to the Lord. Ask Him for help with the inner conflict you're experiencing; to give you peace concerning the dream within you.

And remember—no matter what you achieve, its ability to satisfy you is limited. No amount of success can ever take the place of God. So learn to draw your strength and fulfillment from Him, instead of relying on your own accomplishments.

WHAT DOES EASTER MEAN TO YOU?

Is it nothing to you, all you who pass by?

Lamentations 1:12 NIV

*O*ne day during the1930's, John Griffin, who controlled a railway drawbridge over the Mississippi River, took his young son to work with him. After putting the massive drawbridge up, Griffin was eating lunch when suddenly he heard the whistle of the Memphis Express roaring towards the crossing. Leaping from the observation deck he ran to throw the control switch. Glancing down, his heart stopped! His son had fallen into the gears trapping his leg in the cogs.

Desperately he tried to devise a rescue plan. But there was no time. His son was down there—but there were 400 passengers on the train! Griffin knew what he had to do. Burying his face in his arm, he pushed the master switch just in time to lower the bridge into place as the train thundered across. Then raising his head he looked into the passing windows with tear-filled eyes. There were businessmen casually reading the newspaper, ladies sipping coffee and children eating ice cream. Nobody even looked at the control house or glanced down at the great gearbox. In agony Griffin cried out, "I sacrificed my son for you people. Don't you care?" But as the train rushed by, nobody heard the anguished father's words.

Today as we consider the cross where God sacrificed His Son for each of us, He's asking, "Is it nothing to you, all who pass by?" Our question then becomes: "What . . . shall I do with Jesus who is called Christ?" (Mt 27:22 NKJV). Today, accept Him as your Lord and Savior.

HE DID IT TO BRING YOU TO GOD

He was not guilty, but He suffered for those who are . . .
to bring you to God.

1 Peter 3:18 NCV

*S*oldiers may have nailed Jesus to the cross, but what held Him there? The knowledge that it was necessary for Him to "be sin . . . so that . . . we might become the righteousness of God" (2Co 5:21 NIV). The reason Jesus didn't call an army of angels to save Him was because He'd rather give up His life, than give up on you.

W. A. Criswell writes: "In a dream I saw the Savior. His back was bare and there was a soldier lifting up his hand and bringing down that awful cat-o'-nine-tails . . . I rose and grasped his arm to hold it back. When I did, the soldier turned in astonishment and looked at me. And when I looked back at him I recognized—myself."

In Mel Gibson's movie, *The Passion,* multitudes were moved to tears by the hideous nature of the crucifixion. Underlying it all were 2 clear messages: (1) *This* was the price required to redeem each of us. (2) *This* is what we need to keep before us each time we're tempted to sin by "doing our own thing."

We struggle to comprehend God's love for us because we've nothing to measure it by; nobody has ever loved us like He does, and nobody ever will. The cross made it possible for us, "to walk into God's presence" (See He 10:19). No matter what you've done or how far you've fallen, you can receive God's love and mercy. What makes you a Christian isn't perfection—it's grace!

THE TOMB IS EMPTY!

I am the resurrection, and the life.

John 11:25

Nine-year-old Philip had Down's syndrome. In Sunday school the kids made fun of him because he was different. The Sunday before Easter the teacher gave each child a plastic egg and asked them to look for symbols of new life like seeds and leaves, then place them inside the egg. The idea was to open their eggs the next Sunday and discuss what they'd found. When the kids gathered they'd collected things like flowers, butterflies and rocks. But when the teacher opened Philip's egg it was empty. One kid said, "That's not fair, he didn't do it right!" Philip tugged at the teacher's sleeve and said, "I did do it right. It's empty because the tomb is empty. That's why we have new life." The class gasped—and from then on Philip became part of the group.

But Philip's family knew his time was short; too many problems for one small body. So, that summer he died. As the class of 8-year-olds faced the reality of death they marched up to the altar—but not with flowers. Together with their teacher they each placed an empty plastic egg on their friend's tiny casket.

Jesus said, "I am the resurrection and the life, he that believeth on me though he were dead, yet shall he live." Jesus is the only man ever to make an appointment beyond the grave —and show up for it! And His resurrection guarantees ours. If you live long enough you'll experience the heartache of burying those you love. But Easter guarantees you'll meet them again, alive, immortal, glorified, and just like Jesus!

CHANGING YOUR FAMILY DYNAMICS!

Tear down your father's altar to Baal.

Judges 6:25 NIV

$\mathcal{M}$ark Twain said he spent a lot of money tracing his family tree, then twice as much trying to keep it a secret! That reminds us of the family that wanted its history written, so they hired a professional biographer. However, they were worried about Uncle George, the black sheep of the family who'd been executed in the electric chair for murder. "No problem," said the biographer. "I'll say that Uncle George occupied a chair of applied electronics at an important government institution. He was attached to his position by the strongest of ties, and his death came as a real shock."

When it comes to your upbringing or your family's past, you can't do much except learn from it. But you can do a lot about your future! Your parents may have stumbled in spiritual blindness, but you can walk in the light—and take your family with you! Gideon grew up in a family of idol worshippers. One night God told him, "Tear down your father's altar. . . .Then build a proper kind of altar to the Lord" (Jud 6:25-26 NIV). Was that easy? No, by nature Gideon was very fearful. Furthermore, the townsfolk wanted to stone him for doing it. But he surrendered his life to God, and ended up changing his entire family!

So, who's going to change *your* family dynamics? If not you, who? If not now, when? Gideon discovered that when you work with God, He works with you. So, with God's help you can change the dynamics in your family—starting with yourself!

GUIDANCE (1)

He will be our guide even to the end.

Psalm 48:14 NIV

*H*ow come when someone speaks to God we say, "They're praying," but when they claim that God speaks to them we say "They're flaky?" Has God suddenly stopped speaking to His children? Would you stop speaking to *yours?*

John Calvin described God's guidance as "the inner testimony of the Holy Spirit." Saint Ignatius called it "movements of the soul—thoughts, feelings, or desires . . . given to us by God." These may come as a conviction of sin, an assurance of God's love, or the call to do a certain thing. But they're "a must" for the Spirit-guided life.

To hear from God you must be receptive. And sometimes —desperate! During a rough time in Jacob's life God appeared to him in a dream, saying, "I am with you and will watch over you wherever you go" (Ge 28:15 NIV). When Jacob awoke the next morning he said, "Surely the Lord is in this place, and I was not aware of it" (Ge 28:16 NIV). "Not aware," do those words describe *you?*

As you read these words your thoughts are being guided by a writer. Don't you think God can do the same, or better? Actually, God can guide your thoughts *without* the aid of intervening sounds or images.

Look what happened to Samuel when he was a boy. God spoke to him one night in the temple, but he didn't know it was God speaking. He needed the help of Eli the priest to learn to recognize the voice of God. But when he did, his life changed dramatically—and yours will too!

GUIDANCE (2)

He will be our guide even to the end.

Psalm 48:14 NIV

*B*efore talking about what guidance is, let's understand what it's not:

(1) Insider information. We give little thought to spiritual guidance until we face something major like, who to marry, which house to buy, what stock to invest in. Often what we want isn't guidance it's insider information. The key to knowing whether you really want God's guidance is by asking, "How often do I seek it when I'm not facing difficulties?"

(2) A badge of importance. God once spoke to a donkey. Now, what if the donkey had put on airs and considered itself an exalted spiritual class, above all the other quadrupeds?

(3) Passivity. One man said he decided not to seek a certain job on the grounds that it would be a sign of God's will if he got it without trying. So, does that mean whatever happens as a result of our passivity, is God's will? That's like sitting in the middle of a busy highway saying, "If I don't get run over by a car, I'll know it's God's doing and not me acting in the flesh."

(4) Avoiding risk. Sometimes we don't really want guidance, we want safety! Decision-making can be scary— and lonely! Even small decisions can create anxiety. God wants us to develop good judgment, and there's no way to do it apart from making choices, taking risks, and occasionally failing. Our Father wants mature children, not robots. His purpose in guidance isn't merely to get us to perform the right actions, but to become the right kind of people.

GUIDANCE (3)

He will be our guide even to the end.
Psalm 48:14 NIV

*S*o, how can we be guided by the Holy Spirit?
(1) By listening continually. Thomas Kelly wrote, "There is a way of ordering our mental life on more than one level at once. On one level we may be thinking, discussing, seeing . . . but . . . at a more profound level, we may also be in prayer . . . and a gentle receptiveness to divine breathings."

(2) By being responsive. What use is guidance if you're not willing to follow it? And what about the guidance you've already received through the Scriptures? Frank Laubach, whose life was an experiment in listening to God, wrote, "I never lived until I reached the place where I wholly resolved, and then re-resolved, that I would find God's will, and that I would do it though every fiber in me said no, and that I would win the battle in my thoughts. It was as though some deep artesian well had been struck in my soul . . . money, praise, poverty, opposition—these made no difference, for they will all alike be forgotten in a thousand years, but this spirit which comes to a mind set upon continuous surrender, this spirit is timeless life."

(3) By listening in spite of your doubts. Have the words "I believe the Lord told me" been abused? You bet. Sometimes ministers use them as a ploy to get money. But don't throw out the baby with the bath water! The truth is, we won't grow spiritually if we close ourselves off to the guidance of the Holy Spirit. We must believe—mind-blowing as it sounds—that God really can and does speak to us.

SHORT-CUTS!

*Listen for God's voice . . . he's the one
who will keep you on track.*

Proverbs 3:6 TM

*A*re you tired of waiting for God? Are you tempted to get behind the wheel and take over? Before you do remember this: a short-cut can short-circuit your destiny! It happens on God's timetable, not yours.

After Samuel anointed David to be king, he had to stand back and wait for 7 long years while Saul jeopardized Israel's future and forced him into hiding. Then one of those "short-cuts" showed up. One of David's soldiers discovered Saul defenseless and asleep in his tent, so he came to David and told him, "God has delivered your enemy into your hand . . . Let me strike him."

What an opportunity! Get rid of the man who wants to kill you. Come out of hiding and claim your throne. After all, you're already anointed to be King! It all made sense except for one thing—it wasn't part of God's plan. As much as David wanted to rule Israel he knew that to succeed he must do it God's way, according to God's timetable, or else it wouldn't have God's blessing and approval.

When Abishai offered to kill Saul he had only David's welfare at heart. That's sobering! Well-meaning friends can give you advice that's contrary to God's plan. *That's* when it's hard not to go along with it, or to defend your decision by rationalizing that the end justifies the means. Never let anyone, however well-intentioned, persuade you to do what you know is wrong. Instead, "Listen for God's voice . . . he's the one who will keep you on track."

ARE YOU GENEROUS?

Where your treasure is, there your heart will be also.
Matthew 6:21 NIV

We say that if we *ever* have a lot of money, we'll become generous. Who are we kidding! Prosperity has little to do with generosity. The average personal income in the State of Mississippi is the second lowest in the United States, yet that State is ranked 6th in charitable giving. By contrast, New Hampshire is ranked 6th in average personal income, but guess where they rank in charitable giving—45th!

A big income doesn't mean you have a big heart! Henry Ward Beecher warned that prosperity could actually make us *less* likely to give: "Watch, lest prosperity destroy generosity." People in the United States live in the most prosperous country in the world, during the most prosperous time in its history. Yet only 2.5 percent of their income goes to charity; that's lower than it was during the Great Depression!

If you desire to become a more generous person, don't wait for your income to change, change your heart! Find a reason to give every day. Look for a compelling cause or a worthy ministry. They're all around you. Listen: "When he saw the crowds, he had compassion on them, because they were harassed and helpless, like sheep without a shepherd" (Mt 9:36 NIV). When it comes right down to it, the recipients of our generosity are never churches, causes or institutions. Ultimately, the recipients are people—people loved and valued by God; people for whom Christ died! *So, what are you doing for others? How you answer that question is the measure of your generosity!*

LIVE BY YOUR VALUES

Let the process go on until . . . you . . .
have . . . mature character.

James 1:4 PHP

*Y*our life is a direct result of the values that have fashioned it. And those values are critical, because they function as:

(1) Your anchor. Without values you're adrift. Any storm can take you under, any current can carry you places you don't want to go. But with godly values, you've an anchor that holds you steady, even when the weather gets nasty. *(2) Your faithful friend.* Your core values are your life-long companions. Abraham Lincoln said, "When I lay down the reigns of this administration I want to have one friend left, and that friend is inside myself." *(3) Your compass.* Seasons change. Relationships change. Circumstances change. Goals change. But values don't! Like a compass, they always point toward the magnetic north. Is living this way easy? No! Doubters will discount you as foolish when you "walk by faith." People without family values won't understand your devotion to your family. The carnal minded won't understand your dedication to Christ. Those whose values are different from yours will try to convince you to follow them or lower your standards. Your values will be tested daily!

Speaking about the mid-life crisis that many people experience between the ages of 35-50, Dr. James Dobson says, "I believe mid-life crisis is more of a phenomenon of the wrong value system, than the age of the group in which it occurs. All of a sudden you realize that the ladder you've been climbing is leaning against the wrong wall." *Centering your life around Christ will keep that from happening to you!*

FAITH (1)

Draw near to God and he will draw near to you.

James 4:8 NASB

$\mathcal{J}$ohn Bisagno says, "Faith is at the heart of life. You go to a doctor whose name you cannot pronounce, he gives you a prescription you cannot read, you take it to a pharmacist you don't know, he gives you medication you don't understand— and you take it." *That's faith!*

Heaven help the atheist! When something good happens, who does he give thanks to? When something bad happens, who does he run to? If you wait until you can explain God, you'll never turn to Him. F.B. Mayer said, "Unbelief puts our circumstances between us and God. But faith puts God between us and our circumstances." Who wouldn't like to have the Creator of the universe helping them!

"But I wasn't raised in church. None of my friends or family are particularly religious. How do I find faith?" D.L. Moody said, "I prayed for faith and thought that some day it would come down and strike me like lightning, but faith did not seem to come. Then one day I read the tenth chapter of Romans, 'Faith comes by hearing, and hearing by the word of God.' I closed my Bible and prayed for faith. Then I opened my Bible and began to study—and faith has been growing ever since."

"But I don't know how to pray," you say. Just kneel and say, "Jesus, I accept You as my personal Savior and the Lord of my life." Then begin reading His Word and talking to Him each day. Go ahead, do it now—it's a step you'll never regret!

FAITH (2)

The apostles said to the Lord, "Increase our faith."

Luke 17:5 NIV

S. G. Holland, former Prime Minister of New Zealand, said, "Faith draws the poison from every grief, takes the sting from every loss, and quenches the fire of every pain; and only faith can do it."

Henry Nouwen says that our greatest challenge as disciples is, "to recognize and believe that unexpected events are not just disturbing interruptions . . . but the way in which God molds our hearts and prepares us." The deeper your faith in God, the greater its potential to carry you through the rough times. As Rabbi Abraham Heschel said, "Faith like Job's cannot be shaken, because it is the result of having been shaken."

But faith in Christ alone, gives us the assurance for heaven. When you die—what then? John Maxwell tells of attending the funeral of Jane Chapman, wife of his good friend Tom Chapman. During the service the following poem was read: "I am standing on the seashore. A ship appears, spreads her white sails to the morning breeze and starts for the ocean. She is an object of beauty and I stand watching her till at last she fades away on the horizon. Somebody at my side quietly says, 'She is gone.' Gone where? Gone from my vision, that is all; she is just as large as when I saw her last. The diminished size and loss of sight is in me, not her; and just at the moment when someone at my side says 'She is gone,' there are others who are watching her coming, and voices take up the joyful shout, 'Here she comes!'"

TAKE ACTION—NOW!

And others save with fear.

Jude 23

*W*hen someone you love gets caught up in a situation that has the power to hurt or destroy them, what should you do? Jude says, "And others save with fear." This word *save* is taken from a Greek word, meaning, "to take immediate, decisive and continuous action." The word *fear* is also taken from a Greek word, meaning "a strong dose of respect for something that's life-threatening, dangerous or alarming." Jude lets us know those who continue to disobey God, place themselves in a dangerous position. This is no game. Therefore he commands us to act immediately.

This places a heavy responsibility on us to do whatever we can to bring the misguided or rebellious one back to the place of safety. We don't have a choice—we must act fast, act deliberately and be continuous and unending in our efforts until we are certain that they are back in safe territory again.

So, the word for you today is, "take action—now!" The consequences are too serious to ignore. You must pray for wisdom then do everything within your power to rescue that one who's caught in a web of deceit, and do it as quickly as possible. Why don't you pray this prayer: "Lord help me to know exactly what to say and do. Give me Your heart, Your wisdom and Your boldness to say what needs to be said. Help me to love them enough to speak the truth to them. Use me as an instrument of grace to reach them as soon as possible. In Jesus' name, Amen."

WHY YOU'RE A TARGET!

By this I know that thou favorest me.

Psalm 41:11

*S*atan doesn't want you to know that the favor of God is upon you, that you've been blessed by Him and given all the good things you enjoy. Actually he doesn't want you to think that God's done *anything* for you! His lie is that you've no purpose, no power and no potential. To convince you he'll play the race card. If that doesn't work he'll play the childhood memories card. Finally he'll resort to reminding you of all the broken promises and shattered dreams. If you buy into it you'll have such low self-esteem that you won't believe God has blessed you in any way, or that you have any real possibility for success in life.

Understand this: no matter how limited your ability or lack-luster your accomplishments are to date, you don't have a thing God didn't give you. Your blessings have been made possible *only* because the Lord is on your side. Listen: "By this I know that thou favorest me, because mine enemy doth not triumph over me. And as for me, thou upholdest me in mine integrity, and settest me before thy face for ever" (Ps 41:11-12). David understood that his enemies were attacking him because they could see the favor of God on his life. Do you understand that too? If you don't, you won't expect the attack, understand the reason for the attack, or know how to respond to the attack. You're blessed, that's why you're a target! They're jealous because of what God has done for you. *How come they see it, but you don't?*

RULES TO LIVE BY

Don't live . . . unthinkingly.
Ephesians 5:17 TM

*H*ere are three to live by each day:

(1) Be grateful! Happiness is not about getting what you want, it's about enjoying what you've got! So keep your perspective and be grateful every day. Rudyard Kipling said, "Do not pay too much attention to fame, power or money. Some day you will meet a person who cares for none of these, then you will know how poor you are."

(2) Don't compare! When you see your neighbors buying new furnishings for their home, taking expensive vacations and driving new vehicles, does something stir inside you to do the same? Because someone appears to be in similar circumstances to you, doesn't mean anything. Your neighbors might earn twice as much. Or they may be in debt up to their eyeballs; or be three-quarters of the way to bankruptcy or divorce court. Don't make assumptions and don't try to be like someone else.

(3) Give! Bruce Larsen says, "Money is another pair of hands to heal, feed and bless the desperate families of the earth. In other words, money is my other self." But that's true only if you're willing to part with it! Money's like manure: if you let it pile up it stinks, if you spread it around it helps things grow! Jesus said, "Unto whomsoever much is given, of whom shall much be required" (Lk 12:48). Money gives you options the less fortunate can only pray for. On the other hand, how you *use* your money will be one of the biggest issues you'll face on Judgment Day. Think about it!

HAVING INTEGRITY

Stay close to anything that makes you want to do right.
2 Timothy 2:22 TLB

*C*omedian Red Allen said, "You only live once. But if you work it right, once is enough." So, how can you work it right? By living by your convictions every day; do that, and you'll have few regrets. Living a life of integrity involves: (a) thinking regularly about your values and letting them soak in; (b) constantly measuring your choices against God's Word and whenever it's appropriate, talking about them. This not only cements your values, it also adds a level of safety and accountability.

We get into trouble when our convictions and our impulses collide. When everything's going our way it's not difficult to live by our convictions. But "where the rubber meets the road," is when those convictions demand that we do something that'll *hurt* or *cost* us! Spiritual people do what's right, no matter how they feel about it. You don't *feel* your way into doing what's right; you act first, act scripturally, act consistently—your feelings follow suit. Usually it doesn't involve anything dramatic; the tough decisions are the every day ones. Character is built like a wall, one brick at a time.

Nice guys may appear to finish last, but usually it's because they're running a different race. Running that race involves pausing regularly to examine your life and to pray with the Psalmist, "Search me, O God, and know my heart: try me, and know my thoughts: And see if there be any wicked way in me, and lead me in the way everlasting" (Ps 139:23-24).

EXAMINING YOUR MOTIVES (1)

Diotrephes . . . loves . . . the preeminence.

3 John 9 NKJV

*O*ne pastor writes: "Years ago I wanted to lead a certain ministry. When I wasn't chosen I became angry. Of course I didn't show it. That's not to say I didn't love God. I just wanted to serve *me* more than Him! By saying no, God was correcting a destructive attitude that would destroy any real ministry I might have later. When you represent God so visibly, it's nearly impossible for anyone to detect that you're a fake . . . except God."

Many of us suffer from "approval addiction." The symptoms are: living in bondage to what others think of us; getting easily hurt by what they say; a nagging sense that we aren't good enough; trying to impress important people. And like all addicts we'll go to any lengths for a "fix."

Henri Nouwen writes, "Many of my daily preoccupations suggest that I belong more to the world [than to God]. A little criticism makes me angry . . . a little praise raises my spirits . . . often I am like a small boat on the ocean, completely at the mercy of the waves."

Paul writes, "But with me it is a very small thing that I should be judged by you . . . It is the Lord who judges me" (1Co 4:3-4 NRSV). Imagine receiving criticism as "a very small thing." Imagine being liberated from the need to impress, our self-esteem no longer resting on someone else noticing how smart or attractive we are. Imagine being able to actually feel love toward someone who expresses disapproval of us. *It's not only possible, with God's help and a lot of hard work—it's attainable!*

EXAMINING YOUR MOTIVES (2)

You didn't lie to people. You lied to God!
Acts 5:4 CEV

*O*ne successful pastor writes, "Numerous Sundays I've preached a message that deeply moved the members of my congregation. But ironically I 'prepared' by arguing with my wife on the way to church, or making life miserable for my children. Years of practice came to my rescue and I easily morphed into 'The Pastor,' becoming instantly compassionate, holy and spiritual. I was faking . . . [because] feeling needed, respected and wanted, can become as great a motivation as love for Christ." Wow!

Ananias and Sapphira harbored wrong motives and it cost them dearly. They saw other early-church Christians selling their land to help the poor and thought it was a great idea—in theory! However, when they did the same they withheld part of the money and then lied about it. They wanted increased visibility and spiritual standing without paying retail for it.

But Peter said, "You didn't lie to men, you lied to God." And do you know what? There's more of Ananias and Sapphira in each of us than we care to admit. We want to "look the part." Be careful! Being the center of attention can quickly become addictive! It can also disqualify you in God's eyes! Check out these 2 Scriptures: (1) "The Lord searches every heart and understands every motive behind the thoughts. If you seek him, he will be found by you" (1Ch 28:9 NIV). (2) "I the Lord search the heart and examine the mind, to reward a man according to his conduct, according to what his deeds deserve" (Jer 17:10 NIV).

EXAMINING YOUR MOTIVES (3)

Do not rejoice that the spirits submit to you . . . rejoice that
your names are written in heaven.

Luke 10:20 NIV

*U*nless we're careful, *looking* good can become more important to us than *doing* good. For example, when others praise us for how much we've helped them, it feels good, doesn't it? The disciples were no different. When Jesus sent them on their first mission, they "Returned with joy and said, 'Lord, even the demons submit to us'" (Lk 10:17 NIV). Now while Jesus encouraged them, he also warned them, "Do not rejoice that the spirits submit to you . . . rejoice that your names are written in heaven." God doesn't want us doing the right things for the wrong reasons! Listen: "For the Lord is a God who knows, and by him deeds are weighed" (1Sa 2:3 NIV).

Jesus taught the practice of secrecy. Listen: "Beware of practicing your piety before others to be seen by them" (Mt 6:1 NRSV). The practice of secrecy liberates those of us who are trapped by the desire "to be seen." It enables us to give up on the whole business of "impression management." What's that? Trying to impress others that our motives are pure, our accomplishments stellar, and our life in better shape than it is. The desert fathers had a saying concerning the connection between the practice of secrecy and a heart that's warm for God: "If you want to keep the fire hot, you must not open the door to the furnace too often."

Winston Churchill once called Clement Atlee, "A modest little man, with much to be modest about." And *that* describes each of us, doesn't it?

HANDLING TEMPTATION

Happy is the man who doesn't give in . . . when he is tempted.
James 1:12 TLB

*E*very temptation is an opportunity to grow. Every time you choose to do right instead of wrong, you're growing in the character of Christ. And what are His characteristics? Listen: "Love, joy, peace, patience, kindness, goodness, faithfulness, gentleness, and self-control" (Gal 5:22-23 NLT).

So, will you wake up one day and suddenly start demonstrating these qualities? No, fruit grows slowly. Don't get discouraged if your progress is slower than you'd like it to be. Even Paul confessed, "I have the desire to do what is good, but I cannot carry it out" (Ro 7:18 NIV).

Rick Warren says, "God develops the fruit of the spirit in our lives by allowing us to experience circumstances in which we're tempted to express the exact *opposite* quality. You can't claim to be good if you've never been tempted to be bad. You can't claim to be faithful if you've never had an opportunity to be unfaithful."

One of the secrets to overcoming temptation is to be prepared *before* it comes! Certain situations will make *you* more vulnerable to temptation than others. Those circumstances will cause you to stumble almost immediately, while others don't bother you much at all. Satan targets his temptations to our weakest areas! So, you need to identify them quickly because Satan surely knows them. He knows what trips you up and he's constantly working to get you into those situations. That's why Peter warns, "Stay alert. The Devil is poised to pounce, and would like nothing better than to catch you napping" (1Pe 5:8 TM).

MAKE A START!

An intelligent person aims at wise action . . .
a fool starts off in many directions.

Proverbs 17:24 TEV

*E*verybody wants to be thin, but nobody wants to diet. Everybody wants more money, but nobody wants more work. Successful people form the habit of doing things unsuccessful people don't like to do. The bookends of success are—commitment and consistency! Without commitment you'll never start. Without consistency you'll never finish. Getting started is the hard part. That's because we've so many reasons not to start. So, here are some helpful suggestions: *(1) Start with yourself!* If you want those around you to respond differently, give them a different set of attitudes and actions to respond to. *(2) Start early!* There's an old saying that Noah didn't wait for his ship to come in; he built one! Hard work is just an accumulation of the easy things you didn't do when you should have. The truth is, the work doesn't seem quite so hard when you stop putting it off. *(3) Start small!* Just take the first step. You can't do step two until you've done step one. Taking the first step to prioritize your life focuses you in the right direction. Don't expect to understand all that's required. Listen: "By faith Abraham . . . went out, not knowing" (Heb 11:8). You'll know as you go! Just take the first step. *(4) Start now!* What are you waiting for? Until you finish school? Get married? Have kids? Your kids leave? You retire? You die? If you wait long enough you'll have only one regret— that you didn't start now.

GROWTH (1)

Let the wise listen and add to their learning.

Proverbs 1:5 NIV

*F*ace it, all of us want to find and fulfill our God-given destiny. Yet so many of us don't. Why? Because it requires growth—and:

(1) We think growth is automatic! When we're children we grow naturally. During that time there are adults such as parents and teachers challenging us to grow on a daily basis. So we get used to growing. The problem comes when we get out of school and nobody's pushing us to grow or improve anymore. If you don't take responsibility for your own growth, it won't happen!

(2) We think growth comes from information! The greatest obstacle to growth isn't ignorance—it's the illusion of knowledge! Have you ever known someone who was absolutely brilliant yet couldn't seem to do anything of benefit for God, themselves, or others? Such people are like an encyclopedia—filled with knowledge which has no value because it's never used.

(3) We think growth comes with experience! Believing that growth comes simply from experience is like an archer shooting arrows off-target, believing he's improving because he keeps on shooting. No, experience is profitable only if you learn from it and start hitting your target! Pulitzer prize-winning composer Gian Carlo Menotti said, "Hell begins on the day when God grants us a clear vision of all that we might have achieved, of all the gifts we wasted, of all that we might have done that we did not do." Don't end your life regretting the time and opportunities you wasted. Pray. Read your Bible. Work each day on your personal growth!

GROWTH (2)

Let the wise listen and add to their learning.

Proverbs 1:5 NIV

*I*f you're serious about growth, here are 4 things you must do:

(1) Make a commitment to change. Most of us want things to get better—without having to change anything. To grow, you must commit yourself to not only accepting change—but to seeking it! Listen: "Let us . . . go on to maturity" (Heb 6:1 NIV).

(2) Focus on your strengths. Peter Drucker said, "The great mystery isn't that people do things badly, but that they occasionally do things well. The only thing that's universal is incompetence. Strength is always specific. Nobody ever commented that the great violinist, Jascha Heifetz, couldn't play a trumpet very well." If you try to be good at everything, you'll end up good at nothing. God gave you specific gifts. Find them and use them for His glory!

(3) Put yourself in a growth environment. Certain fish grow according to the size of their environment. Put them in a small aquarium and they remain small. Release them into the ocean and they grow to their intended size. And you are the same! If you spend your time with the wrong crowd in the wrong place doing the wrong things, you'll never experience growth.

(4) Learn to enjoy the journey. Most Grand Masters of chess learn and relearn their moves over a period of 15 years before winning their first world title. That's almost a fifth of their lives! If you're going to spend that much time doing something, you'd better like it. If the destination appeals to you but you're not enjoying the journey, you'd be wise to seek God's guidance and make sure you're heading in the right direction.

POLLUTERS AND PURIFIERS!

Make every effort to do what leads to . . . mutual edification.
Romans 14:19 NIV

*W*e've a tendency to adopt the attitudes of those we spend time with. That's why Paul wrote, "Your faith will help me, and my faith will help you" (Ro 1:12 NCV).

Fred Smith points out that there are 2 kinds of people in any group: polluters and purifiers. The polluters are like smoke stacks belching out dirty smoke all the time. They hate clear skies. No matter how good it gets they find a way to make it gloomy. When the people around them breathe their toxins they feel sicker and sicker. The purifiers, on the other hand, make everything around them better. It doesn't matter what kind of rotten atmosphere they encounter. They take in the toxic words of polluters just as everyone else does, but they filter them before passing them on. What goes in gloomy and negative comes out fresh and clear."

So, are you a polluter or a purifier? When you spend time with others do they walk away feeling better or worse? Do you clear the air giving them fresh perspective and encouragement, or do they leave you feeling hopeless about things? Watch how people respond to you and you'll know which group you belong in.

Bottom line: doubters usually get what they expect. So do believers! Looking for God's best in every situation is not only scriptural, it helps you to see opportunities that you'd otherwise miss. Seeing people through God's eyes causes them to be attracted and open to you. Is that important? Absolutely! Your *attitude* will reach them long before your *message* does.

IT IS WELL!

And she answered, it is well.

2 Kings 4:26

*I*n 1871, when fire ravaged the City of Chicago leaving 300 dead and 100,000 homeless, attorney Horatio Gates Spafford, a friend of D.L. Moody, helped its people get back on their feet. After 2 years of tireless effort he and his family decided to take a much-needed vacation. They planned to travel to England and join Moody in an evangelistic crusade then go on to Europe. When Spafford got delayed he sent his family ahead planning to meet them on the other side of the Atlantic.

But they never made it. Near Newfoundland their ship collided with an English sailing vessel and sank within 20 minutes. Spafford's wife, Anna, survived by clinging to some floating wreckage but all 4 of their daughters drowned. Next day Spafford received this terrible two-word telegram from his wife: Saved Alone! He immediately went to be with her.

Later in the course of relating their story to D.L. Moody, Spafford said quietly, "It is well, the will of God be done." In fact it was those days of overwhelming grief that inspired him to compose the beloved hymn that has comforted so many of us: *When peace like a river attendeth my way, when sorrows like sea-billows roll; whatever my lot, thou hast taught me to say: It is well, it is well with my soul!* Can you sing those words? Have you come to the place in your life where you know for sure that if you were to die today, you'd go to heaven? You can, by accepting Jesus as your personal Savior. Why don't you do it today!

SUCCESS MYTHS (1)

Let the discerning get guidance.

Proverbs 1:5 NIV

*L*et's look at some common success myths:
(1) We believe success is impossible, so we criticize it.
Because we want to believe that life should be easy, we assume
anything that's difficult must be impossible. Then when
success eludes us we're tempted to throw in the towel and say,
"Who wants success anyway?" And if success is achieved by
anyone we consider less worthy than ourselves, we really get
"steamed."
(2) We believe success is mystical, so we search for it. The
problem is, we want the rewards without paying the price. Seth
Grodin says, "We need to stop shopping for lightning bolts. You
don't win an Olympic medal with a few weeks of intensive
training. There's no such thing as an overnight opera sensation.
Great companies [and great churches] don't spring up
overnight . . . every great thing has been built in exactly the
same way: bit by bit, step by step, little by little."
(3) We believe success comes by chance, so we hope for it.
We say, "She just happened to be in the right place at the right
time." Wrong! The chances of that happening are about as good
as your chances of winning the Lottery—50 million to one. If
you're really serious about success, you'll agree with one small
business owner who had a sign posted that read: *"The 57 Rules
of Success. Rule One: Deliver the goods. Rule Two: The other
56 don't matter.* That's why Paul said to Timothy, "Be diligent
in these matters; give yourself wholly to them, so that everyone
may see your progress" (1Ti 4:15 NIV).

SUCCESS MYTHS (2)

Let the discerning get guidance.

Proverbs 1:5 NIV

*H*ere are 3 more success myths that trap us:

(1) We believe success is the result of opportunity, so we wait for it. Many people who work hard but don't seem to get anywhere, believe that the only thing they need is "a break." Their motto is, "if only." If only my boss would cut me some slack . . . if only our church was in a better area of town . . . if only I had start-up capital . . . if only I'd married someone different. Sound familiar? People who do nothing more than wait for opportunity, are neither able to see it or seize it when it comes.

(2) We think success comes from having leverage, so we work for it. This idea is reinforced by the words of people like industrialist Andrew Carnegie: "Success is the power with which to acquire whatever one demands of life." So we take that a step further, assuming all successful people have taken advantage of others to get to where they are, and begin to look for ways to manipulate people too. We believe they can force our way to success, but it doesn't work.

(3) We believe success comes from connections, so we strive to make them. People who believe in connections think they'd "have it made," if only they'd been born into the right family or met the right person. But those beliefs are misplaced. Knowing good people has its rewards. But connections alone won't improve your life if you're off track. For followers of Christ, success comes by seeking God's will and following *His* plan for your life!

BOUNDARY-MARKER RELIGION (1)

Whoever does not love does not know God.
1 John 4:8 NIV

*W*hen it came to "boundary-marker religion" the Pharisees were experts: circumcision, dietary laws, dress codes, etc. These practices allowed them to decide who was "in" and who was "out." And worse, the insiders became judgmental toward the outsiders. Sound familiar? Dallas Willard writes, "How many people are radically and permanently repelled by Christians who are unfeeling, stiff, unapproachable, boringly lifeless and dissatisfied? Yet such Christians are everywhere . . . Spirituality wrongly understood or pursued, is a major source of human misery and rebellion against God."

When our lives are not marked by genuine joy and devotion to Christ, we start looking for substitute ways of distinguishing ourselves from those we classify as "worldly." Jesus didn't do that. When asked to identify what the law was about, He simply replied "Love God and love people." Paul said, "If I speak in the tongues of men and of angels, but have not love, I am only a resounding gong or a clanging cymbal" (1Co 13:1 NIV). It's possible to think you're becoming more spiritual when in fact you're becoming what Mark Twain called "A good man, in the worst sense of the word."

Winston Churchill once had a political opponent called Cripps, a man widely disliked for his smug self-righteousness. One day, so the story goes, Churchill saw Cripps passing by and remarked, "There but for the grace of God, goes God." The strongest argument for Christianity is Christians drawing life from Christ. The strongest argument against Christianity is Christians who are smug, judgmental and complacent. *So, what kind of Christian are you?*

BOUNDARY-MARKER RELIGION (2)

Whoever does not love does not know God.

1 John 4:8 NIV

To know if you suffer from "boundary-marker religion" ask yourself:

(1) Am I real? A little boy in Sunday school knew the sort of answers you're supposed to give. So when the teacher asked, "What's brown, furry, has a long tail and stores up nuts?" he muttered, "I guess the answer is Jesus, but it sure sounds like a squirrel to me." So often we try to say spiritual sounding things to impress each other, when the world hasn't a clue what we're talking about. Be real!

(2) Am I judgmental? John Ortberg writes: "As soon as we start to pursue virtue, we begin to wonder why others aren't as virtuous as we are. It reminds us of the reply Homer Simpson's neighbors gave when Homer asked them where they'd been: 'We went to a Christian camp, we were learning how to be more judgmental.' Have you been to that camp? Does a little voice inside you categorize people: this one's needy and dependent—stay away. That one's bright and has much to offer—try to connect. Why do we constantly find ourselves rating people, as though we were in some kind of contest?"

(3) Am I approachable? Speaking of the Pharisees Jesus said, "they love . . . to have men call them 'Rabbi'" (Mt 23:7 NIV). In Jesus' day, some rabbis had the idea that true spirituality required you to distance yourself from people. Ironically, the only Rabbi the outcasts could touch, turned out to be God Himself. Jesus was the most approachable person they'd ever seen. How about you?

BOUNDARY-MARKER RELIGION (3)

Whoever does not love does not know God.

1 John 4:8 NIV

$\mathscr{B}$efore leaving the subject of "boundary-marker religion," here are 2 more questions:

(1) Am I growing weary of pursuing spiritual growth? Speaking of the Pharisees, Jesus said, "They tie up heavy loads and put them on men's shoulders" (Mt 23:4 NIV). "What is boundary-marker religion?" you ask. Stephen Mosley writes, "Our morality calls out rather feebly. It whines from the corner of a sanctuary; it awkwardly interrupts pleasures; it mumbles excuses at parties; it shuffles along out of step and slightly behind the times . . . it's often regarded by our secular contemporaries as a narrow, even trivial, pursuit." Then he captures the essence of boundary-marker religion in these words, "Tragically, conventional religious goodness manages to be both *intimidating* and *unchallenging* at the same time." Intimidating—because it may involve 101 difficult rules about so-called spirituality. Unchallenging—because we may exhaust ourselves trying to keep all these rules, yet never experience the true joy Jesus offers. This is why people inside the church so often get weary. Conforming to boundary-marker religion is simply not a rewarding enough experience to fill the void in our hearts.

(2) Am I measuring my life in superficial ways? When asked, "How's your spiritual life going?" what's the first thing that comes to mind? Prayer? Bible reading? Church attendance? Tithing? Good answers, but they're by no means the whole story. Jesus said, "I have come that they may have life, and have it to the full" (Jn 10:10 NIV). Nothing attracts the spiritually hungry and hurting, like someone who lives the "Christ-life." So, are you living it?

MAKE THE DECISION!

How long will you waver between two opinions?

1 Kings 18:21 NIV

The "winners" in God's kingdom are those who settle their critical issues early and manage them daily. That way they don't have to keep revisiting them. That's a good idea for 2 reasons:

(1) It takes the emotion out of the decision. If we're not careful we'll make life-altering decisions based on temporary situations, rather than on God's will for us. Or worse, we'll base our decisions on our feelings. By setting our life's priorities before we have to, we can set them without our emotions manipulating and controlling us. When we do that, we're more likely to set them with integrity.

(2) It makes managing your life easier. Once you nail down the important decisions, you can live based on them. Let's say you're a compulsive gambler and you decide to quit. Your task will then be to order your life in the light of that decision. That probably means not hanging out around racetracks or moving to Las Vegas. Or if you want to build a better marriage, it may mean spending less time on the golf course or at work, and planning a date night each week. It takes honesty born in prayer to know what your real issues are, and make good decisions accordingly. It also takes character and perseverance to determine what happens after those decisions are made. The great thing is, once you decide, then commit it to the Lord, He'll give you the strength each day to live by your decisions.

MAINTAINING A GOOD ATTITUDE

Seven times a day I praise you.

Psalm 119:164 NIV

*E*ach morning you have to tell yourself, "Today I'll make whatever adjustment is necessary to keep my attitude right." Here are some guidelines:
(1) Realize that your attitude needs daily adjustment. Anything you don't maintain deteriorates. The stronger your natural inclination to be negative or doubtful, the more you'll have to work at it. So begin each day with an attitude check. And watch for red flags throughout the day, signaling that you're not doing well.
(2) Ask God to help you. Someone sent us this humorous prayer: "Dear Lord, so far today I haven't gossiped, lost my temper, been greedy, grumpy, nasty, selfish or self-indulgent. But in a few minutes I'm going to have to get out of bed, then I'll need all the help I can get." The truth is, you'll need God's help to maintain a good attitude, so seek it!
(3) Always look for what's good. Mother Teresa had only two requirements for those working with her in Calcutta: a desire to work and a joyful attitude. Think: if somebody could be joyful amongst the dying and the poorest of the poor, surely you can too!
(4) Seek out faith-filled people. They're everywhere. You'll find them soaring above the doubters like eagles. If you're having a hard day, get close and "draft" behind them the way racers do. And if they're having difficulty, you be the one to get out front and make things easier. To maintain a good attitude the Psalmist said, "Seven times a day I praise you"—try it!

STAY IN YOUR STRENGTH ZONE

Absolutely everything . . . finds its purpose in him.
Colossians 1:16 TM

*P*eople don't pay for average, they try to avoid it!
You've got to stay in your strength zone! If you're not sure what
your strengths are, here are some suggestions:

(1) Talk to God. After all, who knows the product better
than the manufacturer? Contrary to popular books, guru's and
seminars, you won't discover your life's meaning by looking
within yourself. You've probably tried that. You didn't create
yourself so there's no way you can tell yourself what you were
created for. If someone handed you a gadget you'd never seen
before you wouldn't know its purpose. And the gadget itself
wouldn't be able to tell you either. Only the manufacturer (or
the owner's manual) can tell you that. Are you getting the idea?

(2) Trial and error. Remember how you learned to walk?
You spent more time on your bottom than you did on your feet.
But eventually you succeeded because you were born to walk.
But a word of caution: anytime something seems to be all
"trial" and you never make any progress, consult God, and be
prepared for some new instructions.

(3) The counsel of others. Solomon says, "The way of a
fool seems right to him, but a wise man listens to advice" (Pr
12:15 NIV). Never be too proud to seek help. Asking others for
feedback isn't always fun, but it's essential. But again a word
of caution: choose people who have no agenda other than to
help you. Bottom line: the more you stay in your strength zone,
the more fruit you'll bear for God.

TAKE CONTROL OF YOUR TIME

Teach us to number our days . . . that we may gain . . . wisdom.
Psalm 90:12 NIV

*Y*our priorities determine how you spend your time, so set them prayerfully and maintain them carefully. Wisdom consists in the elimination of non-essentials. You can have certain things, but you can't have *everything!* You've got to choose! Excellence comes from doing the right things right, and letting the rest go. If you're not sure what the right things are, pretend you have only 6 months to live—you'll figure it out!

Let's face it, there are a lot of things vying for your attention. Have you ever noticed that the people with nothing to do, usually want to spend their time with *you?* Advertisers want you to spend your money on their products. Even your own desires can be so diverse and your attention so scattered, that you aren't sure what should get your attention. That's why you need to focus on your God-given purpose—daily.

By focusing on the top 20 percent of your priorities, you generally get an 80 percent return on your effort. So, you need to get up every morning and say, "Today, I'll prioritize my life according to God's will and give my energies to those things that help me fulfill it."

Your greatest possession is your next 24 hours. How will you spend it? Will you allow TV, pointless e-mails, unimportant tasks, telemarketers, the wrong crowd, or other distractions to consume your day? Or will you take control of your time and make today yours? If you don't decide how your day will be spent, count on it—someone else will!

HAPPY BIRTHDAY, AGNES!

The Son of Man came to find lost people and save them.

Luke 19:10 NCV

*L*ate one night while traveling in an unfamiliar city, Tony Campolo wandered into a diner where the only other customers were a group of prostitutes. He overheard one of them say that tomorrow was her birthday. So the next night he came back with a cake and a sign that read, "Happy Birthday, Agnes." Campolo says, "The door swung open and in came Agnes . . . never have I seen a person so flabbergasted. Her eyes moistened . . . and she started to cry. Not knowing what else to do I said, 'What do you say we pray?' Looking back . . . it seems more than strange for a sociologist to be leading a prayer meeting with a bunch of prostitutes in a diner! But it felt like the right thing to do. I prayed for Agnes: for her salvation, that her life would be changed. That God would be good to her. When I finished, the guy behind the counter said, 'What kinda church do you belong to anyway?' I replied, 'The kind that throws birthday parties for prostitutes.' He waited a moment, then answered, "No you don't. There's no church like that. If there was, I'd join!'"

But *that's* the kind of church Jesus came to build. Grace is the one thing it offers that can't be found anywhere else. He "came to find lost people and save them," because He loves to salvage and recycle the hurting, the throw-aways, the left-out, the used-up and the put-down. And that's news they're waiting to hear outside the church doors!

FIXING GOD'S WORD IN YOUR HEART

Fix these words of mine in your hearts.
Deuteronomy 11:18 NIV

$\mathcal{G}$od wants you to fix His Word in your heart. That happens by:

(1) Turning knowledge into action! Your Bible knowledge may be 10 times greater than someone else's, but if you're not 10 times more loving, patient and joyful, what good is it? The right doctrine with the wrong spirit will turn people away from Christ every time.

(2) Taking one thought with you through the day! David says that the way to prosper, is through meditating on Scripture "day and night" (Ps 1:2). But you can't meditate fast! There are no Evelyn Wood courses in speed meditating: "I can meditate 700 words-a-minute with a 90 percent comprehension rate." The Bible likens meditating to a cow chewing cud or roots drawing up moisture from deep well-springs. When God impresses a thought on you, live with it all day. Make it your first thought in the morning and your last thought at night. Try that for 365 days and see what happens. You'll love the results!

(3) Allowing it to wash you daily! Listen: "How can a young man keep his way pure? By living according to your word" (Ps 119:9 NIV). His fellow monks used to ask Martin Luther why he spent so much time in the confessional. After all, he lived in a monastery, what could he have to confess? Chanting off-key? No, Luther was aware of his own cleverness at self-justification. God's Word is the only detergent strong enough to get down into the deepest levels of our thought, imagination and motives and cleanse us.

APPRECIATE YOUR JOB!

O give thanks unto the Lord.

Psalm 105:1

*B*efore you complain about your job, look at the regulations employees at Mt. Corry Carriage and Iron Works were asked to follow in 1782:

(1) Employees will daily sweep the floors, dust the furniture, shelves and show cases. (2) Each day fill lamps, clean chimneys and trim wicks, wash windows once a week. (3) Each clerk will bring a bucket of water and a shovel of coal for the day's business. (4) Make your pens carefully. You may whittle nibs to individual taste. (5) This office will be open at 7 am and close at 8 pm daily, except on the Sabbath. (6) Men employees will be given an evening off each week for courting purposes, and two evenings if they go regularly to church. (7) Every employee should lay aside from each pay, a sum of his earnings for his benefit during his declining years so that he will not become a burden upon the charity of his betters. (8) Any employee who smokes Spanish cigars, uses liquor in any form, gets shaved at a barber's shop or frequents public halls will give good reason to suspect his worth, intentions, integrity and honesty. (9) The employee who has performed his labors faithfully and without fault for a period of five years in my service, and who has been thrifty, attentive to his religious duties, and is looked upon by his fellow man as a substantial law-abiding citizen, will be given an increase of 5 cents per day in his pay, providing that just returns in profits from the business permit. *So, what do you think? Maybe your job isn't so bad after all: "O give thanks unto the Lord."*

COMMITMENT (1)

I run straight to the goal with purpose in every step.
1 Corinthians 9:26 NLT

$\mathcal{T}$o become the person God intends you to be, you'll need commitment. Why? Because: *(1) Commitment can change your life!* Frederic F. Flach writes: "Most people can look back and identify a time and place at which their lives changed significantly. Whether by accident or design, these are the moments when because of a readiness within us and a collaboration of events around us, we are forced to seriously reappraise ourselves and the conditions under which we live, and to make choices that will affect the rest of our lives."

(2) Your commitment will be tested—daily. Too many of us see commitment as an event, like saying, "I do" in a wedding ceremony or shaking hands to close a business deal. In January we buy a treadmill to get in shape, by February we quit because it calls for too much discipline. Any time you make a commitment to something, you'll be tested—daily.

(3) Commitment helps you overcome life's obstacles. Maltbie Babcock said, "One of the most common mistakes and one of the costliest, is thinking that success is due to some genius, some magic something or other which we do not possess. No, success is generally due to holding on, and unwillingness to let go. You 'decide' to learn a language, study music, take a course in reading, train yourself physically, etc. Will it be a success or failure? That depends upon how much pluck and perseverance that word *'decide'* contains. It's the decision that nothing will overrule and the grip that nothing can break, that brings success."

COMMITMENT (2)

I run straight to the goal with purpose in every step.
1 Corinthians 9:26 NLT

*A*nytime you make a commitment to something, your commitment will be tested in 3 ways:

(1) Experiencing failure. The greatest challenge to commitment is failure. Olympic gold medallist Mary Lou Retton says, "Achieving that goal is a good feeling, but to get there you have to get through the failures. You've got to be able to pick yourself up and continue."

(2) Having to stand alone. When you want to accomplish something people will try to distract you, challenge you or get you to settle for less. It may be unintentional, or it may be because they're worried that if you grow and succeed they'll feel left behind. In those moments you must ask: "Who am I trying to please—God or man? When I stand before God what will I be glad I did now?"

(3) Facing deep disappointment. When things go wrong, when life gets tough, when the enemy begins to attack will you be able to carry on? That depends. "On what?" you ask. On your willingness to renew your commitment each day. To keep yourself on track, make a copy of these words by William H. Murray and carry them with you wherever you go: "The moment one definitely commits ones self, then [divine] providence moves too. All sorts of things occur to help one that would never otherwise have occurred. A whole stream of events issue from the decision, raising in ones favor all manner of unforeseen incidents and meetings and material assistance, which no man could have dreamed would come his way."

COMMITMENT (3)

I run straight to the goal with purpose in every step.
1 Corinthians 9:26 NLT

*B*efore you commit to something count the cost, otherwise you won't stick with it.(See Luke 14:28). After the Nazis obtained France's surrender, they were certain that victory was at hand. But they underestimated the commitment of Winston Churchill and the British people. Churchill knew what was at stake, as evidenced by his remarks at the time. "The Battle of Britain is about to begin. Upon this battle depends the survival of Christian civilization. . . . Hitler knows that he will have to break us in this island or lose the war. If we can stand up to him, all Europe may be free . . . but if we fail, then the whole world, including the United States, including all that we have known and cared for, will sink into the abyss of a new dark age . . . let us therefore brace ourselves to our duties, and so bear ourselves that, if the British Empire and its commonwealth last for a thousand years, men will still say 'This was their finest hour.'"

Did victory come easily or without a cost? No, Britain suffered terrible bloodshed and bombing by the Nazis. But they stood. And because they stood the allies won the war. Their resolve was strong, not only because they knew what was at stake—but because they had decided in advance the price they were willing to pay. *Understand this: it's virtually impossible to stand by a commitment naively or thoughtlessly made. Commitment only works when you count the cost and agree in advance to pay the price. So, how committed are you?*

COMMITMENT (4)

I run straight to the goal with purpose in every step.
1 Corinthians 9:26 NLT

*P*eople forget how fast you did a job, they just remember how well you did it. A real craftsman *wants* you to inspect his work. Sloppy people hide their work. If anyone finds fault with it they blame their equipment, their boss, or their environment, etc. "Excellence" for the child of God, means doing it "as unto the Lord" (to be presented to Him).

Talent is important, but it's not enough. You need a strong work ethic. Longfellow wrote: "The heights by great men reached and kept, were not attained by sudden flight. But they, while their companions slept, were toiling upward in the night." We approach commitment in one of two ways: we either focus on the *external* or the *internal.* When we focus on the external, we allow circumstances to determine the outcome. Because circumstances constantly change, our commitment level changes like the wind. But not Jephthah. Listen: "I have opened my mouth unto the Lord, and I cannot go back" (Jud 11:35). *That's* commitment!

Each choice is a crossroad: one that will either confirm or compromise your commitment. When you come to a crossroad you can recognize it because: (a) a personal decision is required; (b) the decision will cost you something; (c) others will likely be influenced by it. Your choices are the only thing you can truly control. You cannot control your circumstances, nor can you control others. But by focusing on your choices and making them with integrity, you control your commitment. *And that is what separates success from failure!*

COMMITMENT (5)

I run straight to the goal with purpose in every step.
1 Corinthians 9:26 NLT

*N*othing stokes the fires of commitment like— single mindedness! Look at William Carey, "the father of modern missions." Although he'd only an elementary education, by the time he was in his teens he could read the Bible in 6 languages. Because of his talent for languages, when he was in his early 30's he was chosen to be a missionary to India. Six years later, he founded the Serampore Mission. A few years after that he became Professor of Oriental Languages at Fort William College in Calcutta. He also used his talent to become a publisher. His press at Serampore printed Bibles in 40 languages and dialects for more than 300 million people. He impacted a nation for God!

So, to what did Carey attribute his success? Noble birth? Unlimited resources? An easy assignment? No, he said it was because he was a plodder. Listen: "I can plod. That is my only genius. I can persevere in any definite pursuit. To this I owe everything."

Thomas A. Buckner said, "To bring one's self to a frame of mind and to add proper energy to accomplish things that require plain hard work continuously, is the one big battle everyone has. But when this battle is won for all time, then everything is easy."

When the Olympic athletes come into the stadium during the opening ceremonies they recite the following: *"I have prepared. I have followed the rules. I will not quit."* When you can say that with integrity, you can feel good about yourself no matter what happens afterward.

A NEW SONG!

They [all] sang a new song.

Revelation 5:9 CEV

We'll never experience real growth in the church if we keep insisting everybody has to do everything *our* way. When it comes to salvation there's only one way—Christ. But when it comes to worship—there are many ways and expressions. There's no "exclusive" way of worshipping God! The music that turns one generation on, turns another off. So let's stop arguing over personal preferences or speaking where God's Word is silent. Listen: "They *all* sang a new song to the Lamb . . . every tribe, language, people, and nation." We all worship the same Lord and the only thing He asks is a sincere heart. God doesn't require us to express our love in identical ways, but He does mind us passing judgment on how others do it.

When the Bible says, "They all sang a new song to the Lamb," do you seriously think they all had the same music style? The great spiritual awakening that took place under the Wesley brothers left us with soul-stirring hymns like, "O, for a thousand tongues to sing." Yet many in their day, while believing the words, condemned the melody as "bar room music." Wow!

The danger with getting old is not just wanting to keep things the way we like them, but insisting that others agree with us—and branding them as unspiritual if they don't. Paul said, "I am made all things to all men, that I might by all means save some" (1Co 9:22). Notice the words "all means." *As long as someone's song is "to the lamb," it's okay!*

J. PAUL GETTY

The world of the stingy gets smaller and smaller.
Proverbs 11:24 TM

J. Paul Getty was once the world's richest man. But his stinginess became as well known as his wealth. He wore rumpled suits. He even installed a pay phone to be used by the guests in his home—Sutton Place, a 16th Century English Manor. But the worst example of his stinginess involved his grandson.

J. Paul Getty III, Getty's 16 year-old grandson, was kidnapped in 1973 by an Italian gang which demanded $17 million in ransom. But Getty refused to pay. Only when part of the boy's right ear was cut off and sent to a newspaper in Rome did Getty relent. But even then he wouldn't give them the entire amount; he agreed only to a fraction, $2.7 million—saying that was all he could raise. Fortunately the boy was eventually found alive near Naples, but he had endured abuse and captivity for 5 long months! When Getty died 3 years later, his children whom he had long ago alienated, and his former wives (he'd married and divorced 5 times) fought in court over his fortune which was valued at $4 billion. Most of the money ultimately went to, guess where? The Getty Museum in Los Angeles!

"But don't I have the right to keep what I earn?" Sure, but we're not talking about your *rights,* we're talking about your *responsibilities* before God. God told Abraham, "I will bless you . . . and you will be a blessing" (Ge 12:2 NIV). You're blessed—to be a blessing! When you have more than you need, it's seed. Start sowing it!

FORGIVE AND LET IT GO!

Forgive whatever grievances you . . .
have against one another . . . as the Lord forgave you.
Colossians 3:13 NIV

A group of doctors was asked which emotions cause the most physical illness. Their answer was "anger and unforgiveness," because over time they release deadly toxins into your body. That's why Paul says, "Do not let the sun go down while you are still angry" (Eph 4:26 NIV). So, when you've been treated unfairly what should you do? Take these 4 steps:

Confront. There's a right time, place and way to do this. Before you do, pray and ask God to guide your thoughts and your words. Then say what's in your heart in a low-key, nonjudgmental way. After that, leave the rest to God; He'll do a better job of changing things than you will.

Release it. Not only does God require us to forgive each other, He gives us the grace to do it. You may let someone off your hook but that doesn't mean they're off God's! He'll deal with them the right way and bring about the right result— something you can't do.

Remember how often God forgives you. Paul says, "Forgive . . . as the Lord forgave you." When you're tempted to lick your wounds or lash out, recall the price Jesus paid to take away your sins. Looking through those eyeglasses will help you to forgive anybody.

Pray for the offender. Forgiveness means refusing to let the wrongdoer keep on hurting you. God said, "Pray for those who hurt you" (Mt 5:44 NCV). Without showing mercy, life becomes an endless cycle of resentment and retaliation. But as you walk in love, you experience freedom.

TAKING RESPONSIBILITY FOR YOUR ATTITUDE

Be joyful always.

1 Thessalonians 5:16 NIV

*S*ome of us complain about everything. The weather's too hot; the job's too hard; the pay's too low; the vacation's too short. And what we think about our mother-in-law isn't fit to print.

In an old *Peanuts* comic strip, Lucy announces, "Boy, do I feel crabby." Her little brother, Linus, always anxious to relieve tension, responds, "Maybe I can be of help. Why don't you just take my place in front of the TV and I'll go fix you a nice snack? Sometimes we all need a little pampering to make us feel better." Then Linus brings her a sandwich, a few chocolate chip cookies and some milk. "Now, is there anything else I can get you? Is there anything I haven't thought of?" he asks. "Yes, there's one thing you haven't thought of," Lucy answers. Then she shouts, *"I don't want to feel better!"*

Face it, some people don't want to feel better—they just want attention! Know anybody like that? It takes uncommon honesty to ask, "How much of what I say focuses on *complaining* about the situation rather than *improving* it? Have I built my life around people who feel the same way, and would probably be upset if I decided to grow and change for the better? Am I living in the past, nursing old wounds, refusing to forgive others and myself?" Time doesn't heal—insight does! Jesus said that *knowing* the truth sets us free. Once you're willing to face the truth about your attitude and do something about it, your life will begin to improve rapidly.

OSCAR WILDE

In all thy ways acknowledge him, and he shall direct thy paths.
Proverbs 3:6

$\mathcal{O}$scar Wilde won scholarships and was educated in Britain's best schools. He was honored as "First in Greats" at Oxford. He was the toast of London. *British Heritage Magazine* called him, "Our most quotable writer after Shakespeare." Yet his undisciplined living landed him in prison. From there he wrote:

"I must say to myself that I ruined myself. Nobody great or small can be ruined except by his own hand. The gods have given me almost everything. But I let myself be lured into long spells of senseless and sensual ease. I surrounded myself with smaller natures and meaner minds. I became the spend-thrift of my own genius. To waste an eternal youth gave me a curious joy. Tired of being on the heights, I deliberately went to the depths in search of new sensations. Desire, at the end, was a malady, or a madness, or both. I forgot that every little action of the common day, makes or unmakes character, and therefore what one has done in the secret chamber, one has someday to cry aloud on the housetop. I allowed pleasure to dominate me. I ended in horrible disgrace. There is only one thing for me now, absolute humility." In the end Oscar Wilde lost his family, his fortune, his self-respect and his will to live. He died bankrupt and broken at age 46.

If you think that couldn't happen to you, you're naive, foolish, or arrogant. That's why Solomon wrote, "In all thy ways acknowledge *him,* and he shall direct thy paths."

MONEY MATTERS

The borrower becomes the lender's slave.

Proverbs 22:7 NASB

*B*uying stuff you don't need, with money you don't have, to impress people you don't know, is no way to live! Here are 2 simple truths about your money that you need to keep in mind:

(1) Money won't make you happy! Now most of us agree, yet we act like it will. We're better paid, better fed and better educated than ever. Yet the divorce rate has doubled, the teen suicide rate has tripled, and depression has soared in the last 30 years. Two thousand years ago Seneca wrote, "Money, of itself, has yet to make anyone rich." Why? Because you are what you are—no matter how much or how little you have.

(2) Debt will make you unhappy! Samuel Butler, who satirized Victorian life in England, wrote, "All progress seems based upon a universal desire . . . to live beyond one's income." That's why Solomon wrote, "The borrower becomes the lender's slave." Do you want to be a slave? If not, work toward getting out of debt!

Now purchasing a home, buying a car, improving your education or investing in a business are good things—as long as you manage them well. But too many of us incur debt for frivolous stuff. When you're still paying for something you didn't need, no longer use or even have, you're not being wise. To reduce your debt: (a) honor God with your giving; (b) live on a budget; (c) don't expect instant miracles; (d) seek professional help. Don't let your possessions possess you. If you're a slave to debt, find a way to free yourself!

DEEPENING YOUR HUNGER
FOR GOD'S WORD

Crave pure spiritual milk . . . that . . . you may grow.
1 Peter 2:2 NIV

*H*ave your daily devotions become more duty than desire? God says, "Crave pure spiritual milk . . . that . . . you may grow." The word crave means "asking earnestly; longing eagerly; feeling in great need of." So:

(1) Ask God to meet you in the Scriptures. As you read, expect Him to show up. Remember, your goal is to build a relationship, not turn in a book report! Listen: "The kingdom of heaven is at hand" (Mt 4:17). As you read, become aware that Jesus is present. Ask Him to wash your mind—even if the cleanser stings a bit. Expect to be moved by His love for you, convicted of some sin or prompted to make changes in your life.

(2) Read your Bible with a repentant heart. Be vulnerable! What you're after isn't information but transformation. Being unchanged by your Bible is worse than having no Bible at all! Jesus said, "Now ye are clean through the word which I have spoken unto you" (Jn 15:3).

(3) Meditate on a brief passage or a word. This may mean adjusting your attitude from "getting through the Bible," to hearing God speak to you. Success isn't in the number of pages you read; God doesn't have a big behavior modification chart on His refrigerator and each time you read another chapter you get a gold star. Your goal is not to get through the Scriptures, it's to get the Scriptures through you! If you're serious about deepening your hunger for God's Word, take a moment and reread today's devotion.

KEEPING YOUR PRIORITIES

Be very careful, then, how you live.

Ephesians 5:15 NIV

*T*he purposes of God in your life must be continually revisited—and guarded! What does that mean?
(1) Stay flexible. Conditions constantly change; so do methods of getting things done. So, to fulfill your God-given priorities you must stay flexible.
(2) Plan your time carefully. To be effective, you must be able to plan your day. Only one in three people do. John Maxwell says, "It's a rare day that I get up in the morning wondering what I will be doing that day." Can you say that?
(3) Follow your plan. Most of us don't get to our most important tasks until mid-afternoon. We tend to finish off low-priority tasks first, so that we'll have a sense of accomplishment. That's not wise. Do first things first. If you plan your day but don't follow through, your results will be the same as those who don't plan at all. Gothe said, "Things that matter most must never be at the mercy of things that matter least."
(4) Delegate whenever possible. People fall into two categories: clingers or dumpers. Clingers refuse to let go of anything they think important, whether they're the best person to do it or not. Their goal is perfection. Dumpers, on the other hand, are quick to get rid of tasks, yet give little thought to how well the job will get done. Their goal is to get things off their desk. Proper delegation calls for being wise, secure in who you are before God, and generous toward others. It also means that the job gets done right. And isn't that what you want?

A FRIEND IN HIGH PLACES!

Whenever we are in need, we should come bravely
before the throne of . . . God.

Hebrews 4:16 CEV

*S*cientists say our Milky Way, the galaxy to which our sun belongs, is part of more than100 billion stars. And there may be as many as 100 billion other galaxies, billions of which may have hundreds of millions of planets like ours. The moon and stars which are visible on a clear night are mere drops in the vast sea of the universe. In fact, the Hubble Telescope relays images of galaxies as far away as 12 billion light years—*that's 12 billion times 6 trillion miles!* Blows your mind, doesn't it? And all this from God's one-sentence command in Genesis! No wonder Job says, "Stand still and consider the wondrous works of God" (Job 37:14 AMP).

But do you know what's even more amazing? The One who created it all, who said: "All authority has been given to Me in heaven and on earth" (Mt 28:18 NASB)—cares about every detail of your life. He really does! Listen: "We have an Advocate with the Father, Jesus Christ" (1Jn 2:1 NASB). Imagine the most powerful force in the universe going to bat for you! When you're weak, He's strong. When you blow it, He covers you! The Bible says, "Come bravely before the throne of . . . God . . . be treated with undeserved kindness, and . . . find help" (He 4:16 CEV). God's grace is amazing! And you don't have to do anything to deserve it! Because God's your Father you can call home anytime and find a welcome, plus "grace to help . . . in your times of need." What could be better!

FAMILY MATTERS (1)

God sets the lonely in families.

Psalm 68:6 NIV

A strong Christian family is like:
(1) A safe haven! The workplace is demanding. The schoolyard is an increasingly hostile environment. The pace of life is out of control. Where can you find a shelter? If not at home, then probably nowhere. President Theodore Roosevelt said, "I'd rather spend time with my family than with any of the world's notables." His home was a safe haven in the midst of life's storms. Is yours?

(2) A crucible of character! A Christ-centered home not only helps to form the character of your children, it also continues to strengthen your own character as well. Character is little more than the collection of choices you make and habits you cultivate every day. Since your family creates your primary environment, it influences those choices and habits. Strong, Christian families encourage us to make good choices, develop the right disciplines, and pay the price today for success tomorrow.

(3) A mirror of truth! To grow, you must be able to look at yourself realistically. And where's the best place to do that? In a home filled with unconditional love. It allows you to be open about your mistakes and shortcomings. It's a safe place to fail. It creates a listening environment filled with understanding and support. Those closest to us—form us. When Mother Teresa received the Nobel Peace Prize she was asked, "What can we do to promote world peace?" Her answer was, "Go home and love your family." If you want to make a real impact, start at home! Treasure your family!

FAMILY MATTERS (2)

God sets the lonely in families.

Psalm 68:6 NIV

*I*f you go into marriage thinking it'll be easy, you've probably seen too many movies. Within 5 years, 20 percent of all first marriages end in divorce. Within 10, that number almost doubles. So, how can you keep from being one of those statistics?

(1) Put your family first on your calendar! If you feel like you ought to be at work when you're with your family or be with your family when you're at work, your priorities are screwed up. Call a conference! Figure out and agree on how much time you should spend together. And protect those times, otherwise you're not serious about it!

(2) Keep your relationship strong! Theodore Hesburgh said, "The most important thing a father can do for his children, is to love their mother" (and vice versa). A successful marriage is one that can go from crisis to crisis and keep getting stronger. Commitment, not emotion, is what carries you through. If you intend to stay married only as long as you *feel* like you're in love, you might as well quit now. Like anything else in life, a good marriage requires constant attention.

(3) Express affection for each other! William James said, "In every person there's a deep craving to be appreciated. If we don't receive it at home there's a good chance we won't get it because, in general, the world doesn't fulfill that desire." One of the best things you can do for your marriage partner and your children, is get to know them and love them simply because they're yours—not based on performance.

BEING HONEST ABOUT SIN!

Wash me thoroughly from mine iniquity.

Psalm 51:2

We don't talk much about sin anymore. It's no big deal. In the past Christians hated it, feared it, fled from it, and grieved over it. The truth is, we need a new way of looking at our sin; a new understanding of it. All sin involves denial! One of the worst things about sin is that it carries with it a certain moral myopia—nearsightedness. We need a new lens. We need to begin to see our sin through the eyes of the One we've sinned against. David prayed, "Against thee . . . have I sinned" (Ps 51:4).

One Christian college professor got honest and put it like this: "I'm nice to my students, respectful to my colleagues, love my family, don't steal, commit adultery, use drugs or swear, and I floss regularly! But when I look at myself honestly I see that I harbor bitterness, hoard my time and resent others intruding on me. I'm vain and consumed with how others perceive me. I wrestle with my sexuality and have strayed with my eyes and my heart. I pretend to listen but I don't. I think more about being great than being good. I act more spiritual than I am. I'm a mess—broken in every way—and my only hope is God's mercy."

A realization of our sinfulness can begin as a gentle nudge, or knock us down with hurricane-force. What's important is how we respond. Regardless of how often we've fallen, God offers us cleansing and a chance to begin again—if we're willing to acknowledge our sin and receive forgiveness.

A WORD TO SINGLES

Commit everything . . . to the Lord . . . and He will help you.
Psalm 37:5 NLT

*W*hen you meet that "someone special," here are 5 questions you should consider:

(1) Is the relationship based on honesty? The Bible speaks about, "Telling each other the truth" (Eph 4:25 CEV). Relationships thrive on openness and trust. When deceit creeps in, it's time to get truthful in a hurry, or call it quits.

(2) Can you be yourself? Paul writes, "Each of us is an original" (Ga 5:26 TM), and "Let's . . . be what we were made to be" (Ro 12:6 TM). If you feel like you constantly need to reinvent yourself or walk on your tip-toes, you're in the wrong relationship. Wise up! If they disapprove of you now, do you seriously think marriage will improve things?

(3) Is either of you possessive? The Bible says, "Love is . . . never jealous" (1Co 13:4 CEV). If one of you can't make a move without the other's permission, it's a red flag, back off!

(4) Have you established physical boundaries? If the relationship ended today would you regret your level of involvement? You may know that the Bible says, "Run . . . from sexual sin" (1Co 6:18 NLT), but do you understand why God says He made sex as a commitment specifically for marriage? And why it can otherwise leave you feeling "used?"

(5) Do you plan your time together? Without a specific plan it's easy to get more physically involved than you should. That's why it's good to agree up front as to your boundaries. Listen: "Commit everything . . . to the Lord . . . He will help you." Lasting relationships always put God first—always!

THINK! (1)

The wisdom of the prudent is to give thought to their ways.

Proverbs 14:8 NIV

$\mathcal{G}$od gave you a brain—use it! If you're serious about becoming a better thinker, understand this: great thinking comes from *good* thinking!

One night at dinner, a friend of John Kilcullen's described something he overheard in a bookstore. A customer asked the clerk, "Do you have any simple books on Microsoft DOS—something like DOS for dummies?" It was only a passing comment meant as a joke, but it stuck with Kilcullen and he did something with it. He launched the "Dummies" books. Some unknown customer had a good idea and it went nowhere. In fact, they probably didn't even know at the time that it was a good idea. But in the hands of a thinker, that good idea became a great idea. Then it became a bunch of great ideas. The "Dummies" books now encompass a product line of 370 titles, in 31 languages, with sales of more than 60 million copies.

So, if you want to become a great thinker, concentrate on becoming a good thinker. But before becoming a good thinker, you need to become a thinker. And in order to become a thinker, you need to be willing to produce a bunch of mediocre and downright bad ideas. Only by practicing and developing your thinking daily, will your ideas get better.

Your thinking ability is determined not by your desire to think, but by your past thinking. So, to become a good thinker, do more thinking. Once the ideas start flowing, they get better. And once they get better, they keep improving. And so does your life!

THINK! (2)

The wisdom of the prudent is to give thought to their ways.

Proverbs 14:8 NIV

*I*n order to become a better thinker, you need to:
(1) Do what works for you. Immanuel Kant used to stare out his window at a tower in order to think creatively; when trees grew up threatening to block his view, he chopped them down. Samuel Johnson said he needed a purring cat, an orange peel and a cup of tea in order to write. Some of us like music, some do better at a computer, some must write in long hand. Do whatever works for you!

(2) Write down your thoughts. If you don't write down your ideas you'll lose them. In *Bird By Bird,* Anne Lamott says, "I have an index card and pens all over the house—by the bed, in the bathroom, in the kitchen, by the phones . . . I used to think that if something was important enough I'd remember it . . . but then I wouldn't . . . [writing down your ideas right away is] not cheating. It doesn't say anything about your character."

(3) Put your thoughts into action quickly. Dave Goetz, founder of CustomZigns.com says, "For me, when an idea hits it strikes fire . . . the more time that passes after the idea strikes, the less heat it gives off. I forget parts of it, it doesn't seem so great. Ideas have a short shelf life." Author Alfred Montapert says, "Every time a person puts an idea across, he finds ten people who thought about it before he did—but they only thought about it." Don't just think creatively, put those God-given ideas into action and make a difference in His world!

RESTING IN GOD

If you are tired from carrying heavy burdens,
come to me and I will give you rest.
Matthew 11:28 CEV

*F*rank Laubach said, "If you are weary of some sleepy form of devotion, probably God is as weary of it as you are." Walking with Jesus shouldn't bore you or drain you, it should energize you! Are you feeling burned out? He said: "If you are tired from carrying heavy burdens, [that I didn't give you] come to me and I will give you rest."

Nobody was busier than Jesus, yet He was never in a hurry. He had a lot more to do than you, yet He never seemed to do it in a way that severed the life-giving connection between Him and the Father, or interfered with His ability to give love when love was required. He regularly withdrew from activity to the place of solitude and prayer. And when His disciples returned, flushed with success, their adrenaline pumping from a busy time of ministry, He told them "Come away . . . all by yourselves and rest a while" (Mk 6:31 NRSV). Mark explains that "Many were coming and going, and they had no leisure even to eat." Sound familiar? Constant hurry is the mark of an un-prioritized life. It's a sign that second and third things have become first things.

We want microwave maturity. We try to exchange wisdom for information and depth for breadth—and it doesn't work. Depth comes slowly. Following Jesus can't be done at a sprint; you can't go faster than the one who's leading. So, slow down. Don't just work for God—spend time with Him!

LEADERSHIP

Have a sane estimate of your capabilities.

Romans 12:3–4 PHPS

*W*ithout a "sane estimate" of your capabilities as a leader, you set yourself up for trouble. So ask:

(1) Am I a control freak? You empower others by being willing to relinquish power. That requires security; the kind that comes from knowing who you are before God. If you have one pencil and you think it's the only one you'll ever have, you'll hold on to it. But when you know you've dozens you can say, "Here, take what you need!"

(2) Do I inspire loyalty? In the past people were loyal to you because you were the leader. Nowadays they won't be loyal to anybody they don't respect, and who doesn't respect them. They need to feel, "I'm a better person because of your leadership."

(3) Am I willing to develop myself? Paul writes: "Work hard so God can approve you" (2Ti 2:15 NLT). It takes time to accomplish anything of significance. But it's never too late to grow. Leaders who recognize the importance of their assignment, keep developing themselves.

(4) Am I passionate, or driven? There's a difference. When you're driven, you seek other people's approval by focusing strictly on the goal. When you're passionate, you relish the journey as much as the destination. Driven people burn out, passionate people don't.

(5) Can I accept my limitations? By acknowledging your limitations you encourage the same openness in others. John Maxwell says, "I no longer believe that the most spiritual people build the biggest churches or work the hardest. Fatigue is no indication of spiritual maturity . . . it just makes me vulnerable to sin and error."

TWO QUESTIONS

Make the most of every opportunity.
Colossians 4:5 NIV

*A*uthor Myers Barnes said, "Time management is an oxymoron. It cannot be managed. You cannot save time, lose time, turn back the hands of time, or have more time tomorrow than today. Time is unemotional, uncontrolled, unencumbered. It moves forward regardless of circumstances, and in the game of life, creates a level playing field for everyone. Since you can't change time, you must change how you approach it." Once your goals have been set in prayer and you're certain your steps are being directed by the Lord, ask yourself each day:

(1) What's required of me? Any realistic assessment of your priorities must start with questions like: "What must I do to be a better Christian, or marriage partner, or parent, or worker? If you lead others the question should be, "What must I personally do that cannot be delegated to somebody else?" Always start with the requirement question. Give it careful thought before moving to the next question.

(2) What brings me the greatest fulfillment? If you do only what you must and what's effective, you'll be highly productive but you may not be fulfilled. But a note of caution: some of us want to start with the *fulfillment* question before we've answered the *requirement* question. Don't! You'll never succeed if you don't have the discipline to take care of the first question, before addressing the second. William James said, "Being wise, is the art of knowing what to overlook." If you bring your priorities into focus by constantly asking these two questions, you've a good chance of fulfilling God's purposes for your life.

ONLY A MOM

Mary treasured all these things . . . in her heart.
Luke 2:19 NIV

*W*hen a preacher stopped by a home in England and asked to speak to the mother, her little boy said, "You can't see her right now, she's praying." That's because Susanna Wesley spent one hour every day praying for each of her 17 children. Eventually two of her sons, John and Charles, were used by God to bring a great spiritual awakening to the U.K. and to establish the Methodist Church. Such is the influence of a praying mother.

Max Lucado writes: "Some things only a mom can *do . . .* like powdering a baby's bottom with one hand while holding the phone with the other . . . spending the day wiping noses, laundering socks, balancing a checkbook, and still mean it when she thanks God for her kids.

"Some things only a mom can *fix* . . . like the cabinet door her husband couldn't, and his bruised ego when he found out she could! Broken shoelaces . . . broken hearts . . . breaking up with your sweetheart.

"Some things only a mom can *know* . . . Like how long it takes to drive from piano lessons to ball practice . . . how many pizzas you need for a sleepover . . . the number of days left in a semester. The rest of us can only wonder . . . 'Mom, what was it like when that infant's cry first filled the room? Or the day the school bus pulled to a stop, you placed a kiss on a five-year-old's cheek, waved goodbye and then saw the tricycle—silent and still? How did you feel? Did you cry? Did you smile?'" The Bible says, "Mary treasured all these things . . . in her heart," because there are some things only a Mom understands.

"ONLY ONE THING!"

You are worried . . . about many things,
but only one thing is needed.

Luke 10:41–42 NIV

$\mathcal{S}$ometimes the reason we approach God with a list of requests the length of our arm, is because we're more interested in His "presents" than His presence. What we consider needs, are often wants. Can you imagine having "only one thing" on your agenda; like just wanting to be *with* Him? David said, "One thing have I asked of the Lord...that I may dwell . . . [in his presence] all . . . my life" (Ps 27:4 AMP).

Speaking of His presence, Jesus told Martha, "You are worried . . . about many things, but only one thing is needed." No doubt, Martha loved Jesus. In fact she couldn't do enough for Him. The problem was, she was so busy serving Him that she didn't know how to relax and just enjoy just being with Him! Sound familiar?

If you're not spending time enjoying God's presence, you're way over-scheduled! Maybe like Martha you think that unless you do the job yourself it won't get done right. And who knows, you may be right! But remember this: God will never ask you to do anything that hinders your relationship with Him. He wants that to be your top priority!

So, if you're so busy serving God that you're not doing the "one thing" He really wants from you, right now would be a good time to heed the words of the old hymn *"Turn your eyes upon Jesus; look full in His wonderful face. And the things of earth will grow strangely dim, in the light of his glory and grace."* So, how about it?

THE BLAME GAME

The man said, "The woman whom You gave . . . me
. . . gave me of the tree, and I ate."

Genesis 3:12 NKJV

*T*he blame-game is just another way of avoiding responsibility for our actions. It started when Adam blamed Eve: *"She* gave me of the tree and I ate." Next Adam blamed God, "The woman whom *You* gave . . . me." And Eve? Well, she said, "The *serpent* deceived me" (Ge 3:13 NKJV).

It's our genes! We'll do anything to avoid taking the rap! One blame-gamer, a recovering alcoholic and addict, admitted, "Each time I was pulled over for drunk driving I'd reason that the police were out to get me because I drove a sports car. Or, if my doctor hadn't prescribed those pain pills I'd never have gotten hooked. Or, if they hadn't served champagne at my brother's wedding I wouldn't have ended up in jail."

Understand this: you can fix the problem or fix the blame —but you can't do both! Nowhere in Scripture does God excuse you because of somebody else's behavior. Listen: "We'll all have to . . . take what's coming to us as a result of our actions" (2 Co 5:10 TM).

God didn't buy Adam and Eve's excuses, and He won't buy yours either. Others may have contributed to the mess you're in today, but it's your choice to stay there! What do you want—sympathy or solutions? Do you want to justify your past or change your future? Come on, it's time to clean up your act and admit, "Lord, *I'm* the problem. Please fix me by showing me what to do to be forgiven, healed and restored."

PEOPLE-PLEASING

Fear of man is a dangerous trap.

Proverbs 29:25 TLB

*I*t's sometimes called peer pressure, codependency, or people-pleasing, but God's word says, "Fear of man is a dangerous trap." And it generally takes 2 forms: you turn yourself into a pretzel trying to make others happy or you quietly make all your decisions based on getting their approval.

Maybe you became a people-pleaser early in life to get the love and attention you craved, or because you weren't taught to trust your own judgment. Either way it always backfires. Not only do others get annoyed with you, you end up disliking *yourself* when things don't work out. So why do we do it? Because it's always easier to listen to the people we can see, than to the God we can't see.

Peter struggled with people pleasing. One night when a girl asked him if he was a friend of Jesus he replied, "I don't even know that man!" (Mt 26:72 CEV). When the prophet Samuel confronted King Saul for failing to destroy the Amalekites, "Saul . . . admitted . . . 'I was afraid of the people and did what they demanded'" (1Sa 15:24 NLT). On the other hand, Paul said, "I am not trying to please people . . . If I were . . . I would not be a servant of Christ" (Gal 1:10 CEV).

God makes no allowance for people-pleasing. The Bible says He hasn't "given us a spirit of timidity, but of power" (2Ti 1:7 NASB). When you yield to the fear of others, you allow them—not God—to control you. God doesn't want you to serve others out of fear, but because you love them—and Him!

STOP YOUR COMPLAINING!

Stay away from complaining and arguing.
Philippians 2:14 TLB

*C*ounselors say that complainers are the hardest people in the world to help. You can't satisfy them, but they won't let you stop trying, so you end up feeling trapped. Once you earn a reputation as a complainer, people will avoid you like the plague!

Attitudes don't just happen, you choose them. Paul says, "Rejoice in the Lord always" (Php 4:4). Joy is a command. It's non-optional and non-negotiable. Joylessness is a sin: one that church folks are particularly prone to indulge in; one that seems to be readily tolerated amongst us; one that's never the object of church discipline. Even televangelists don't get cancelled for displaying too much of it.

The Psalmist writes, "This is the day the Lord has made; let us rejoice and be glad in it" (Ps 118:24 NIV). He doesn't say "yesterday was God's day, how happy I was then," or "tomorrow will be God's day, I'll endure until then." No, *"This day with its blessings and challenges is a gift from God, so I'm not going to insult Him by complaining."* Complaining is usually self-centered. It focuses on what *you* don't like. Get over yourself! True joy is a choice; one that comes to those who have devoted themselves to something greater than their own personal happiness. Listen: "For we have sinned and grown old, and our father is younger than we." A life of gratitude and service to others will keep you young till you die. But a life of complaining will age you prematurely and possibly hasten your death. *So—stop your complaining!*

THAT'S HOW MUCH HE LOVES US!

He . . . made himself nothing.

Philippians 2:7 NCV

*D*r. Maxwell Maltz tells of a man who was severely burned attempting to rescue his parents from a fire. But he didn't succeed and they died. Depressed and disfigured, he went into seclusion refusing to let anyone see him—not even his wife. Desperately looking for help she came to Maltz, a prominent plastic surgeon. Even though he told her he could probably restore her husband's face, the man stubbornly refused treatment. So when the woman came back to see Maltz he was surprised. But this time her question blew him away. She asked, "Can you disfigure my face, so I can be like my husband and share his pain? That way maybe he'll let me back into his life again!" That's how much she loved him! Maltz was so moved, he prevailed on the woman's husband to accept his help and thankfully the story has a happy ending.

The Bible says before Jesus left heaven He "was like God in every thing . . . But gave up his place . . . and made himself nothing. He was born to be a man and became like a servant." Our limited human minds can't begin to comprehend the world Jesus left. The homes of the rich and famous are like run-down shacks by comparison, and our finest clothes like dirty rags! The Bible says, "The Word became flesh and lived among us" (Jn 1:14 NRSV). Just think: the God of the universe willingly left the splendor of heaven, was born into poverty and died on a cruel cross for wayward humanity. Why? *Because that's how much He loves us!*

MAKE TIME TO DREAM

*I will give my spirit to everyone . . . your young men will see
visions and your old men will have dreams.*

Acts 2:17 CEV

One day H.C. Booth was sitting in a rocker
watching the sunset. Living in the Midwest he was also
watching the dust blow. As he contemplated the scene he began
to wonder, "What if we could reverse the wind so that it sucks
dust instead of blowing it? Later that year he invented the
vacuum cleaner!

Edison said, "The thoughts that come unsought and drop
into the mind, are commonly the most valuable." God said, "I
will give my spirit to everyone [not just a selected few!] . . .
your young men will see visions and your old men will have
dreams." Did you get that? Regardless of your age, God's spirit
can birth in your heart a dream, a vision of "what can be." Stop
putting yourself down, thinking "others are more worthy and
more qualified than me." Listen: "For it is God who works in
you to will and to act according to his good purpose" (Php 2:13
NIV). You may be flawed and limited, but the God who lives
and works in you is *not!* Don't allow fear to make you settle for
less than the life God intends you to live. Go ahead, risk, reach,
for "It is God who works in you," and longs to be glorifed
through you.

Historian Henry J. Taylor reminds us that "Vision lit every
lamp, built every church and business, performed every act of
kindness, and created more and better things for more people.
It's the priceless ingredient of a better day." *So start dreaming
and don't stop!*

BUILDING GREAT RELATIONSHIPS (1)

Do the hard work of getting along with each other.
James 3:18 TM

*T*o build great relationships and influence others for God, you must do 2 things:

Place a high value on people. Face it: if you're self-absorbed, you won't make building good relationships a priority. You've got to place a high value on people—because God does! That means expecting the best of them; assuming their motives are good unless they prove otherwise; valuing them by their best moments, not their worst; giving them your friendship with no strings attached, rather than asking for theirs.

Try to understand people. Many of us care about others, yet we still remain out of touch. Often that's because we don't try to understand them. Surveys consistently show that the number one problem in churches (and companies) that fail to grow, is leadership that's out of touch with people's needs. To improve your understanding of people and build great relationships, keep in mind the following truths and actions you can take to bridge the gap caused by them. (a) People are insecure, so give them confidence. (b) People want to feel special, so sincerely compliment them. (c) People desire a better tomorrow, so offer them hope. (d) People need to be understood, so listen to them. (e) People are basically self-centered, so speak to their needs first. (f) People get emotionally low, so encourage them. (g) People want to be associated with success, so help them to win. When you try to understand people and help them to succeed, you lay the groundwork for great relationships—and you influence people for God!

BUILDING GREAT RELATIONSHIPS (2)

Do the hard work of getting along with each other.

James 3:18 TM

A man arriving at an airport saw a well-dressed businessman (a professing Christian) yelling at a porter about the way he was handling his luggage. The angrier the businessman became the calmer the porter remained. After the businessman left, the first man complimented the porter on his restraint: "Oh, it was nothing," he said. "You know, that man's going to Miami, but his bags—they're going to Kalamazoo." When you disrespect others you not only hurt your testimony, you hurt yourself. In God's eyes *everyone* has value. So giving people respect is one of the most effective ways of reaching them. Now, that doesn't mean you can demand respect in return. No, you must earn it! But if you genuinely respect others and show them God's love, they'll almost always give you back respect.

The trouble is, some of us approach our dealings with others as a transaction. We're willing to give, only if we expect to get something back in return. Check your heart motives! Be sure you're not trying to manipulate others for your own gain. Jesus said, "Freely ye have received, freely give" (Mt 10:8).

Always start a relationship by asking: do I have ulterior motives for wanting to relate to this person? Is my caring conditional? Am I planning to use them? Do I need them to help me make up for a deficiency in myself? If your answer to any of these questions is "Yes," leave them alone; they're better off without you!

A WORD TO HUSBANDS AND WIVES

*Husbands, love your wives, even as Christ also
loved the church, and gave Himself for it.*

Ephesians 5:25

*S*o many wives complain: "I just don't know what
my husband wants!" There's a reason. Their husbands don't tell
them—at least not in a loving way. When a wife understands
what her husband desires and sees that he loves her unselfishly,
she's usually eager to respond and quick to do all she can to
meet his needs. Wives often say to their husbands: "I need to
talk to you." That's because wives often need to talk, more than
husbands feel a need to talk. What a wife means when she says,
"I need to talk," is that she needs her husband to listen to her—
then respond. She needs to know that she's loved, that he
understands how she feels, that he recognizes the problems that
she faces and wants to do something about them.

And when a husband talks to his wife it's extremely
important that she listen. Many women don't understand how
difficult it is for a man to trust a woman with his heart. That
trust is so fragile. He can be turned off by one insensitive
comment. So, when he opens up, listen with your heart—and
don't interrupt. Don't move to fill a silence that might occur for
a few seconds or even minutes. The more he's allowed to
articulate the vision he has for your family, the faith he has in
the Lord and the desires he has for you as a couple, the more
secure you're going to feel in your marriage.

KEEP IT SIMPLE

They think they will be heard because of their many words.
Matthew 6:7 NIV

$\mathcal{O}$ne Christian author writes: "The purpose of prayer is to release our faith—not repeat phrases over and over. For example, if I need forgiveness I can pray: 'Lord, I lost my temper and I'm sorry. By faith I receive your forgiveness, Amen.' Or I can pray: 'Lord, I'm so wretched. I can't seem to do anything right. No matter how hard I try I'm always screwing up. I don't know what I'm going to do—I've gotta stop getting mad. Please forgive me. I'll never do it again. I feel so guilty, so bad; I don't see how you can use me. Well Lord I don't feel much better but I'll try to believe I'm forgiven.' You'll agree that the first prayer is much more effective than the second."

Then she continues: "My problem was I didn't have faith that my prayer would get through if it was simple, short and to the point. I'd fallen into the trap of the-longer-the-better. Most of the time I felt confused and unsure, as though I still hadn't gotten the job done. But not anymore. Now I 'keep it simple' and I experience a much greater release of faith, plus I've confidence that God has heard and will answer."

Be honest with yourself about your prayer life and make adjustments. If you're not praying enough, pray more. If your prayers are too complicated, simplify them. If you need to keep them more of a secret, quit talking about them to everybody you meet. *In other words—keep it simple!*

DEALING WITH FAULT-FINDERS

Bless those who curse you, pray for those who mistreat you.
Luke 6:28 NASB

*H*ow does God want us to treat the fault-finders in our lives? Those who, when they don't win, act "hurt" and blame others for everything that's gone wrong. Know anybody like that? The Bible says, "Speaking the truth in love . . . grow up . . . into . . . Christ" (Eph 4:15 NASB). Here are some pointers to help you:

(1) Never confront with power, only with love! Recognize that the outward bravado of the fault-finder usually disguises deep insecurity; it lets them shift the focus off their own fears and on to the faults of others. *(2) Move towards, not away from.* Our first inclination is to ignore or isolate difficult people. Don't! Difficult people often want to be ignored, so avoiding them just provides emotional distance for them to hide. Plus it confirms their belief that you don't care, that you won't listen because you think they're wrong and you're right. *(3) Engage relationally.* Show genuine interest in their family, their work and their well-being. Fault-finders usually struggle with giving and receiving love. They're inclined to elevate opinion and loyalty, above communication and reconciliation. Nowhere is this more evident than in their personal lives. So be prepared to empathize with the trail of broken relationships you're likely to find. *(4) Bless and affirm.* Mark Twain said, "Kindness is the language which the deaf can hear and the blind can see." Fault-finders generally get more kicks than kisses. So, "Bless those who curse you, pray for those who mistreat you." Avoiding them doesn't work; neither does arguing. But "love *never* fails."

PRAYER SNARES

You do not receive because the reason you ask is wrong.
James 4:3 NCV

*H*ere are some prayers you may want to reconsider:
The manipulative. Direct your prayers to God, not others! For example, don't turn the blessing at mealtimes into a venting of your frustrations, or try to bounce your prayer off God and hit an unsaved loved one across the dinner table. God gets enough bad PR without that! Jesus said whenever we pray "don't turn [it] into a theatrical production" (Mt 6:5 TM).

The judgmental. In one church a childless couple was praying for a baby but some members of the prayer group decided that the husband wasn't godly enough to be a father, so they spent their time asking God to change him. Listen: "We do not ask because we deserve help, but because you are so merciful" (Dan 9:18 NLT). If God only gave children to perfect parents, the human race would be extinct!

The mass-produced. Maybe you think there's a better chance of getting answers to your prayers if you involve a lot of people. And sometimes you will. But with God, what matters is the faith with which you pray, not the size of the team. Jesus said, "If two of you on earth agree about anything you ask for, it will be done for you by my Father in heaven" (Mt 18:19 NIV). When you face a situation too big to handle alone, reach for someone who really knows God and begin to pray in agreement with them. *By the way, do you have any prayer partners?*

TAKE A STAND!

Let everything you say be . . . an encouragement.

Ephesians 4:29 NLT

*G*ossip by its very nature is destructive, regardless of your rationalization. It's a sick form of entertainment—and a major sign of insecurity! Let's be honest, knowledge is power; the reason we gossip is to impress others with what "we know." A student who was the subject of vicious rumors writes: "I remember it like it was yesterday. The queasy stomach, the tears, the hurt. I thought I'd be sick as I sank to my knees on the cold concrete floor . . . I knew I didn't deserve this. But that didn't make it any easier. I felt like I didn't have a friend in the world. All because of gossip." God says, "Evil people relish malicious conversation" (Pr 17:4 TM). Did you get that? Gossip isn't just frivolous, it's downright evil! So, how should you respond to those who whisper in your ear, "Have you heard about so 'n so?"

(1) Speak up. Listen: "Fire goes out for lack of fuel, and quarrels disappear when gossip stops." Tell your friends kindly but firmly that gossip is hurtful. If that doesn't work, vote with your feet. Walk away! *(2) Consider the consequences.* Wise up! Smart people know if you'll gossip to them, you'll gossip about them! And what's worse, you're dishonoring God and degrading your testimony! The Bible says, "Whatever you . . . say, let it be as a representative of . . . Jesus" (Col 3:17 NLT). You're representing—whom? *(3) Be an encourager.* Paul says, "Let everything you say be . . . an encouragement." So whenever you hear somebody being criticized, turn the conversation around and say something nice.

"A-W-E-SOME" PARENTING (1)

A father deals with his . . . children, encouraging, comforting
and urging [them] to live . . . worthy of God.
1 Thessalonians 2:11–12 NIV

*T*he mother of four teens says, "I used to have lots
of theories about raising kids; now I have lots of kids—and no
theories!" Adolescents are like hormones with feet, and there's
not much you can do about that. However, if your goal is to
raise responsible, godly adults, here's an effective strategy. It's
called "A-W-E-some parenting," because it encourages you to
create a home environment that's:

A-ffectionate: Teens aren't too excited about displays of
parental affection—especially in front of their peers!
Nevertheless God wants you to interact with them by,
"encouraging, comforting, and urging [them] to live . . . worthy
of God." As part of that, affectionate gestures and supportive
comments at the right time, work wonders.

W-arm: Dorothy Parker said, "The best way to keep your
kids home is to make the atmosphere pleasant—or let the air
out of their tires!" Seriously, what kind of home are you
creating? Do your kids enjoy being there? Do their friends? Or
is it a war zone? There are no conflict-free families, but
working to reduce stress can create a healthier atmosphere. And
if that means fewer activities, less travel and shorter work hours
—do it, you won't regret it!

E-ncouragement: Kids need discipline and consistency,
but they also need parents who believe in them no matter what.
The Bible says, "Harsh words stir up anger" (Pr 15:1 NLT).
Kids respond better to encouragement than they do to insults
and angry putdowns. Think about it!

"A-W-E-SOME PARENTING (2)

Memorize his laws . . . tell them to your children.
Deuteronomy 6:6–7 CEV

*R*obert Orben jokes, "I take my kids everywhere; but they always find their way back home!" And while we may smile, the truth is most of us didn't come to the job of parenting with an instruction manual. We learned from watching our own parents give it their best shot. Sometimes it worked, sometimes it didn't.

But God's principles *always* work; that's why the Bible says, "Memorize his laws . . . tell them to your children." Even model-parents who seem to have it all together, still fall short. The only One who never fails is our Heavenly Father; He's the ultimate parent. Here are some examples of His parenting style that can help you think like He does.

He's got high expectations, but He's also tolerant (Ro 2:4 NCV). He always tempers His judgment with mercy (Is 30:18 CEV). He teaches us through values, and rewards us for results (Gal 6:7 CEV). He exercises His authority, but He's willing to share His power (Ps 115:16 NIV). He insists on "His way," but also gives us the freedom to fail, recover and do it better next time (Gal 5:1). He protects us as we go through life, but still teaches us about reality (Mt 10:16 TM). He knows when to keep His distance, and when to connect (1Sa 12:22).

There's no way to be a *perfect* parent, but with God's help you can be a *good* one! So cut yourself some slack. You'll learn by trial-and-(mostly) error. Just take your kids with one hand and God with the other, and keep growing!

SEEING OTHERS THROUGH GOD'S EYES

We bless God . . . with the same tongues we curse . . .
men and women he made in his image.

James 3:9 TM

*W*hen you see a drug addict or a homeless person on the street do you think: "There but for the grace of God, go I?" Or do you secretly feel you're better than them? Come on, be honest! Our society admires beauty, power and money, including those who flaunt God's laws to get it; they think net-worth equals self-worth. Seeing others through God's eyes switches your focus from the package to the contents.

God says, "Pride lands you flat on your face" (Pr 29:23 TM). Why? Because it blinds you to the truth. Pride made Adam and Eve want to play God (Ge 3:5). Wounded pride caused Joseph's brothers to sell him into slavery (Ge 37:8). Pride made King Saul so jealous, he wanted to kill David, "the competition" (1Sa 18:8). Pride made Hezekiah reveal his nation's wealth to the enemy (Isa 39:2). Pride caused the disciples to compete for the top spot in God's Kingdom (Lk 9:46). Pride is why "We bless God . . . with the same tongues we curse [look down on] . . . men and women he made in his image." Next time you see someone caught in a trap of their own making, remember, the only difference between them and you—is God!

Listen: "When he saw the multitudes, he was moved with compassion . . . because they fainted . . . as sheep having no shepherd" (Mt 9:36). Jesus didn't see people as *bad,* He saw them as *lost!* Once you begin to do that, you're seeing them through God's eyes.

REBUILDING YOUR INTEGRITY!

Let me be weighed on honest scales,
that God may know my integrity.

Job 31:6 NKJV

Integrity. It's not a word you hear much nowadays. Bill Hybels says, "People who never use the word . . . look around them at promiscuity . . . abortion . . . sexually transmitted diseases, and mourn its passing. They see officials taking bribes, business leaders demanding kickbacks . . . investors parlaying inside information into untold wealth, and they lament the demise of integrity. They read about battered wives, jobless husbands and abused children, and wonder what happened to caring."

Unlike your reputation which is how others see you, integrity is who you are when they're not looking. Listen: "The integrity of the upright shall guide them" (Pr 11:3). What does that mean? Rebuilding your integrity means acknowledging, "Often my thoughts aren't fit to print," or, "I've hurt that person, I need to go back and make things right," or, "I've cheated on my taxes and I need to make restitution." (It's estimated that 50 percent of evangelical Christians fudge on their tax returns).

After Zacchaeus met Jesus he said, "If I have cheated anybody out of anything, I will pay back four times the amount" (Lk 19:8 NIV). Integrity doesn't stop with regret, seek to minimize painful consequences, or attempt damage control. It calls for honest repentance, making amends when possible and living in an accountable way that guarantees you'll do things differently in the future. Job said, "Does He not see my ways . . . If I have walked with falsehood, or my foot has hastened to deceit? Let me be weighed on honest scales, that God may know my integrity."

BE COURAGEOUS!

Be . . . of good courage.

Deuteronomy 31:6 NKJV

$\mathcal{T}$he times we're most likely to hear about courage nowadays, is when the media reports how somebody was rescued from a burning building or pulled from a frozen lake.

Being a Christian is not for the weak-kneed! It takes courage to 'fess up,' admit you're a sinner and commit your life to Christ. And it takes even *more* courage to live for Him when the going gets tough. It's always easier to quit a job you hate, bail out on a strife-torn marriage, settle for being a popular parent instead of a godly one, stay home and watch TV instead of going to church, or not bother sharing your faith.

Every day you must choose between doing what's right or what's convenient; living by your convictions or compromising for the sake of greed and approval; taking a risk or staying in your comfort zone. In other words, you must decide between trusting God (even when you don't understand His ways), or living in doubt and second-guessing Him.

Abraham's trip up Mount Moriah to sacrifice the son he loved more than his own life, begins with the words, "God tested Abraham's [faith and obedience]" (Ge 22:1 TLB). God's tests will stretch you to your limits! They'll demand every ounce of courage you've got—and then some! But you can't have a testimony without the test! Just like God told Joshua, "Be . . . of good courage," He'll give you strength to equal the test. The road may be rough and the enemy powerful, but remember, God "goes before you . . . [and] will not . . . forsake you."

A NEW WAY OF THINKING

I will put a new way of thinking inside you.

Ezekiel 36:26 NCV

*W*hen Jesus talked about being "born again" (Jn 3:3), Nicodemus couldn't get his head around the idea that a new birth must come from a new source. It doesn't matter how religious you are, Jesus said, "No one can enter the Kingdom . . . without being born of water and the Spirit" (Jn 3:5 NLT). "Water," as in the breaking of water, refers to your natural birth. "Spirit," as in being convicted by the Holy Spirit of sin and drawn to Christ, refers to your new birth. But the new birth doesn't merely blot out your past and give you a fresh start. God says, "I will put a new way of thinking inside you . . . and . . . give you obedient hearts. I will put my Spirit inside you and help you live by my rules." God doesn't just tell you what to do, He gives you the power to do it!

"But if that's true why do I keep falling?" Why did you keep falling after your first birth? Because you weren't born wearing walking shoes! No, you had to learn. And when you did you stumbled more than you walked. *"Yes, but I fall so often."* When you tripped as a toddler you didn't say, "Oops, I've fallen again, maybe I was never born in the first place." Mistakes don't invalidate your spiritual birth, they're part of growing up. Some of us just grow up faster than others. So be encouraged! "He who began a good work in you will [He guarantees it] carry it on to completion" (Php 1:6 NIV).

START BELIEVING

I know the plans I have for you.

Jeremiah 29:11 NIV

*H*ead-faith says, "I believe!" Heart-faith says, "I believe it's so for me," then acts on it. God says, "I know the plans I have for you . . . plans to prosper you . . . to give you hope and a future" (Jer 29:11 NIV). The Lord will take every negative thing that's happened to you and turn it into something positive, if you'll only work with Him and trust Him. He offers you beauty in exchange for ashes.

One lady wrote, "A lot of very painful and abusive things happened to me that soured my attitude toward life. I was trapped in my past and I didn't believe I had a future. But as soon as I believed God's Word, I was released from my pain and began making progress toward the future God always had in mind for me."

When Lazarus died, his sister Martha doubted that Jesus could do anything about it, so He told her, "Did I not tell you that if you believed, you would see the glory of God?" (Jn 11:40 NIV). Well, God's saying the same thing to *you!* He's asking you to put your trust in Him and believe that you can do whatever He asks you to do.

His Word says, "Let the weak say, I am strong" (Joel 3:10). Change what's coming out of your mouth! When you begin to say with conviction that you're strong, even though you're feeling weak, the Lord will be strong in you. Paul was practicing this principle when he wrote, "I can do everything *through him* who gives me strength" (Php 4:13 NIV).

"LOOK CAREFULLY!"

Looking carefully . . . lest any root of bitterness
springing up cause trouble.

Hebrews 12:15 NKJV

*H*arboring bitterness won't change the other person, but it'll sure change you—and not for the better! The heaviest thing you'll ever carry is a grudge. It'll make you sour and miserable to be around because your only desire will be to see the guilty party punished; especially when you or someone you love is the perceived victim.

What happens is this: Satan enters the picture and convinces you it's okay to harbor resentment. After all, you're only "protecting yourself" from getting hurt again, right? When that happens you dig in, justify your position and get comfortable living with resentment. That is—until it destroys you! The reason God says "look carefully," is because our bitterness has many sources: like an absentee or abusive parent we can't forgive; a nasty divorce we keep reliving; the careless words of a friend who's not even aware of their effect; the boss who passed us up for a promotion. By harboring grudges we let bitterness live rent-free in our head!

What's the answer? Forgive—before the problem becomes embedded in your emotions and starts feeding off your memories. Rehearsing old hurts drives them deeper until they take root and resist all attempts to weed them out. Paul said, "Make a clean break . . . Forgive one another as quickly . . . as . . . Christ forgave you" (Ep 4:31-32 TM). And the sooner you do it the better! Remember, there's no emotion so deeply rooted that God's grace can't reach down and remove it. *The question today is—are you ready to let Him?*

FOR PARENTS

Obey his laws . . . that things will go well
for you and your children.

Deuteronomy 4:40 NCV

*S*piritual values are more "caught" than taught. As a parent, you're constantly transmitting your values to your children. So:

Teach them to pray. Help your child to understand that prayer is how we build a life-long friendship with God. And they'll need His friendship, especially when you're not around to help them. Let them know that God is on "speed-dial," that He's available 24-7.

Don't tell them, show them. You form your child's concept of God. Whether you're loving and protective or distant and cold, your children grow up seeing God through the experiences they have with you. For example, God's never too busy to be interrupted, He constantly says He loves us, He's never abusive. Getting the idea?

Teach them to see God in others. Once your children see God at work in their own lives, they'll begin to see Him at work in the lives of others too. When that happens they'll value and respect others, and be valued and respected by them—that'll make them secure!

Don't send them, take them. Your children need to believe —and belong! Teach them that just as an organ disconnected from a body dies, they'll die spiritually unless they're connected to a local church. "Belonging" means they'll always have a place to go! The Bible says, "Teach your children to choose the right path, and when they are older, they will remain upon it" (Pr 22:6 NLT). Showing them the right path is the greatest thing you can do!

IT'S TIME TO MOVE ON!

Tarry . . . in . . . Jerusalem, until ye be endued with power.
Luke 24:49

 *J*esus never intended His disciples to stay in Jerusalem. He told them, "repentance . . . would be proclaimed . . . beginning from Jerusalem" (Lk 24:47 NAS). They were just to "tarry," remain there temporarily until they received power from heaven, then use it to take the Gospel to the world. After this we read that they "Returned to Jerusalem . . . were continually in the temple praising and blessing God" (Lk 24:52-53 NKJV). Now it's one thing to wait on God for directions and the power to carry them out, it's another to keep trying to relive some earlier experience you've had with Him. So, how did God get them out of town? Listen: "At that time the church in Jerusalem suffered terribly . . . the Lord's followers . . . were scattered . . . Saul started . . . arresting men and women and putting them in jail" (Acts 8:2-3 CEV).

When God has a mission for you He'll do whatever it takes to get you there! Before He'll let you miss out on your destiny, He'll permit trouble to uproot you. In fact, you may be going through certain difficulties right now because you're trying to stay where you're not supposed to be! You can't freeze-frame your past or relive it. When God moves, you must learn to move with Him.

Philip finally ended up in Samaria where he was used by God to bring revival to the entire city. The chances are, you may be going through certain trials and tests right now because God wants to use you too! So, tune in—know when it's time to move on with God!

ANGELS WATCHING OVER YOU

Angels are . . . spirits sent from God
to care for those who will receive salvation.
Hebrews 1:14 NLT

*S*ome of us struggle with the idea of angels watching over us. And what's the result? Listen: "Don't forget to show hospitality to strangers, for some who have done this have entertained angels without realizing it!" (He 13:2 NLT). Is it possible you have missed them?

"Tell me again what angels are supposed to do," you say. Okay, but keep an open mind; you're about to come into a new awareness! *(a) Angels are God's protective detail watching over you constantly.* Your early cancer detection! That narrow escape! Those were more than just lucky breaks. Listen: "He orders his angels to protect you wherever you go" (Ps 91:11 NLT). *(b) Special angels are assigned to watch over our children.* Now you know why kids survive things that make parents go weak at the knees. Listen: "Don't despise a single one of these little ones. For I tell you that in heaven their angels are always in the presence of my heavenly Father" (Mt 18:10 NLT). An angel went before Israel's army guaranteeing their victory. An angel shut the mouths of the lions for Daniel. An angel opened prison doors for Peter, saving his life on the eve of his execution. An angel showed up in a storm to let Paul know that he'd be okay.

So, did God suddenly do away with His Secret Service Department? Are they drawing unemployment somewhere in heaven? No, they're still on the job. We just need to become wise enough and humble enough to acknowledge them.

FULFILLING YOUR CALLING

Let every man abide in the . . . calling wherein he was called.
1 Corinthians 7:20

*W*hen Peter preached at Pentecost, 3,000 souls came to Christ. But when Paul preached a guy nodded off, broke his neck and killed himself by falling out of a third story window. Hardly an encouraging sign! But Paul admitted that preaching wasn't his chief calling: "I came to you . . . timid and trembling . . . my message and my preaching were very plain" (1Co 2:3-4 NLT). Yet while he mightn't have been the most dynamic speaker in town, God empowered him to raise the man from the dead after he fell out of the window!

Listen: "Let every man abide in the . . . calling wherein he was called." What Paul lacked as a speaker, he more than compensated for as a writer. His pen changed the world. He was responsible for more New Testament doctrine than those who spent every waking minute with Jesus. He judged cities, straightened out fornicators, stopped incest, rebuked idolatry, and established truth. Paul didn't *need* to preach; he wrote the inspired Word that enabled others to do it.

Something so powerful was released through Paul's writings that even when they threw him in jail he didn't ask for a lawyer or a gourmet meal because he was tired of prison food. No, he asked for more paper so that he could keep writing. In fact, Paul wrote all the way to the end of his life. And because he did, souls are still being reached today! What a legacy! And all because one man devoted himself to his calling! Now for the question—are you devoting yourself to yours?

HEARING FROM GOD (1)

Speak, Lord, for your servant is listening.
1 Samuel 3:9 NIV

*T*oo many of us think of prayer as just talking to God, rarely stopping to wonder if He might want to talk to us. How does God speak to us? *(1) Through His Word.* A familiar verse jumps off the page and takes on new meaning. *(2) Through people.* But you can't be so preoccupied, or selective, that you don't recognize them. *(3) Through His Spirit.* The Holy Spirit leads, rebukes, encourages, comforts, and stretches us.

A lot of us, however, don't seem to expect God to speak to us at all. By our actions you'd think that Jesus packed up and went back to heaven 40 days after His resurrection and hasn't been heard from since. No, the Bible is *full* of accounts of God speaking to His children. If the essence of Christianity is a personal relationship with God, then God must still speak today. But you can't build a relationship on one-way speeches; you need regular, intimate contact between two persons, both of whom speak and both of whom listen.

Hearing God speak to us through His Spirit is not only normal, it's essential. Paul wrote, "You . . . are controlled . . . by the Spirit, if the Spirit of God lives in you" (Ro 8:9 NIV). Once you turn your life over to Jesus, it can't be business as usual. Life no longer consists only of that which can be seen, felt or figured out. It includes walking by faith! Trusting God! Constantly opening yourself to His voice and to the leadings of His Spirit!

HEARING FROM GOD (2)

Speak, Lord, for your servant is listening.
1 Samuel 3:9 NIV

*S*ome of us are reluctant to open ourselves to God's leadings. Why? Because we know people who claim to be doing this, but their approach scares us. These people seem to have performed a kind of intellectual lobotomy on themselves; now they expect God to choose their socks in the morning and their restaurant for dinner. They claim to experience a leading an hour, a vision a day, a miracle a week. In reaction to this, some of us run in the opposite direction. To us, the Holy Spirit's promptings seem to go against human nature and conventional thought. Accustomed to steering our own ship, we're squeamish about letting Him lead. We wish the package was a little neater; it seems too illusive and mysterious. It unnerves us. So when we sense the Spirit's leading, we resist it, analyze it, and conclude it isn't logical; therefore we don't pay attention to it. What a loss!

Some of us want to obey the Spirit, but we're not sure we know when He's really speaking. "Am I hearing my own desires or God's voice?" Not wanting to go off the deep end, we avoid the water altogether. All these reactions are understandable. We've all experienced them. Yet Paul writes, "Since we live by the Spirit, let us keep in step with the Spirit" (Gal 5:25 NIV). When you fail to open yourself to God's Spirit and keep in step with Him, your Christian life becomes cerebral, boring, and worst of all—unfruitful. Don't let that happen to you!

HEARING FROM GOD (3)

Speak, Lord, for your servant is listening.

1 Samuel 3:9 NIV

*W*hy is it important to recognize the Holy Spirit's leadings in your life? Because:

(1) Your eternal destiny is determined by it! If you're a Christian, no doubt you can remember that inner tug which first drew you to God, enabling you to acknowledge Christ as your Savior. Well, even after you become a Christian, God still keeps tugging.

(2) Your assurance depends on it! When you're in an airport, notice the difference between passengers who hold confirmed tickets and those who are on stand-by. One reads the newspaper, chats with their friends or sleeps, while the other hangs around the ticket counter, pacing anxiously. What's the difference? Confidence! If you knew that in 15 minutes you'd have to stand before God, what would your reaction be? Would you pace nervously or say to yourself, "I can't wait?" Paul writes: "The Spirit himself testifies with our spirit that we are God's children" (Ro 8:16 NIV). In other words, the Spirit whispers, "Relax, you've trusted Christ, you're on the flight to heaven."

(3) Your growth as a Christian depends on it! Listen: "When he, the Spirit of truth, comes, he will guide you into all truth" (Jn 16:13 NIV). As believers we are responsible to read God's entire Word. But the Bible's a big book, we can't swallow it all at once. So, as we read it, God feeds us His truth, one bite-sized piece at a time. The Holy Spirit has a wonderful way of emphasizing different truths at different stages of growth. Aren't you glad?

TAKE THE PRESSURE OFF!

They tie up heavy loads and put them on men's shoulders.
Matthew 23:4 NIV

*Y*ou can demand perfection in others, *only* when your own perfection is complete. Ouch! Stop expecting more out of people than they're able to give! Continued pressure causes relationships to collapse.

We all need the freedom to be who we are. That doesn't mean we don't need or want to change, but we don't like people giving us the message, even subtly, that we must change in order to be "in." We're more likely to change for those who are willing to accept us with our flaws, than for those who expect us to live by their rules and regulations. One thing's for sure, God won't change the people we are trying to change; He has a "hands off" policy. We must get out of His way and allow Him to work!

Even when we think we're hiding our disapproval, people still feel it. It's in our voice and body language. Prayer is the great change agent, not pressure! If we truly love people and pray for them, God will work.

Many of those who irritate us are simply being themselves; their personality just doesn't mesh with ours. Sometimes we want others to change when actually we need to change. Often the things we need in other people are already available for us to enjoy, if we'll just stop judging them. For change to be lasting it must come from the inside out, and only God can affect that kind of change. So, who do you need to take the pressure off today?

TAKE THAT FIRST STEP!

The whole nation . . . completed the crossing on dry ground.

Joshua 3:17 NIV

*J*ust inside the Promised Land the children of Israel came face to face with a huge obstacle: the River Jordan. It was flood season so the river was impassable. God said He'd provide a path through, but they'd never seen anything like that happen before because most of them weren't born when the Red Sea was parted. Now, God could've made the river subside before their eyes or thrown a bridge across it. But He didn't, He gave Joshua some strange orders, which he in turn passed on to the people: "Command the priests to pick up the Ark and go stand in the river." Then He told the people to follow. Finally, He said to expect amazing things.

When you come up against a difficult situation, here are 3 things you must do: (a) Pray and stand on the Scriptures, bringing God into the situation. (b) Seek out godly leadership and fall into line with it. (c) Begin expecting and claiming great things from the Lord.

Notice, nothing happened until they stepped into the water. There's a lesson here for you: nothing will change until you step out in faith. There's a new relationship waiting to be formed—a successful business or ministry to be launched, a break through to be experienced—but nothing will happen until you move. The moment you quit holding back God will move to meet you, doors will open, the right people will show up and the resources will be provided. But you've got to take the first step!

ARE YOU COVETOUS? (1)

Thou shalt not covet.

Exodus 20:17

$\mathcal{G}$od said: "Thou shalt not covet" because covetousness can shipwreck you. "What is covetousness?" you ask. Here's a 4-part definition: *(1) Wanting the wrong things.* Wanting power without a willingness to serve. Wanting control so that I can be at the center. Wanting wealth strictly for myself. Wanting glory and praise from others. *(2) Wanting the right things for the wrong reasons.* Paul writes, "If a man desires the position of a bishop [an elder], he desires a good work" (1Ti 3:1-7). Wanting to make an impact—that's a good thing; but you have to want it for the right reasons. If you want it for egocentric purposes like personal recognition or power over others—that's covetousness. *(3) Wanting the right things at the wrong time.* A young couple says, "We love Christ and each other. We've committed ourselves to a lifetime together; we're going to get married in 3 months. But we want to sleep together now." They want the right things for the right reasons, but they want them at the wrong time—that's covetousness. *(4) Wanting the right things but in the wrong amount.* How much is enough? We don't know so we answer, "More!" Covetousness is wanting more than is required to provide for your needs and fulfill your God-given assignment. *Get this: more of anything other than God, will never satisfy the longing for fulfillment He's placed within you.* Only when you acknowledge that and bring your life's choices into alignment with it, will you discover the key to true and lasting happiness.

ARE YOU COVETOUS? (2)

Thou shalt not covet.

Exodus 20:17

*W*hy do you keep caving in to sinful desires? (1) Because you've 2 natures. Like 2 cars approaching an intersection at the same time, your old and new natures are constantly on a collision course. (2) When you dwell on a desire, yielding is only a matter of time. Ever go to your fridge when you weren't hungry but weren't really satisfied, sort of looking for something to grab you? As bad as that is, it's worse when you do it in life. Sort of like surfing the web of behavior options, looking for something to make you happier than you are at this particular moment. When you covet something, you make it more attractive and accessible than it really is. Eating too much? "I'll diet tomorrow." Smoking? "I know people who've smoked for 50 years and are still healthy." A one-night stand? "Nobody will ever know!" Covetousness maximizes the desire while it minimizes the danger.

Understand this: it's impossible to *dwell* on a desire for any length of time without rationalizing a way to get it. Like starting the countdown on the Space Shuttle, it's just a matter of time until lift off. So, if you're dwelling on it, set the clock: yielding is inevitable. What's the answer? Change your focus! Listen: "Those who live according to the flesh *set their minds* on the things of the flesh, but those who live according to the Spirit, the things of the Spirit" (Ro 8:5 NKJV).

ARE YOU COVETOUS? (3)

Thou shalt not covet.

Exodus 20:17

*B*e *careful what you beg God for; in time you may come to hate the thing you had to have!* Listen: "The Lord will give you meat . . . until it comes out of your nostrils" (Nu 11:18-20 NIV). God was pretty ticked off with this bunch. Why? Because they thought something else could satisfy them in a way that He couldn't. So He gave them so much, they choked on it. David writes, "He gave them their request; but sent leanness into their soul" (Ps 106:15). Try to understand this: *with* God, you can be satisfied with very little; *without* Him, all your accomplishments will leave you empty.

What are you craving? Putting your life on hold for? Continually begging God for? Nothing is essential but God. *Things* were never designed to take His place! When we covet something and make it essential—then beg God to give it to us —we're asking Him to replace Himself with something we consider more important. When we do this, God may allow us to experience the consequences. And they're not pretty! Don't reach the end of your life only to look back with regret on a shattered marriage, prodigal children, a blighted conscience, and the pain of having missed God's will. Our problem is not that we don't want God; it's that we want God and . . . the perfect spouse, an impressive career, the house by the lake, or whatever catches our fancy next. *What will it take for us to come to that settled place where the central desire of our lives is "God, I just want You."*

GOD IS DEVELOPING YOUR PATIENCE!

*Patient endurance is what you need now, so you will . . .
receive all . . . he has promised.*
Hebrews 10:36 NLT

*P*atience isn't just the ability to wait, it's the ability to keep a good attitude while you're doing it. God knows the exact time for everything, and while your impatience can make you and everybody else around you miserable, it won't rush Him. Listen: "In due season we shall reap" (Gal 6:9). "Due season" is God's season, not ours. We're in a hurry, He isn't. He takes the time to do things right. We may not know what He's doing but He does, and that'll have to be good enough for us.

God's timing seems to be His own business. He's never late but He usually isn't early either. He takes every opportunity to develop in us the fruit of patience. But other fruits are being developed in us as well. There are several things that must arrive at the finish line at the same time in order for us to win the race! Developed potential without character doesn't glorify God one bit. If we were to become a huge success yet be harsh with people, that wouldn't be pleasing to the Lord. Therefore, if we get ahead of ourselves in one area, He gently but firmly blocks our progress in that area until the others catch up. We don't appreciate any of this while it's happening, but later on we realize what an awful mess we'd have made if things had been done on our timetable instead of God's.

TO LOVE IS TO WIN

Love never fails.

1 Corinthians 13:8 NIV

*O*ne of Abraham Lincoln's earliest political enemies was Edward Stanton. In one speech he called Lincoln a "low, cunning clown." In another he said, "It's ridiculous to go to Africa to see a gorilla when you can find one just as easily in Springfield, Illinois." Yet Lincoln never responded. Why? Because "Love is patient, love is kind" (1Co 13:4 NIV). This kind of love is not passive endurance, it's active good will. It's not just standing across the room saying, "That person drives me bananas so I'm going to steer clear of them." No, it's crossing the room and finding a way to physically or in conversation embrace them. Lincoln did that. When he was elected President and needed a Secretary of War, guess who he chose? Edward Stanton. When friends asked why, Lincoln said, "Because he's the best man for the job." Years later as the slain President's body lay in state, Edward Stanton looked into the casket and said through his tears, "There lies the greatest ruler of men the world has ever seen." His animosity had been broken by Lincoln's long-suffering, non-retaliatory spirit.

Is someone injuring you? Have they chosen a place of opposition in your life? How are you responding? Do you want victory over your critical attitude? Then by an act of your will—forgive them, move toward them with grace and begin to love them. Then watch God bring victory in a way you never could, because "Love [the God kind] never fails."

PRAY FOR THOSE YOU RESENT

Love your enemies. Let them bring out the best in you . . .
respond with . . . prayer for that person.
Luke 6:27-28 TM

*I*s there someone you really resent? Maybe they're in your life to teach you something! Melody Beattie writes: "Years ago I felt I was meant to work at the *Stillwater Gazette,* but when a job opened up they hired Abigail. I'd always been taught to pray for those you resent, so I prayed for her. Sometimes 3-4 times a day—that's how much I disliked her! Eventually I landed a job at the *Gazette,* but not the one I wanted. Abigail had that—plus all the best assignments! So I kept praying, 'God bless Abigail;' it's all I knew to do. Then after watching her I realized she was quick, efficient, a good interviewer, so I began to push myself, thinking, "If she can do it, so can I!" Abigail was actually inspiring me! Eventually I stopped resenting her and we became friends. Soon afterwards I got an offer from a publisher to write a book and when it became a *New York Times* best-seller, I was glad I hadn't gotten Abigail's job or I'd never have had the time to write my book!"

God says, "Love your enemies. Let them bring out the best in you . . . respond with . . . prayer for that person." Certain people are in your life to show you what you're capable of. The ones you perceive as your "thorn" actually teach you things you need to learn. So stop resenting them, start praying for them and watch what happens!

VISION (1)

Where there is no vision, [we] perish.

Proverbs 29:18

*E*verybody ends up somewhere. A few end up somewhere on purpose; they're the ones with vision. A clear vision along with the courage to follow through, dramatically increases your chances of coming to the end of your life, looking back with satisfaction and thinking, "I succeeded. I finished well. My life counted; I made a difference." But without a clear vision, odds are you'll reach the end and wonder if your life really mattered at all. Vision gives meaning to otherwise meaningless details. Let's face it, much of what we do each day doesn't appear to matter a lot when evaluated apart from the bigger picture. But take the minutiae of any given day, drop them into the cauldron of a God-ordained vision, stir them around and suddenly there's purpose! Worth! Adrenaline!

It's the difference between filling bags with dirt or building a dike to save the town. There's nothing glamorous about filling bags with dirt, but saving the town is something else altogether. Building a dike gives meaning to the drudgery of filling bags with dirt. And so it is with vision. Too many times the routines of life begin to feel like shoveling dirt. But take those same routines and view them through the lens of a God-given purpose, and suddenly everything looks different. Vision brings your world into focus. It brings order to chaos. It enables you to see everything differently. *So, do you have a clear vision for your life?*

VISION (2)

Where there is no vision, [we] perish.

Proverbs 29:18

*V*ision weaves 4 essential things into our daily living:

(1) Passion. A clear, focused vision, allows you to experience ahead of time the emotions associated with an anticipated future. These emotions serve to reinforce your commitment to the vision. How? By providing a sneak preview of things to come.

(2) Motivation. Vision is the reason you completed college. Think of all the seemingly wasted hours of study: science labs, European history, research papers. Much of what you were memorizing seemed like a waste of time and effort. But you did it. Why? Because of what could be. A degree: and beyond that, a dream fulfilled.

(3) Direction. Vision serves as a roadmap. It simplifies the decision-making process. Anything that moves us closer to our vision gets a green light, everything else is approached with caution. Vision will prioritize your values, bring what's important to the surface and weed out anything that stands in your way. Without vision, good things will keep you from achieving great things. People without clear vision are easily distracted. They've a tendency to drift from one thing to another. They've no spiritual, relational, financial, or moral compass; consequently, they make decisions that rob them of their dreams.

(4) Purpose. Vision gives you a reason to get out of bed in the morning. If you don't show up, something important won't happen. Suddenly your life matters! It matters a lot! Without you, what could be—won't be. So, protect your vision!

VISION (3)

Where there is no vision, [we] perish.

Proverbs 29:18

*I*n a democracy every person has the right to dream his or her own dreams about the future. But at the cross, those of us who have sworn allegiance to Christ have surrendered that right. Listen: "You are not your own; you were bought at a price. Therefore honor God" (1Co 6:19-20 NIV). Honor God? What does that mean? It means discovering His purpose for your life and refusing to march to the beat of any other drummer.

With that in mind, consider these words: "For we are God's workmanship, created in Christ Jesus to do good works, which God prepared *in advance* for us to do" (Eph 2:10 NIV). Your life's been pre-planned. You can't just take your talents, experiences, opportunities and education and run off in any direction you please. No, you lost that right at Calvary. But then why would you dream of doing such a thing? What could possibly be more fulfilling than God's purpose for your life? And what could be more tragic than missing out on it?

Maybe up until now your vision has been making money, but it's the kind of vision that finds you at the end of life wondering what you could've done, should've done, with your brief stay on this planet. You cannot wring enough meaning out of secular accomplishments to satisfy your soul. The hole you're trying to fill has an eternal dimension that only Christ can satisfy. That's why it's imperative for you to pray, "Lord, help me to discover and fulfill *Your* vision for my life."

LEARNING TO RECEIVE

That we may receive.

Hebrews 4:16 NIV

*W*e're so accustomed to "working" for everything, that we struggle to get what God wants us to freely receive. God's always pouring out His blessing. As empty, thirsty vessels we must learn to open our hearts to what He freely offers. Listen: "Let us then approach the throne of grace with confidence, so that we may receive mercy and find grace" (Heb 4:16 NIV). To "get" is to obtain by effort. To "receive" is simply to accept what's being offered.

Jesus came to deliver us from struggling, not invite us to a new way of struggling under the banner of Christianity. We need to realize that all of God's blessings are given because of grace, and received by faith. One noted Bible teacher writes: "Every time I became frustrated it was because I was trying to do something in my own strength instead of putting my trust in God and receiving His grace (help). I was always trying to 'do' something and leaving God out of the loop. I tried to change myself, my family, circumstances I didn't like, even make my ministry grow. But God will never permit us to succeed without Him. If He did, we'd take all the credit. Finally I learned to pray for what I needed and allowed God to provide it His way, in His timing. When I did, I entered into His rest."

If we're to live victoriously, we must: (a) realize our importance to God; (b) learn to count on His grace. He is more than willing to help us, if we'll only let go of our independent attitudes.

QUIT YOUR COMPLAINING (1)

The people became like those who complain of adversity.
Numbers 11:1 NAS

*L*isten: "Now the people became like those who complain of adversity in the hearing of the Lord; and . . . His anger was kindled . . . and consumed some of the outskirts of the camp" (Nu 11:1 NAS). If that doesn't convince you of how God feels about complaining, nothing will!

"But who am I really hurting when I complain?" *(a) Yourself.* Complaining leads to anger, bitterness, even depression. God loves you. He doesn't want you hurting yourself. *(b) God.* Complaining questions His character. It says in effect: "God, you blew it! You'd a chance to meet my demands but you chose not to." *(c) Others.* Nobody enjoys being around a member of the Cold Water Bucket Brigade. Your stinking thinking affects those around you. Have you ever wondered why complaining is so popular, yet it changes nothing? Because it satisfies our selfish nature!

But there's good news. Listen: "The people *became* like those who complain." Note the word *"became,"* they developed a way of thinking about things, a way of approaching life. So, if you can *become* a complainer, then by God's grace you can *become* a thanks-giver! By acknowledging, "I choose my attitude," it becomes possible to choose a better one. If you're serious about changing, begin to pray: "Lord, I want the landscape of my life to be different; to experience the joy You give to those who leave the wilderness of ingratitude and move into the Promised Land of thanksgiving."

QUIT YOUR COMPLAINING (2)

Now the people became like those who complain of adversity.
Numbers 11:1 NAS

*T*here's a particular kind of complaining that really grates on the ears of God. Listen: "Now the people became like those who complain of adversity in the hearing of the Lord."

For some of us, adversity is a health situation. For others it's a struggling career and continuous job changes. For others it's a family situation that happened years ago; now we shoulder responsibility that seems unfair. Some of us made poor decisions and our marriage fell apart; now we struggle with blended families and the consequences of our choices. We all have to deal with some level of adversity. Each of us has something in our lives that God doesn't want to hear us complain about!

It's hard to live with adversity, but understand this—you forfeit the grace that'll get you through it, when you complain about it. The strength and joy needed to experience victory is available to you, but by choosing to complain or cling to the idol of a perfect life, you forfeit it.

"But what can I do?" Ask yourself 2 questions: (a) Am I a complainer? Think about that! Why? Because complaining is hard to see in ourselves but easy to see in others. (b) Am I willing to repent? If you're serious about putting this wilderness attitude behind you, think about why you're in the wilderness to begin with. If God reveals complaining as a problem in your life, acknowledge it—then turn from it! Otherwise, expect more wilderness ahead.

BEATITUDES (1)

Blessed are the poor in spirit,
for theirs is the kingdom of heaven.
Matthew 5:3 NKJV

The Beatitudes are simply what your attitudes
should be! We think of being poor as having very little, yet
Jesus says, "Blessed are the poor in spirit, for theirs is the
kingdom of heaven." What did He mean? That self-sufficiency
can keep you from experiencing *God's* sufficiency!

Old John B. Rockefeller, a Christian multi-millionaire,
once said, "I've made many millions but they brought me no
real happiness. I'd barter them all for the days I sat on an office
stool in Cleveland and counted myself rich on $3 a week." W.
H. Vanderbilt said, "The care of $200 million is too great a load
for any brain or back to bear. It's enough to kill anyone. There's
no pleasure left in it." John Jacob Astor, who spent his life as a
victim of ulcers and depression, said, "I'm the most miserable
man on earth." Henry Ford, the automobile king, said, "Work is
my only pleasure. It keeps me alive and makes life worth living.
I was happier doing a mechanic's job." Andrew Carnegie noted
that, "Millionaires seldom ever smile."

So when Jesus says, "It is easier for a camel to go through
the eye of a needle than for a rich person to enter the kingdom"
(Mt 19:24 NCV), does that mean He's against us being
successful? No, He's just saying, "Be careful how you order
your priorities. Don't let your possessions obscure your
relationship with Me, or keep you from fulfilling the purpose
for which I put you on this earth."

BEATITUDES (2)

Blessed are those who mourn, for they shall be comforted.
Matthew 5:4 NKJV

Grief is the price we pay for love! To love deeply is to grieve our losses deeply. Henri Nouwen writes: "We wonder when grief hits hard, 'why did this happen? To remind us of the brevity and fragility of life? To deepen the faith of those who carry on?' It's hard to answer 'Yes,' when everything seems dark. The important thing to us at that moment is to be relieved of the pain. But when we move through adversity rather than avoid it, we greet it differently. We become willing to let it teach us. Like Joseph, we see how God can use it for some larger end. *Ultimately, mourning means facing what wounds us, in the presence of the only One who can heal us!*"

David writes: "Weeping may endure for a night, but joy cometh in the morning" (Ps 30:5). Morning always comes! Your grief will ease with time. Your willingness to embrace the pain rather than escape it, guarantees that. It's not that you'll forget, it's that you'll remember it differently: with more gratitude and less grief.

Your tomorrows aren't in the hands of your employer, your banker, your broker, or even your family. No, they're in *God's* hands, and He'll be there for you when every other support has gone. Hasn't He *always* protected, provided for, and comforted you? Times and seasons change, but not "the God of all comfort." He's promised never to leave you. So, be encouraged, today He'll be with you wherever you go!

BEATITUDES (3)

Blessed are the meek, for they shall inherit the earth.
Matthew 5:5 NKJV

Meekness is not weakness; it's strength harnessed for service! Jesus' definition of meekness is one of a powerful, majestic stallion that's been brought into submission. It hasn't lost any of its stamina. It's just that whereas it once had a will of its own, now it yields to the will of another. The breaking process is complete; now all it needs is a gentle tug on the reins.

At Calvary, Jesus could have called down legions of angels to save Him, but instead He chose to submit to His Father's will. And He is our example. That means submitting each decision to God, taking direction from Him, trusting Him to provide for you, letting Him make whatever changes He deems necessary—all the stuff your carnal nature rebels against.

Elaborating on his pet proverb, "Speak softly and carry a big stick," Teddy Roosevelt said, "If a man continually blusters a big stick will not save him; neither will speaking softly—unless there's strength behind it." That's the same principle Jesus is applying here. So, whether you're stepping out into a new opportunity or just faithfully doing what's given you to do, go about it with quiet confidence, knowing you're backed up by, and infused with, the strength of God. Meekness says, "Lord, I gladly receive what You give and surrender what You demand. You not only know what's needed; You'll provide it. So I surrender my all to You."

BEATITUDES (4)

Blessed are those who hunger and thirst for righteousness,
for they shall be filled.

Matthew 5:6 NKJV

*W*hen Jesus said, "Those who hunger and thirst for righteousness . . . shall be filled," He was letting us know that we've a spiritual hunger only He can satisfy. But He can't if we're full of ourselves, or the things of the world. Sadly, society has come to associate righteousness with being a "do-gooder" or having "a holier-than-thou attitude!" That's not righteousness, it's a religious pride and Paul calls it "dung" (Php 3:8). Jesus condemned it by saying, "You . . . outwardly appear righteous . . . but inside you are full of hypocrisy" (Mt 23:28 NKJV).

On our own we could never be good enough to satisfy the requirements of a Holy God. That's why He sent Jesus to die for us on the cross, "So that there may be righteousness for everyone who believes" (Ro 10:4 NIV). The moment you accept Jesus as your Savior, you become righteous in God's eyes.

But Paul says "Count yourselves dead to sin but alive to God" (Ro 6:11 NIV). Why? Because it's not just about a *position* of righteousness that we hold before God, but a *condition* of righteousness that we demonstrate before the world in our daily living. Jesus said to "Seek . . . first the kingdom of God, and his righteousness" (Mt 6:33). "How do I do that?" (1) By valuing God's opinion more than anybody else's (See Pr 3:5). (2) By seeking Him before making important decisions (See Jer 29:13). (3) By replacing selfishness with the Fruits of the Spirit (See Gal 5:19-23). (4) By modeling your life on Jesus. (See 1Pe 2:21).

BEATITUDES (5)

Blessed are the merciful, for they shall receive mercy.
Matthew 5:7 NAS

*R*evenge only *looks* sweet, in reality it's bitter. That's why Paul writes: "Never avenge yourselves. Leave that to God" (Ro 12:19 NLT). Satan wants to keep you in a constant stew so that you'll forfeit God's blessings. Don't let him! Instead choose to:

(1) Be gracious instead of always having to be "right." Jesus said, "The merciful . . . receive mercy." Unforgiveness keeps you on the merry-go-round of resentment. Is it that important to make others wrong and yourself right? Listen: "You can't get forgiveness . . . without . . . forgiving others. If you refuse . . . you cut yourself off" (Mt 6:14-15 TM). Is that a price you're prepared to pay?

(2) Go to the source! Often the root of your anger is hidden from you. That is, until you whack your elbow or get stuck in traffic—then you turn the air blue! Exaggerated anger is often displaced anger; something deeper's at work. Ask God to show you what it is.

(3) Refuse to be a victim. Mercy heals; unforgiveness makes you a perpetual victim. Plus, while you're busy ulcerating and planning your payback, the other guy's out enjoying life! God's already promised you justice, so forgive your enemies! In fact, the only people you should consider getting even with—are those who've helped you! William Stoddard says, "Forgiving the unforgivable is hard. But so was the cross: hard words, hard wood, hard nails." Weak people seek retribution; mercy is always a characteristic of the strong. So be strong!

BEATITUDES (6)

Blessed are the pure in heart, for they shall see God.

Matthew 5:8 NAS

*D*escribing how as a child he accompanied his dad to the Texas oil fields, Max Lucado writes: "The countryside was flat and predictable, that's why the refinery stood out like a science-fiction city. The function of that maze of machinery is defined by its name. A refinery takes whatever comes in and purifies it, so it's ready to go out. It does for petroleum what your heart should do for you—remove the bad and utilize the good."

Listen: "The good man brings good things out of the good stored up in his heart" (Lk 6:45 NIV). When you're criticized or ignored, do you bite back or bite your tongue? When you're on overload, do you blow your top or stay cool? When you hear gossip do you entertain it, silence it, or spread it? When somebody offends you, do you harbor a grudge or choose to forgive? That all depends on the state of your heart.

Jesus said, "The pure in heart . . . shall see God." When your heart's been purified, you'll begin to see God at work in *people* and in *ways* you never noticed before. We do the reverse by cleaning up the outside first, but it doesn't work; superficial change is only skin deep. A dirty "refinery" will always produce an impure product. You only change your life by working with God to develop a state-of-the art heart.

BEATITUDES (7)

Blessed are the peacemakers,
for they shall be called sons of God.
Matthew 5:9 NAS

*I*n June, 2003, the historic feud that began 125 years ago between the *Hatfields* and the *McCoys* over a stolen pig, finally ended! Their descendants gathered in Kentucky to sign a peacemaking agreement that read: "We declare an end to all hostilities, now and forevermore. We ask that by God's grace we forever be remembered as those that bound together the hearts of two families." Conversely, a newspaper recently reported that a group of Texas firefighters deliberately set over 40 fires! When they were caught they said, "We'd nothing to do; we just wanted to get the red lights flashing and the bells clanging!" Jesus said, "Peacemakers . . . shall be called sons of God," because just as the job of those firefighters was to *extinguish* fires not start them, your job is to resolve conflict not add to it.

This principle inspired St. Francis of Assisi to pen his famous prayer: "Lord make me an instrument of Your peace! Where there is hatred, let me sow love. Where there is injury, pardon. Where there is doubt, faith. Where there is despair, hope. Where there is darkness, light. Where there is sadness, joy. Divine Master grant that I may not so much seek to be consoled as to console. To be understood, as to understand. To be loved, as to love. For in giving we receive. In pardoning we are pardoned. In dying we are born to eternal life." Jesus was called "The Prince of Peace." To be like Him—start sowing seeds of peace.

BEATITUDES (8)

Blessed are those who are persecuted for righteousness.
Matthew 5:10 NJKV

*I*n Yellowstone National Park there's a tree called a *Lodgepole Pine.* Its cones can hang on for years before falling off. Even then they remain tightly closed. They open only when they're in contact with intense heat. Whenever forest fires are raging and all the trees are being destroyed, the heat opens these particular pine cones. That way they're the first to assist nature in re-populating the forest. How's that for divine wisdom?

Jesus said, "Blessed are those who are persecuted for righteousness." Why? Because there's potential in you that's only released when "the heat is on." Job discovered this truth when God permitted Satan to test him. He lost everything, including his seven sons. To add insult to injury, he was forced to endure the scorn of his wife and friends because of his unwavering faith. Finally Job said, "I have heard of You by the hearing of the ear, but now my eye sees You" (Job 42:5 NKJV).

It's one thing to hear how God works based on somebody else's testimony, it's another to see it firsthand when you're wondering, "What did I do to deserve this?" Or asking, "If God's really there, why am I here?" Why? (a) Because in the fire you discover new aspects of God's care and character. (b) What turns worthless carbon into diamonds? Heat! Pressure! (c) In the fire you discover that when others abandon you, God remains faithful.

SPLASHES

Without faith it is impossible to please God.
Hebrews 11:6 NIV

*W*ith God, it usually comes down to one question: "Are you going to trust Me?" If not, expect a rough ride!

You can't tell by looking at a person how much faith they really have. Faith's like a bucket of water—you find out how much is inside when you bump it. When circumstances bump you, you spill out what you're full of. Maybe you've just lost your job or had a financial reversal—bump! What spilled out, doubt or faith? Maybe you got some bad news from the doctor and you're going for tests—bump! What splashed over the side? While you can't tell by looking at people how much faith they really have, you can by *listening* to them.

Bumps are going to happen; to expect otherwise is to set yourself up for disappointment. Count on it, you'll be tested. And the purpose of the test isn't just to reveal your faith, it's to refine it. God doesn't test your faith in order to know how much is there—He already knows. He tests it so that *we* can know—and work on it! Think of the hardest thing that's going on in your life right now, then ask yourself, "Is this circumstance shrinking or stretching my faith?"

If you want to impress the Lord, really impress Him, think carefully about these words: "Without faith it is impossible to please God."

WHEN JESUS COMES!

A man . . . with an unclean spirit met him . . .
screaming . . . and gashing himself with stones.
Mark 5:2 & 5 NASB

*T*his wild man was Satan's poster boy—a tribute to the work of the enemy. He was more comfortable among the dead than the living. Ordinary people were terrified of him. Notice: *(a) He repeatedly hurt himself.* Now, he used stones, but Satan's just as happy when you use drugs, sex, alcohol, gluttony and overwork. *(b) He was preoccupied with death.* Why would someone choose to live among the tombs? Perhaps at a certain point in the past something caused him to give up, to stop living. *(c) He'd no peace.* The Bible says, "The evil spirit . . . wanders . . . looking for rest" (Mt 12:43 Phps). The downside to godlessness is restlessness; nothing's ever enough. *(d) He lived in seclusion.* Satan's continually "seeking someone to devour" (See 1Pe 5:8). And His job's much easier when you don't have a support system. Fellowship wrecks his plans.

But when Jesus spoke, hell went into retreat and the tormenting demons submitted. They "begged Him, saying, 'Send us to the swine' . . . And . . . Jesus gave them permission" (Mk 5:12-13 NKJV). Think: Satan can't even occupy a *pig* without God's clearance!

No séances, chants, candles or crystals; just one word from the Master and he's restored to "his right mind" (v.15). No wonder the songwriter wrote, *"When Jesus comes the tempter's power is broken. When Jesus comes all tears are wiped away. He takes the gloom and fills the life with glory. For all is changed when Jesus comes to stay!"*

UNHURRIED, UNINTERRUPTED TIME WITH GOD

Their delight is in the law of the Lord,
and on his law they meditate day and night.

Psalm 1:2 NRSV

A real Christian stands out in the crowd! Their character is deeper, their ideas fresher, their spirit softer, their courage greater, their leadership better, their concerns wider, their compassion more genuine, their convictions more concrete. They're joyful in spite of difficult circumstances and show wisdom far beyond their years. And they're full of surprises: you think you have them boxed in, but they turn out to be unpredictable. When you're around them you feel slightly off balance because you don't know what to expect next. Over time you realize that their unexpected ideas and actions can be trusted.

Why? Because these people have a strong relationship with the Lord—one that's renewed day by day. David said: "Their delight is in the law of the Lord, and on his law they meditate day and night." They have a spiritual root system that reaches down to streams of living water, consequently, what they put their hand to prospers. Too few of us ever reach this level. How come? Because we're just too busy! The arch enemy of spiritual growth is business, which is closely tied to something the Bible calls "worldliness"—getting caught up with society's agenda, to the neglect of walking with God. Any way you cut it, a key ingredient in real Christianity is—time. Not left over time, not throw away time, but quality time. Time for contemplation. Time for meditation. Time for reflection. Unhurried, uninterrupted time with God.

IS HE LORD?

What do you think about . . . Christ?

Matthew 22:42 NIV

$\mathcal{O}$ne day Jesus climbed a mountain with His disciples. Listen: "Moses and Elijah, appeared and began talking with [Him] . . . Peter . . . blurted out, "Master . . . We will make three shrines—one for you, one for Moses and one for Elijah" (Lk 9:30-33 NLT). Peter's intentions were good, but his thinking was off. Three shrines would have made Moses and Elijah equal with Jesus. When God spoke from heaven, Moses the law-giver, Elijah the prophet, Peter the preacher, James the apostle and John the Revelator were all present. But God didn't say, "Listen to them." No, He said, "This is my beloved Son: hear him" (Lk 9:35).

Jesus knew exactly who He was. When His accusers shouted, "You claim you're the Son of God?" He replied, "Yes." (Lk 22:70). He also said, "He that hath seen me hath seen the Father" (Jn 14:9). Then He really blew their minds: "I've power to lay down my life—and take it up again" (Jn 10:18).

You can discount Jesus as a phony or worship Him as God, but please don't call Him just another historic figure. C. S. Lewis said: "A [mere] man who said the things Jesus said wouldn't be a great moral teacher. He'd either be a lunatic or the Devil. You can spit at Him, kill Him, or fall at His feet and call Him Lord, but let's not come up with patronizing nonsense about His being a great human teacher." He's God! So, what do *you* think about Christ? Is He Lord of your life? He wants to be!

HE'S PULLING STRINGS FOR YOU

Who worketh all things after the counsel of his own will.

Ephesians 1:11

*D*id you ever go to a puppet show when you were a kid? You've learned a thing or two since then, right? Now you understand that the puppet was powerless to make anything happen. It was the Puppet Master who pulled the strings and made the puppets dance and sing. He's the one who closed and opened the curtain at just the right time. Are you getting the idea?

Your success at work, your early detection, your favorable treatment—that was just God pulling strings for you. Like an architect working from a well thought out blueprint, God blesses you because He *loves* to, *wants* to, and *decides* to. Before Israel ever set foot in the Promised Land, God told them He'd already given it to them: all they had to do was go in and possess it. There's a lesson here: we simply carry out on earth what God's *already* decided in heaven. That's also why Jesus said, "Without me, ye can do nothing" (Jn 15:5). That is—nothing of eternal worth. Before He responded to others, Jesus first consulted His Father. Listen: "As I hear I [decide]" (Jn 5:30). He understood that "getting everything done" means little, unless it's what *God* wants done!

Listen: "Having made known unto us the mystery of his will" (Eph 1:9). Imagine living in such a way that God's will is no longer a mystery to you. That kind of life is possible—God pulling the strings and you making the moves!

HE SAID IT—SO YOU'D NEVER HAVE TO!

My God, why did you abandon me?
Matthew 27:46 TEV

*H*ow would you feel about having to stand on a stage and watch a video of every sin you've ever committed? The angry outbursts. Selfish motives. Critical attitudes. Jealous intentions. Secret addictions. You'd probably want to crawl under a rock! Well, Jesus endured much worse. The Bible says He, "carried our sins in his body on the cross so we would stop living for sin and start living for what is right" (1Pe 2:24 NCV).

Now, it's bad enough to die for sins you didn't commit, but can you imagine being forsaken by God? Abandoned! It's the same word Paul used when he wrote, "Demas hath forsaken me . . . and . . . departed" (2Ti 4:10). Paul looked for Demas and couldn't find him; and Jesus looked for His Father that day and couldn't find Him either.

So was David wrong then when He wrote, "I have never seen the righteous forsaken" (Ps 37:25 NIV)? No, because at that moment Jesus was anything but righteous. When you look at Him on the cross you'll see the gossiper, the liar, the cheater, the alcoholic, the porn addict, the child abuser, the murderer. Does it bother you to see His name linked with theirs? Well, Jesus did even *more!* He put Himself in their place—and yours! In a move that broke God's heart, He poured out all His righteous judgment on His only Son. So, when Jesus cried from the cross, "My God, my God, why did you abandon me?" He said it—so you'd never have to!

LEADERSHIP PRINCIPLES (1)

Don't begin until you count the cost.
Luke 14:28 NLT

*Y*ou don't demand leadership you earn it—every day. To be a leader worth following, you must:

(1) Learn to control your impulsiveness! Short-term solutions create long-term problems. Listen: "Be swift to hear, slow to speak" (Jas 1:19). Don't let knee-jerk reactions blind you to sound judgment. Always ask, "Do I have to decide this minute?" Usually you don't. This is important because your leadership is only as good as your track record.

(2) Put the right people in the right slot! We put people in certain slots because there's no one else to fill them at the time. That's understandable. But what happens when the job outgrows them? There's more at stake here than sparing somebody's feelings. Your fear of confrontation is permitting people to languish in the wrong slot, slowing down your vision and discouraging the gifted folks around you who keep wondering, "How long are you going to permit this?"

(3) Consider all your options, then accept final responsibility. By learning to wait a little longer and getting more information before making a decision, you can avoid the heartache of ending up with second best. What looks good today, or in somebody's polished sales pitch, may not look so good tomorrow when you're presented with better options. Don't pay twice for the same information. Talk to someone you respect—someone who's already done what you want to do, particularly when your decision affects others and will be called upon to stand the test of time.

LEADERSHIP PRINCIPLES (2)

Be with wise men and become wise.

Proverbs 13:20 TLB

*B*efore you make the decision, be sure you can *live with the consequences!* Ask yourself, "Do I have what it takes to handle this?" If you can barely cope now, how will you handle more? Check the record; before God builds the ministry He builds the man, because added success brings added pressure. If your success makes you unavailable to God and your family, it's not success, it's failure.

Never allow your expectations to exceed your practical potential! Get rid of the myth that you can do anything if you just put your mind to it. Dogs can walk on their hind legs, but it's not their calling. Be honest with yourself. Only do what you do well. "But what about all the other stuff that needs doing?" Learn to delegate, then let the church (or the business) roll on!

If the return isn't greater than the investment, it isn't worth your time! Time is your most valuable and limited resource; you don't have any to waste. Wasted time is the leading cause of failure, so get away from people and habits that waste your time. Become more focused and goal-oriented. Live every day as though it were your last—it might be!

Survive in order to thrive! Let nothing take you out. David said, "Weeping may endure for the night, but joy cometh in the morning" (Ps 30:5). If you can just survive today, you can thrive tomorrow; and with God on your side, go on to greater things.

IT'S A MATTER OF CHARACTER

I will . . . make your name great; and you shall be a blessing.
Genesis 12:2 NKJV

*G*eorge spent his early years shuffled between foster homes till one day Maria Watkins, a childless washerwoman, found him asleep in her barn. But she didn't just take him in, she took him to church and introduced him to Jesus. When eventually he left her home, he took with him the Bible she'd given him. Maria left her mark on his life—and George Washington Carver left *his* mark on the world. This father of modern agriculture was a friend to 3 Presidents as well as Henry Ford and Gandhi. He's credited with over 300 inventions!

And the remarkable thing is, despite his early disadvantages this orphaned boy never became bitter or spent so much as a minute getting even. Instead, when he went into his lab each morning he prayed, "Lord, open my eyes that I may see" (Read Ps 119:18). How could God fail to bless someone with that attitude?

Great challenge requires great maturity, so God takes the time necessary to develop our character to match the assignment. After telling Abraham, "I will . . . make your name great," it took 25 more years of testing before God finally entrusted him with a son to establish the Jewish nation. So, if you're waiting for "the call," could it be that your character needs more work? That the task God has in mind for you requires a bigger person than you are right now?

WHY DOES DOUBT COME SO EASILY?

Lord, increase our faith!

Luke 17:5 NIV

*B*ecause *doubters are easy to find.* How many real friends of faith do you have? Probably not enough. The people around us usually tend to focus on the obstacles, opening the door to doubt. Once that wave gets going, everybody rides it.

Because doubting satisfies our need for self-protection. Nobody likes to be wrong, to get hurt, to fail, so our subconscious reasoning goes like this, "It's easier not to trust God, to lower my expectations, then I won't be disappointed." But you are disappointed, aren't you? Why? Because of your doubt!

Because doubting is passive. You don't wake up in the morning and say, "Today I'm going to doubt God." No, doubt moves into a vacuum. It takes over when you don't do the right things. Listen: "Faith cometh by hearing, and hearing by the word of God" (Ro 10:17). If you don't keep your nose in God's Word you'll constantly be assailed by doubts.

Because doubting is contagious. It's easier to catch than the common cold. Its carriers are words. Solomon writes, "You are trapped by your own words" (Pr 6:2 CEV). Words either build you up or tear you down. For example: (a) "What'll I do?" versus "In God's strength I can handle it." (b) "It's awful!" versus "It's a learning experience!" (c) "I see no way out!" versus "It's not too big for God." Your words determine the spiritual climate of your life. So, to move from doubt to faith, start eliminating any unscriptural sentiment from your vocabulary.

WHAT IT MEANS TO LOVE

[Love] . . . believes all things, hopes all things,
endures all things.
1 Corinthians 13:7 NAS

*L*ove . . . "believes all things." Love believes the best about others—always! When someone you care about is called into question, love says: "You don't know what you're talking about; that's not the kind of person he is. That's not what she meant." Listen again: "[Love] hopes all things." Love sees people not as they are, but as they will be by God's grace. Wouldn't it be great if God could download that kind of love into all our hearts? Then Paul adds that love "endures all things." *Endure* is a military term. It means driving a stake into the ground—isn't that great? It's like, "I'll stand my ground in loving you."

In his book *Love, Acceptance & Forgiveness,* Jerry Cook describes a church in Washington state that grew in 14 years to more than 4,000 people. The book includes a commitment the people at that church made to each other. It says: "You'll never knowingly suffer at my hands. I'll never knowingly say or do anything to hurt you. I'll always, in every circumstance, seek to help and support you. If you're down and I can lift you, I'll do that. If you need something and I have it, I'll share it with you. If I need to, I'll give it to you. No matter what I find out about you, no matter what happens in the future—either good or bad —my commitment to you will never change. And there's nothing you can do about it!" Today pray, "Lord help me to love like that."

EXCEPTIONAL PARENTING

Bring them up in the . . . instruction of the Lord.
Ephesians 6:4 NIV

A minister's son who'd just gotten his driver's license wanted to borrow the car. His dad said, "First, get your hair cut." "But dad," he protested, "Moses and Noah had long hair!" "Yeah," replied his father, "and they both walked everywhere they went!" Kids can be exasperating, but they're also God's greatest gifts! Here are 6 principles to help you raise yours right:

(1) Don't try to make them carbon copies of you. God made each of your children a genuine "one-of," with their own genetic make-up and personality. Don't try to make them into something that God and the rest of us don't need one more of.

(2) Develop their potential. That means listening, observing, and once their talents and interests are identified, helping to maximize them.

(3) Love them unconditionally. Your kids need to know that their worth is never in question, that they're loved for who they are; that your love is not given or withdrawn because of behavior, appearance, or achievement.

(4) Establish boundaries and be consistent in maintaining them. Boundaries give kids a sense of security; without them, they're headed into a life of trouble.

(5) Help them pursue their dreams. Just like you, your children need goals to shoot for, to stimulate and inspire them.

(6) Help them develop strong character and godly values. These are the all-important intangibles that'll help them to go the distance.

AVOIDING BURNOUT

I've never been this low!

Psalm 142:5–6 TM

We talk about the straw that broke the camel's back. But usually the load's not the problem; camels were built to carry those—it's the overload. Whenever David bottomed out he told God, "I've never been this low." Before you reach that point, here are some suggestions:

Lose the red cape. You're not superman (or woman!) Dr. Faye Crosby says, "Learn to recognize your pressure release points so that your mistakes don't get blown out of proportion. Mismatched silverware at a dinner party doesn't signal the end of civilization. Handing in your report a day late won't push the company into bankruptcy!" In other words—lighten up; don't sweat the small stuff!

Acknowledge your limits. Jesus didn't try to personally minister to every person in Israel, so how come you think you can do it all? When you're planning your schedule build in a little down-time. The daily grind can deplete you, but a few minutes of quiet time with God can refresh and refocus you.

Just say . . . no! Usually we feel guilty and worry that people won't like us if we say no. The problem is, when we don't, we end up resentful, not liking ourselves. Dr. H.B. London writes, "It's easy to say no to a root canal or colonoscopy. It's more difficult to say it when things are interesting and enjoyable. Yet, even if everything we're doing is enjoyable, if we don't learn to say no, overload will overwhelm us."

PRAYER HABITS (1)

Peter and John went . . . to take part
in the three o'clock daily prayer meeting.
Acts 3:1 TLB

*H*ow can I make prayer a daily habit? Before answering, you need to heed 2 warnings:

(1) To those who love formulas! Jesus said, "They think they will be heard because of their many words" (Mt 6:7 NIV). These folks take notes in church, underline when they read, practice a rigorous spiritual regimen—maybe you're one of them. If so, before you lengthen your list, back off! Do you need more habits—or more effective ones? Too often spiritual discipline turns into a straight jacket filled with requirements that squeeze the joy out of life. Most of us can't live that way very long; and some who really work at it, develop such a self-righteous attitude that the rest of us wish they'd fail.

(2) To those who don't think they need any structure at all! You cannot grow without structure anymore than you can lower your body fat or increase your net worth by just sitting back and waiting for whatever happens. You don't wait to exercise until you feel like doing it. Be honest, how many days do you *feel* like it? "Not today, my bio-rhythms are down, it's a little chilly outside, it's going to rain, it's too sunny, my knees ache, the couch looks inviting." The list is endless. Maintaining good prayer habits is non-negotiable. No disciple will, in and of himself, create a relationship with God. But you'll *never* develop a rich rewarding prayer life, if you try it without discipline.

PRAYER HABITS (2)

When you pray.

Matthew 6:5 NIV

*T*he America's Cup team from New Zealand practiced for 2 years, 6 days a week, 8 hours a day, and brought sailing to a new level. People who are serious about something always make room for it in their schedule. When the disciples asked Jesus about prayer, He began by saying, *"When* you pray."* He assumed they'd have a regular time for prayer. Could He assume that about you?

He also said, "When you pray, go into your room, close the door" (Mt 6:6 NIV). Why the emphasis on privacy? Because voices, noise, music, phones, computers, TV, kids, dogs, birds—even a ticking clock can cause you to lose your concentration. So He counseled, "Don't bother fighting distractions because you'll lose. Just find a quiet place where you can pray without interruption."

But there's another reason: once you identify your "secret place" and begin to use it regularly, a kind of *aura* surrounds it. Married couples often have a favorite restaurant where they go for important nights out; they love its atmosphere; its memories draw them back like a magnet. It's easy to be open and intimate there. And when *you* create such a meeting place with God, you'll look forward to going there too. You'll grow to love it and eventually it'll become the most important place in your life. *"When* should I go there?"* you ask. In the morning if you're a lark; at night if you're an owl! In other words, when you can really "get into it."

PRAYER HABITS (3)

When you pray, do not keep on babbling.
Matthew 6:7 NIV

*C*ertain phrases sound so pious that we string them together and call it prayer. Much of the time we don't even *think* about what we're saying: "Lord, be with me as I go on this trip." Jesus said, "Surely I am with you always" (Mt 28:20 NIV). We don't need to ask God to be with us if we're members of His family; we just need to become more *aware* of His presence. Asking God to be with us when He's already there, is a kind of "babbling."

Another kind is heard at the dinner table. We sit down to a nutritional nightmare: the grease is bubbling, the salt is glistening, the food is piled up like a mountain, the sugared drink stands ready to slosh it all down. "Bless this food to the strength and nourishment of our body." Are you kidding? We are to "honor God with our body" (See 1Co 6:20). Asking God to bless junk food and give it nutritional value is like asking Him to make Detroit the capitol of California.

God doesn't want you to pile up impressive phrases or use words without thinking about their meaning. He wants you to talk from your *heart*—as you would to a parent you love and trust. Listen: "You will seek me and find me when you seek me with all your heart" (Jer 29:13 NIV). God knows how you feel —and He cares. Nothing matters as much to Him as what's going on in your life right now. So talk to Him—from your heart!

HOW LOVE ACTS

Love . . . is not rude . . . not self seeking . . .
not easily angered . . . keeps no record of wrongs.
1 Corinthians 13:4–5 NIV

*A*t what point should I confront somebody? Only after you've answered these questions: *(1) Is it critical?* If it involves a major doctrinal error, marital unfaithfulness, a criminal act, an abusive behavior or a situation that could hurt them, it's critical—get involved. *(2) Is it chronic?* If you observe the same thing happening over and over, it doesn't have to be big to get your love in gear. *(3) How close are you to the situation?* If you saw a casual acquaintance making a purchase that was unwise, that's probably not your business. But if someone close to you does it, it's both appropriate and loving to say, "We can't afford that. It's just going to give us problems down the road."

Here's how love takes action. Love: (a) "is not rude." It doesn't use the "open-wide-while-I-jam-this-down-your-throat" approach; (b) "is not self seeking." Love forgets about the need to be accepted and makes sure that what the other person hears is filtered only by kindness. It refuses to walk away having spoken only half the truth; (c) "is not easily angered." When you confront someone in love, don't be upset if you get an angry response like, "Who are you to tell me?" (d) "keeps no record of wrongs." When you've been hurt, it's critical that you deal with the hurt and get it behind you. Only then can you confront someone for their own good. That's love in action—and it's powerful!

A "SPECIAL" RESTORATION

Breathe upon these slain, that they may live . . .
and the breath came into them.

Ezekiel 37:9–10 NRS

*A*nytime you see someone greatly used of God, chances are that along the way they've experienced some hurt and rejection. Ezekiel prayed, "Breathe upon these slain, that they might live . . . and the breath came into them." God has a "special" restoration for those who've been wounded, condemned and left to die. (1) After he was thrown out of the city, stoned, and left for dead, Paul speaks of being taken up into the third heaven and experiencing things too wonderful to speak of on earth. (See 2Co 12:2&4). In fact it was so profound, he couldn't explain whether it had happened to him in the body or out of it! (2) When John was exiled on the penal colony of Patmos, they chained his body but they couldn't incarcerate his spirit. Abandoned and ostracized, he penned these words: "On the Lord's Day I was in the Spirit, and heard behind me a loud voice like a trumpet" (Rev 1:10 NIV). As a result, he wrote the Book of Revelation.

David said, "In the day of trouble . . . my head will be exalted above the enemies who surround me . . . I will sing . . . to the Lord" (Ps 27:5-6 NIV). Now *that's* how you glory in tribulation, then looking back be able to say, "Thank you for the experience. Without it I'd never have gotten to know God like I do today." In fact, once you start seeing things in that light, you might even be tempted to phone up your enemies and thank them for how they treated you!

BEFORE YOU TIE THE KNOT!

Can two people walk together without agreeing?
Amos 3:3 NLT

*S*am and Hilda had been married for 50 years, yet they still fought continuously. One day Hilda said, "Sam, I've got the answer! Let's ask God to take one of us home—then I can go live with my sister!" Just because you're both Christians doesn't guarantee harmony. Here are some practical areas you need to E-V-A-L-U-A-T-E:

Enjoy. Do you enjoy the same things? Maybe it's no big deal now, but later when he's glued to the ballgame and you want a little conversation—it will be! *Values.* The Bible asks: "Can two people walk together without agreeing?" Are you able to agree on child raising, finances, in-laws, goals, and your relationship with God? Those are make-or-break issues! *Accessibility.* Are you both emotionally accessible, or is he the strong silent type who doesn't communicate—or understand your need to? *Love.* Do you really love each other? Not the Hollywood version, but the kind that: listens to your partner's opinions and concerns? Overlooks their faults and failings? Values them? Expresses itself through kindness? *Understanding.* You won't agree on everything, but can you understand and handle each other's point of view? *Appreciation.* Dave McIntye says, "Appreciation is like an insurance policy, it has to be renewed every now and then." Do you make a habit of expressing yours? *Temperament.* Are your personalities compatible? If you're naturally upbeat but they're moody and introverted, you may have an oil and water mix. *Environment.* If you're from different backgrounds, are you comfortable in the same spiritual and social settings? Before you tie the knot— think carefully about these things!

EXPANDING YOUR COMFORT ZONE

The Lord . . . set me . . . in a large place.

Psalm 118:5 AMP

*W*hat you enjoy today is a direct result of what you invested in yesterday. So, if you want the future to be different, start changing what you're doing. Each of us has a comfort zone. We make most of our decisions based on it. Outside of it we begin to feel uneasy. For example, some of us lack self-confidence unless we wear name-brand clothes; others wouldn't know an Armani suit from a tracksuit! Some of us are intimidated by those higher up the food chain; others would be comfortable having tea with the Queen.

Accomplishing anything worthwhile generally means— expanding your comfort zone. That can be scary. It takes guts to leave the ruts! In a rut you learn to tolerate even unbearable situations, which makes change difficult. It takes courage to examine your life, decide what isn't working and change it; especially when it involves changing jobs, locations, habits, and relationships.

But if you want the fruit, you've got to get out on the limb. Behold the turtle: he makes progress only by sticking his neck out. David said, "The Lord . . . set me . . . in a large place." Taking a risk every day empowers you; it widens your space. So go ahead, talk to that person who intimidates you, ask your boss for a raise if you deserve it! Seize that opportunity; invest in that business; eat at a nice restaurant, even if it means dining alone! Each night before you go to sleep, plan tomorrow's "risk." Why? Because the wider your comfort zone, the less fear can control you.

PRACTICE BEING CONTENT

I have learned to be content.

Philippians 4:11 NAS

*H*ow can you find true contentment? By observing these 3 simple principles:

(1) Seek it. Make contentment a daily choice. Come to the place where you really believe that *more* doesn't equal *happier.* To find contentment—simplify!

(2) Say it. Cultivate the ability to say, "I have enough." Push back from the table and say, "I've had enough." Stand with the surprise bonus in your hand considering what you might buy and say, "I have enough; Lord, how can I use this for You?"

(3) Settle it. David writes, "If riches increase, do not set your heart upon them" (Ps 62:10 NAS). Don't let your income dictate your lifestyle. Choose a realistic level of living and don't compromise by spending more just because more arrives. If you don't choose your lifestyle the world will choose it for you, and it'll probably be one beyond your means. Let your lifestyle be biblically based; make it eternally focused!

Consider this: if all the grains of sand on all the beaches of the world represented eternity, then you could say that one grain of sand represents your lifespan. Now think: you're over here grinding your one grain day and night to get everything you can out of it, while ignoring all the beaches of eternity that God has in store for you. Not too bright, eh? To be content, focus on eternity. Let enough be enough. Paul did! He said: "I have learned to be content in whatever circumstances I am." Contentment is something you learn; you have to work at it—daily!

BURIED TREASURE

We have this treasure in earthen vessels . . . that . . .
the power will be of God . . . not . . . ourselves.

2 Corinthians 4:7 NAS

$\mathcal{G}$od's given each of us a talent that He wants to use for His purposes. It may be lying dormant under layers of failure, fear and low self-esteem. You may be aware of your talent yet not know how to put it to work. Maybe you've been going from place to place or relationship to relationship hoping to find someone who'll acknowledge it and draw it out. If so, listen: "We have this treasure in earthen vessels . . . that . . . the power will be of God and not ourselves." Only the One who placed your talent within you, knows where it's hidden and how to release it.

Delayed destiny is the Devil's delight. By not allowing God to develop your talent, you end up frustrated, living far below your potential, making poor decisions. The fact is, you've so much treasure buried within you that the enemy's out to steal it. You never have to wonder about his motive. Jesus says he "comes only to rob" (Jn 10:10 CEV). Now, you don't rob somebody unless they've something worth taking, right? Your talent may be raw and undeveloped, or buried under years of self-doubt, unconfessed sin, bad habits, regret and despair. But God can take something that looks like nothing, and create something wonderful with it. Just think, He made the earth from *nothing*—so imagine what He can do when He has something to start with! Today begin to pray, "Father, help me to recognize and release the talents You've placed within me, and begin using them for Your glory."

HOW TO CHANGE YOUR THINKING

God has . . . given us . . . power . . . love . . .
and . . . a sound mind.

2 Timothy 1:7 NKJV

*W*hen somebody says, "This is off the top of my head," expect dandruff! Einstein said, "Thinking is hard work, that's why so few of us do it." To become a better thinker you must change 2 things:

(1) Your thought processes. Gordon MacDonald says, "People who are out of shape mentally, fall victim to ideas and systems that are destructive to the human spirit. They've not been taught how to think, nor have they set themselves to the life-long pursuit of the growth of the mind, so they grow dependent upon the thoughts and opinions of others. Rather than deal with ideas and issues, they reduce themselves to lives filled with rules, regulations and programs."

(2) Your expectations. A man went to a fortune teller who told him, "You'll be poor and unhappy until you're 45." He asked the fortune teller, "What will happen then?" She replied, "Then you'll get used to it." How many successful people do you know who are apathetic or negative? None! Real faith produces excitement, commitment, energy—characteristics that help you achieve success. If you'd like to possess these qualities, then raise your expectation level. Bring it into alignment with God's promises.

Do you want to succeed where you've failed before? To become the person you always hoped to be? Don't start by trying to change your *actions,* start by changing your *mind.* Renew it daily with God's Word. Nothing you do will have as great an impact.

GOD'S GRACIOUS TREATMENT

Grace be unto you, and peace, from God.
1 Corinthians 1:3

*M*any of the Epistles open with, "Grace be unto you, and peace." Why? Because we cannot experience God's peace unless we first know how to receive His grace and walk in it. There are 3 things about grace you need to understand: (a) It cannot be earned. (b) It's God doing for you what you cannot do for yourself. (c) It usually doesn't kick in until you stop struggling, trying to do it your own way.

James writes: "God opposes the proud but gives grace to the humble" (Jas 4:6 NIV). The humble are those who admit their total inability to succeed without God's help. But the proud are always trying to take credit. They like to think it's *their* ability that gets the job done, so they've difficulty asking, and even more difficulty receiving. That's why Peter writes, "Grow in grace" (2Pe 3:18). We only learn to trust God by doing it. We grow in grace by practicing putting our trust in Him, counting on His gracious provision for each day, and His intervention in situations that are difficult or impossible for us.

Face it: there'll never be a day when you won't need God's grace. And if you're willing to acknowledge that you need it and receive it by faith, there'll be no shortage of it. Listen: "For out of His fullness (abundance) we have all received [all had a share and we were all supplied with] one grace after another and spiritual blessing upon spiritual blessing and even favor upon favor and gift [heaped] upon gift" (Jn 1:16 AMP).

WHAT IS FAITH?

Now faith is the substance of things hoped for,
the evidence of things not seen.

Hebrews 11:1

Faith is a substance! We don't tend to see it that way, we look at it as being very ethereal. But it's not; we use faith every day. For example: you pick up the phone, call a department store to place an order and they ask for your credit card number. Then they send you a receipt. Now that receipt is what you hold on to while you're waiting for the item to arrive; it gives you assurance that the product is on the way. And the same is true in the spiritual world. God promises to answer your prayer. You believe Him. But your faith is the "substance" you hold on to while you're waiting.

Faith is also evidence! Why would you believe that somebody you can't see on the other end of a phone line would send you something just because you order it. Because it happens every day for others, and because it's happened to you before. Therefore, you're not being presumptuous or silly when you go to your door expecting it to be there. You're not the first person to trust God and you won't be the last. Listen: "Lord, You have been our dwelling place in all generations" (Ps 90:1 NAS). People have been trusting God for thousands of years and has He ever let them down? Never! His past faithfulness is all the "evidence" you need. So, it's not foolish at all to put your confidence in a God like that, is it?

THE PERFORMANCE/ACCEPTANCE
TREADMILL (1)

For in Him we live, and move, and have our being.

Acts 17:28

$\mathcal{G}$od loves you as much on your bad days as He does on your good ones. Really? How's that possible? Because His acceptance of you is based on your *position* (in Christ) not your *condition* (in the flesh). Listen: "For our sake He made Christ [virtually] to be sin Who knew no sin, so that in and through Him we might become [endued with, viewed as being in, and examples of] the righteousness of God [what we ought to be, approved and acceptable and in right relationship with Him, by His (not our) goodness]" (2Co 5:21 AMP).

At Calvary God took every sin you could ever commit and laid it upon His Son. When you come to the cross as a sinner, He takes all of Christ's righteousness and wraps you up in it. From that point on He sees you only one way—in Christ! How liberating!

Liberating—yes! Because now we see that our worth isn't based on what we *do,* but on who we *are* in Christ. God actually *assigned* value to you by allowing Jesus to die for you. "But I can't believe that God doesn't care about what I do?" You're right! God wants you to do good works—but He doesn't want you to depend on them; He wants you to do them out of love for Him. Once you understand your position, who you are in Christ, you can get off the performance/acceptance treadmill and begin doing the right things for the right reasons.

THE PERFORMANCE/ACCEPTANCE TREADMILL (2)

> *A man is . . . made upright by faith*
> *independent of . . . good deeds.*
>
> Romans 3:28 AMP

*I*t's essential that you understand what makes you acceptable in the eyes of God. If you've real faith you'll do good works, but you won't depend on them. No, you'll do them as an act of loving obedience—rather than a "work of the flesh" by which you hope to gain right standing with Him.

We spend our lives feeling wrong about ourselves. And unfortunately the world confirms this by promoting the idea that our value is somehow connected to our "doing." Growing up, we're constantly compared. When asked why we were not doing as well as our brother or sister or the child next door, we felt we were doing our best so we'd no answer. Therefore we determined to try harder; but no matter how hard we tried somebody still wasn't satisfied with us. We were still getting the message "something's wrong with you." This leaves us burned out, confused, turned-off, and in some cases mentally ill. It drives multitudes into therapy, when really all they need is—God's unconditional love. *Get this: your wrong behaviors won't be permanently changed until you know that you're loved by God apart from what you do. All of us need that—and that's what Jesus made possible through the cross!*

Why is this important to believe? Because until you know who you are in Christ, you'll stumble along believing that your acceptance with God is performance-based. Your acceptance with God is based on performance, but not yours—Christ's! Grasp that, and you'll begin enjoying your Christian life!

THE PERFORMANCE/ACCEPTANCE
TREADMILL (3)

We do not have a High Priest Who is unable to understand.

Hebrews 4:15 AMP

esus loves you unconditionally and is committed to working with you. And the best part is—He doesn't condemn you while He's doing it! Listen: "For we do not have a High Priest Who is unable to understand . . . have a shared feeling with our weaknesses . . . and [our] liability to the assaults of temptation" (Heb 4:15 AMP).

Notice the word "understand." Jesus understands us when nobody else does. He even understands us when we don't understand ourselves! People see what we do and want to know why we're not doing it better— or even why we're doing it at all. But Jesus understands why we behave as we do. He understands the emotional wounds in our past. He understands what we were created for. He understands the temperament given to us at birth. He understands our struggles. He even understands the faulty foundation upon which we base our self-worth.

And He not only understands, He cares! Once we enter into a personal relationship with Him, Jesus begins a process of relieving our pain, revealing our true value, and releasing our gifts. Bit by bit He restores everything Satan has stolen from us. And while all this is happening, God has positioned us securely "in Christ;" therefore, we're always acceptable to Him. Salvation, including complete acceptance with God, which Jesus earned for us on the cross, becomes ours at the point of believing faith. Knowing that, makes life wonderful!

A WORD TO WOMEN

My people will dwell in a peaceful habitation.
Isaiah 32:18 NKJV

*I*n the past stress was considered mostly a male problem, but women are catching up fast—stress that stems from pursuing perfection, looking a certain way, attempting to do it all, isolating yourself, never saying no, being unable to relax, having no time with God. This isn't how God wants you to live! He said, "My people will dwell in a peaceful habitation." So, if you want to reduce your stress levels, try these 2 things:

(1) Pad your schedule. Since everything takes longer than you think, having enough time to complete the job helps reduce anxiety. Whenever you're under the gun, a good rule of thumb is to allow 20 percent more time than you think you'll need.

(2) Trade the Mercedes for a Ford! A study of 8,000 British households found that those who maintained lifestyles beyond their means, were more prone to stress-related illness. Solomon says, "He that is greedy of gain troubleth his own house" (Pr 15:27). And Paul adds: "Some people want money so much that they have given up their faith and caused themselves . . . pain" (1Ti 6:10 CEV). "Does that mean God doesn't want me to get ahead in life?" No, He just wants you to keep your priorities straight and learn to enjoy where you are, on your way to where you're going. Today, if you're feeling stressed out, pray: "Lord, I need to be renewed. This business of living has drained me. Thank You for ordaining quiet times in the midst of hectic schedules. Help me to always put You first, and to find my place of rest in You. Amen."

START SHOWING SOME GRATITUDE

Oh, that men would give thanks to the Lord.
Psalm 107:8 NKJV

*D*avid writes: "Oh, that men would give thanks to the Lord." Notice the word *would;* a thankful attitude is a choice you make. You choose your attitude just like you choose your diet or your underwear. There's plenty to be grateful for. "Yeah, but there's plenty to complain about too." The point exactly—you've a choice to make.

Robinson Crusoe spent 27 years shipwrecked on a tropical island. Here's part of his journal entry (paraphrased). We'll call his lists, The Gripe List & The Gratitude List. *Gripe:* "I'm stuck on this desert island without hope." *Gratitude:* "I wasn't drowned like the rest of my ship's company." *Gripe:* "I've no clothes." *Gratitude:* "I'm in a hot climate, if I'd clothes I couldn't wear them." *Gripe:* "I've no way to protect myself from man or beast." *Gratitude:* "I see no wild beasts here to hurt me as I saw on the coast of Africa. What if I'd been shipwrecked there?" *Gripe:* "I've nobody to talk to." *Gratitude:* "God sent the ship in near enough to the shore that I've gotten out so many necessary things as will enable me to supply myself as long as I live."

That's powerful stuff! If you can grasp it and put it into practice, it'll keep you from becoming a card-carrying member of the Old Testament wilderness club known as "The Murmurers." Our attitude is just a decision we make about how we're going to approach things. It isn't Disney World-thinking to focus on the good things of life—it's wisdom!

A GREATER AWARENESS

That . . . which we have heard . . . seen . . . touched—
this we proclaim.

1 John 1:1 NIV

*C*ultivating a greater awareness of God's presence brings 3 great benefits:
(1) Companionship. At some point we all realize that human companionship is limited; even the best of friends can't always "be there" for us. They move, fade away, or die. Sometimes they don't understand. Sometimes they aren't faithful. If you try to meet all your companionship needs through others, no matter how wonderful they are, you're in for a life of frustration. But, "There is a friend who sticks closer than a brother" (Pr 18:24 NIV). And since He's been "tempted in every way, just as we are" (see Heb 4:15 NIV), He understands us completely. John says this friend who can "be heard, seen and touched," always listens, always communicates, always expresses affection, is patient with us, forgives us whenever we wrong Him, and stays committed even though we ignore Him for long periods of time.
(2) Confidence. Your journey won't be free of storms. Nobody's is: But an awareness of God's presence will enable you to face those storms, confident that life can't throw anything at you that you won't be able to handle in God's strength.
(3) Compassion. The more time you spend with Christ, the more like Him you become. Look what happened to John. As a young disciple he wanted to destroy a town because some of its residents didn't want Jesus to stay there (See Lk 9:54). But after a lifetime in God's presence he wrote: "Whoever does not love does not know God, because God is love" (1Jn 4:8 NIV).

UNREALISTIC EXPECTATIONS (1)

He . . . knew what was in human nature.
John 2:25 AMP

*O*ur expectations of others often set us up for disappointment. "Are you saying I shouldn't expect anything of them?" No, you should expect the best and encourage it, but never forget that they're just people. When Jesus' disciples disappointed Him, it didn't devastate Him. Listen: "He . . . [needed no evidence from anyone about men], for He Himself knew what was in human nature" (John 2:25 AMP). Jesus expected His disciples to do their best, but He knew that even their best would still be imperfect. And you need to understand that about your loved ones too, and treat them accordingly.

The perfect marriage, the perfect friend, the perfect job, the perfect neighborhood, the perfect church don't exist! God knew that, so He gave us instructions on how to handle people who disappoint us. Listen: "Bear (endure, carry) one another's burdens and troublesome moral faults, and in this way fulfill and observe . . . the law of Christ" (Gal 6:2 AMP). "What is the law of Christ?" you ask. Jesus answers: "I give you a new commandment . . . Just as I have loved you, so you too should love one another" (Jn 13:34 AMP). We must love *His* way—without condition and without pressure. Admittedly, it's easier to *talk* about how to treat the irritating people in our lives than it is to *do* it. But God never commands you to do what He won't give you the grace to carry out. *And the great thing is, in the process of carrying it out, you'll become more like Jesus!*

UNREALISTIC EXPECTATIONS (2)

He . . . knew what was in human nature.

John 2:25 AMP

*U*nrealistic expectations affect us in different areas. First, we have unrealistic expectations of *ourselves.* When we do things poorly we feel bad. That sets in motion a never-ending cycle of reaching for things that are out of our reach, hoping to prove something we don't have to prove in the first place. We think we should be able to do what others do, yet if we're not similarly gifted we cannot excel in it. You don't need to prove anything! Just obey God and allow Him to take care of your reputation. As long as you expect to excel outside of your gifting and calling, you're setting yourself up for disappointment.

Unrealistic expectations also affect us in our relationships with *others.* To make somebody else responsible for your happiness, or you for theirs, is a huge mistake. Abraham Lincoln said, "Most people are about as happy as they make up their mind to be." If people don't have the right outlook on life, you, and 100 others like you, won't make them happy.

Unrealistic expectations concerning *circumstances* also set us up for disappointment. Listen: "In the world you will have tribulation; but be of good cheer, I have overcome the world" (Jn 16:33 NKJV). Here Jesus is saying, "As long as you're in the world you'll have problems. Nobody gets a free pass. But don't worry, I've got everything under control." So learn to be realistic. You'll always have to deal with unpleasant situations and difficult people. *But your attitude (not theirs), is what will determine whether or not you enjoy life!*

BE GENUINE!

I opposed him . . . because he was . . . wrong.

Galatians 2:11 NIV

A well-known manufacturer once asked Will Rogers to write a testimonial for his pianos. Rogers, who never endorsed products he didn't believe in, wrote, "Dear Sir: Your piano is the best I've ever leaned against!" The long-term benefits of shunning hypocrisy far outweigh any short-term comfort level. Here's why: *(1) Your life influences others.* Never underestimate the effect that genuineness has on your family, your co-workers and your friends. As the world tries to squeeze us all into its mold, a life of integrity stands out in sharp contrast. *(2) Hypocrisy destroys your testimony.* We all know people who say they don't attend church because, "They're all hypocrites." How sad! When we preach cream and live skimmed milk, people lose respect for us and the One we represent.

Paul could never be dubbed a phony because he made a practice of calling it like it is. Remember his big confrontation with Peter? Listen: "When Peter came to Antioch, I opposed him . . . because he was . . . wrong . . . he used to eat with the Gentiles. But . . . he began to . . . separate himself . . . because he was afraid of those [in] the circumcision group . . . other Jews joined him in his hypocrisy . . . even Barnabas was led astray" (Gal 2:11 NIV). It takes backbone to speak out like that!

Throughout history, those known for character and integrity were the most admired and influential. Plato said, "He who would be blessed and happy should first be a partaker of truth, then he can be trusted." Do you want to inspire confidence and respect in everybody who knows you? Be genuine!

PERSONAL GROWTH (1)

Let the wise listen and add to their learning.

Proverbs 1:5 NIV

$\mathcal{H}$ere are some things you need to know about growth:

(1) Growth isn't automatic. You're only young once, but you can be immature indefinitely. Each year the lobster is forced to shed its shell; it's a pity we aren't! Come on, if you don't make personal growth your responsibility it'll never happen. The road to anything worthwhile is always uphill, so the sooner you start climbing the closer to reaching your God-ordained potential you'll be.

(2) Growth today brings success tomorrow. What you sow today determines what you reap tomorrow. Oliver Wendell Holmes said, "Once stretched by a new idea, a man's mind never regains its original dimensions." So what are you doing today to become more successful tomorrow?

(3) Growth is your responsibility. When you were a child your parents were responsible for your growth, now you are. Robert Browning wrote, "Why stay we on earth except to grow?" Good question! Yet few of us dedicate ourselves to the process. Why? Because growth requires change and most of us are uncomfortable with change. Gail Sheehy writes, "If we don't change, we won't grow, and if we don't grow, we're not really living. Growth demands the temporary surrender of security. It means a giving up of familiar but limiting patterns, safe but unrewarding work, values no longer believed in, relationships that have lost their meaning. Taking a new step is what we fear most, yet our real fear should be the opposite." Can you *think* of anything worse than living a life devoid of growth and improvement? I can't!

PERSONAL GROWTH (2)

Get understanding. Esteem her, and she will exalt you.
Proverbs 4:7–8 NIV

Be teachable. The famous football coach John Wooden said, "What counts, is what you learn after you know it all." That's because the more you learn, the less you think you have to learn. When that happens you become—unteachable!

Never stay satisfied with your current accomplishments. The greatest enemy of tomorrow's success is today's success. Thinking you've "arrived" because you accomplished certain things is fatal! It takes away your desire for continued growth. Successful people don't sit back and rest on their laurels. They know that wins, like losses, are temporary. They understand that they have to keep growing if they want to stay productive. Some things get you to the top, other things keep you there. You must stay hungry. Refuse to settle in the comfort zone or let success go to your head. Enjoy it briefly, then move on to greater things.

Become a continual learner. A university study done a few years ago found that almost one-third of all physicians were so busy working, they were 2 years behind in the latest developments in their field. Heaven help their patients! If you want to be a continual learner, you must carve out time to do it! Henry Ford said, "It's been my observation that successful people get ahead during the time other people waste." Carry your Bible, tapes and CD's when you travel. Seize every opportunity to keep growing. The secret to becoming a learner —is to learn something new every day! Listen, "Get understanding. Esteem her and she will exalt you."

PERSONAL GROWTH (3)

I will guide you in the way of wisdom.
Proverbs 4:11 NIV

*B*efore we leave the subject of personal growth, let's look at 3 more things:

(1) Refuse to plateau. It's tempting to find a plateau with comfortable stress, adequate finances and enjoyable relationships, without the intimidation of making new ones or entering unfamiliar situations. We all need to plateau for a time: to climb, rest and assimilate. But once we've assimilated what we've learned we must climb again. It's tragic when we've made our last climb. When that happens we're old, whether we're 9—or 99!

(2) Pay the price. You'll always have to trade something you have in order to get something you want—like time spent on leisure activities; the price of further instruction; constant change and constant risks. Sometimes growth is just plain lonely. That's why so many of us stop growing; the cost gets too high! Solomon says: "Though it cost all you have, get understanding." Teddy Roosevelt said, "There's never been a person in history that led a life of ease, whose name is worth remembering." Can you think of one?

(3) Find a way to apply what you learn. Don't let learning lead to knowledge—let it lead to action! If you're not changing as a result of what you're learning, it's because: (a) you're not giving your personal growth plan enough attention; (b) you're focusing on your liabilities instead of your possibilities; (c) you're not applying what you're learning. You've forgotten the all-important principle which says, "When you only listen and do nothing, you are fooling yourselves" (Jas 1:22 NCV).

GETTING THE MOST OUT OF IT!

Let God transform you . . . by changing the way you think.
Then you will know what God wants you to do.
Romans 12:2 NLT

$\mathcal{D}$on't just read this devotional—interact with it. Underline it. Write down your thoughts in the margins. Make it your book! Personalize it. To get the most out of it you need:

(1) A point to ponder. This is a nugget of truth you can reflect on throughout the day. Paul told Timothy, "Reflect on what I am saying, for the Lord will give you insight into all this" (2Ti 2:7 NIV). The more you reflect, the more God will reveal!

(2) A verse to remember. This verse should encapsulate the truth you've just read. If you really want to improve your life, memorizing Scripture may be the most important habit you can begin. Write the verse down on a small card, carry it with you throughout the day, and read it every chance you get.

(3) A question to consider. This question should help you think about the implications of what you've just read and how it applies to you personally. Writing your thoughts down is the best way to clarify and reinforce them.

(4) An action to take. Information only turns to transformation when you do something about what you've just read. James writes, "But the man who looks intently into the perfect law that gives freedom, and continues to do this, not forgetting what he has heard, but doing it—he will be blessed in what he does" (Jas 1:25 NIV). *Your life is worth taking time to think about!* So make an appointment each day to do these 4 things.

CHANGE YOUR AUTOPILOT

Be careful how you think; your life is shaped by your thoughts.
Proverbs 4:23 TEV

*B*ehind everything you do—there's a thought! So
if you want to change your life, you have to change your
thinking. Imagine riding in a speedboat with an automatic pilot
set to go east. If you suddenly decide to head west, you've 2
possible options: one is to grab the wheel and *force* it to head
in the opposite direction from where it's programmed to go. By
sheer will power you could overcome the autopilot, but you'd
feel constant resistance. Your arms would eventually tire, you'd
let go of the wheel, and guess what? The boat would instantly
head back east, the way it's internally programmed to go.

*That's what happens when you try to change your life
through will power:* "I'll force myself to eat less, exercise
more, quit being disorganized, etc." Yep, will power can
produce short-term change, but it creates constant stress
because you haven't dealt with the root cause. The change
doesn't feel natural, so eventually you give up, go off your diet,
quit exercising, and revert to your old patterns.

*Thank God, there's a better way! Change your autopilot—
the way you think!* Listen: "Let God transform you into a new
person by changing the way you think" (Ro 12:2 NLT). Change
always starts in your mind. The way you *think* determines the
way you *feel,* and the way you *feel* determines the way you
act. "But how can I change the way I think?" you ask. By
reprogramming your mind with God's Word. Try it, it works!

AT BEST, IT'S TEMPORARY!

Live your time as temporary residents on earth.
1 Peter 1:17 GWT

*I*magine being an ambassador in a hostile nation. You'd have to learn its language and adapt to its customs. And you couldn't isolate yourself! To fulfill your mission you'd have to be in constant contact, relating to those around you. But what if you fell in love with that country, preferring it to your own? Your loyalty and commitment would be compromised. Instead of representing your country, you'd start acting like a traitor. Listen: "We are Christ's ambassadors" (2Co 5:20 NLT). Don't get too attached to what's around you, it's temporary! Listen: "Those in frequent contact with the things of the world should make good use of them without becoming attached to them, for this world and all it contains will pass away" (1Co 7:31 NLT). Use it—but don't fall in love with it!

The fact that this world is not our ultimate home explains why we experience difficulty, sorrow, and rejection. It also explains why some promises seem *unfulfilled,* some prayers *unanswered,* and some circumstances *unfair.* This is not the end of the story! In order to keep us from becoming too attached to this world, God allows us to feel a certain amount of discontent —longings that will never be fulfilled this side of heaven.

We're not completely happy here because we're not *supposed* to be. We won't be in heaven two seconds before we'll cry out, "Why did I place such importance on temporal things? What was I thinking?" *The truth is, at death you don't leave home—you go home!*

WHAT DRIVES YOU?

*You, Lord, give perfect peace to those
who keep their purpose firm.*

Isaiah 26:3 TEV

*E*verybody's driven by something. What drives you?
(1) Guilt? Guilt-ridden people are manipulated by their memories. They allow their past to control their future. They unconsciously sabotage their own success by thinking, "I don't deserve this blessing." We're all products of our past, but we don't have to be prisoners of it. God says, "Do not dwell on the past" (Is 43:18 NIV). Heed what He says!

(2) Anger and resentment? Instead of releasing the pain through forgiveness, do you constantly rehearse it in your mind? Those who've hurt you can only *keep* hurting you if you hold on to the pain through resentment. For your own sake, forgive, learn from it and move on.

(3) Fear? Many of our fears are the result of a traumatic experience, unrealistic expectations, growing up in a high-control home, or genetic predisposition. Regardless of the cause, fear is a self-imposed prison that'll keep you from becoming what God intends you to be. Rise up; move against it with the weapons of faith and love, for "Well-formed love banishes fear" (1Jn 4:18 TM).

(4) Materialism? Do you think if you had more, you'd be more important? Wrong! Net-worth doesn't bring self-worth! Your value isn't determined by your valuables! The most common lie about money, is that having more of it will make you more secure. No, real security can only be found in that which can never be taken away—your relationship with God. So what's the answer? *A life controlled, and directed by God's purposes.*

THE LORD'S PRAYER (1)

Our Father [Abba] who art in heaven.
Matthew 6:9 RSV

*F*or the next few days, let's look at The Lord's Prayer. The name "Abba" simply means, "Daddy." No Jew would've dared address God that way, yet Jesus did it constantly. And He invites us to do it too.

Max Lucado writes: "One afternoon in old Jerusalem, as my daughter Jenna and I were exiting the Jaffa Gate, we found ourselves behind a Jewish family—a father and his 3 little girls. The 4 year-old fell a few steps behind and couldn't see him. *"Abba!"* she called. He stopped immediately. Only then did he realize they were separated. *"Abba!"* she called again. Immediately he extended his hand and she took it. I made mental notes. I wanted to see the actions of an *"Abba."* He held her hand tightly as they descended the ramp. When they stopped at a busy street, she stepped off the curb and he pulled her back. When the signal changed he led her and her sisters through the busy intersection. In the middle of the street, he reached down, swept her up into his arms and continued their journey."

Isn't that what we all need—an *"Abba"* who'll hear when we call? Who'll take our hand when we're weak? Who'll guide us through the hectic intersections of life? Who'll swing us up into His arms and carry us home? Well, the good news is—we've got one. No matter what you're facing today, all you have to do is pause, reach up and whisper, *"Abba,"* and He'll be there for you!

THE LORD'S PRAYER (2)

Hallowed be thy name.

Matthew 6:9

*Y*esterday we saw God as a child sees her daddy. But with the words "Hallowed be thy name" we're ushered into the throne room where we are awed and silenced by His majesty and power. *At some point in your walk with God, He'll teach you intimacy—and reverence!*

It happened to Moses: "Take off your sandals, for the place where you are standing is holy ground" (Ex 3:5 NIV). The word for such moments is reverence. The phrase is "Hallowed be thy name." As we read further we discover that no time is spent convincing Moses what Moses can do, but much time is spent explaining to Moses what God can do. We'd have done the opposite. We'd have explained to Moses how he was ideally suited to return to Egypt. After all, who better understood the culture of the palace? Then we'd remind him how perfect he was for wilderness travel. Who knows the desert better than a shepherd? Then we'd spend time reviewing his resume and strengths. But God doesn't. The strength of Moses is never considered. Not one word is spoken to recruit Moses, but many words are used to reveal God. Why? *Because the strength of Moses is not the issue; the strength of God is!*

Let's repeat that last sentence, and let you fill in the blank. Replace the name of Moses with your name. *Today, the strength of _____ is not the issue; the strength of God is!* The words "Hallowed be *thy* name" takes the focus off you, and places it where it must always be—on Him!

THE LORD'S PRAYER (3)

Thy kingdom come. Thy will be done in earth, as it is in heaven.

Matthew 6:10

*E*ach time you *obey* God, His "kingdom" is operating in your life just as it does in heaven. Can you imagine anybody in heaven telling God, "I'll think about it?" Or turning a deaf ear? The last employee to try that was Satan.

"Thy kingdom come, thy will be done" simply means, "Be fully in control. My steps are ordered by You. My decisions are based on Your approval alone. My choices are subject to Your veto. If You're not Lord over all, then You're not Lord at all."

Be honest; as you re-examine your greatest mistakes, *whose* will were you operating in—His or yours? Did you even consult Him? Did you linger in His presence long enough to hear what He had to say? Or did you not like the direction He gave you, so you launched out on your own?

God's will can be painful, because He has only one plan for your flesh—death. Paul wrote, "I die daily" (1Co 15:31). Yet the end result of dying to self is "abundant living." When you pray, "Thy will be done," you're seeking the heart of God. Would He hide from you what's in His heart? Never! Could He have done more than send His Son to redeem you? Or His Word to teach you? Or events to awaken and mold you? Or His Spirit to counsel and comfort you? No, when you pray, "Thy kingdom come, thy will be done in earth, as it is in heaven," rest assured, that's a prayer He'll answer!

THE LORD'S PRAYER (4)

Give us this day our daily bread.
Matthew 6:11

$\mathcal{P}$aul says that a man who won't feed his own family, is worse than an unbeliever (See 1Ti 5:8). So would God do less for us? No, how can we fulfill our mission, unless our needs are met? How can we teach, or minister, or influence others, if we ourselves are not provided for? Listen: "God . . . will give you *every* good thing you need so you can do what he wants" (Heb 13:20 NCV).

We pray, "Give us this day our daily bread," only to find our prayer *already* answered. We're like the high school senior who decides to go to college, then learns the cost of tuition. He says to his dad, "I'm sorry to ask so much, but I've no one else to turn to." His father smiles and says, "Don't worry, son. The day you were born I began saving for your education. I've already provided everything you need."

At some point, it occurs to us that *somebody else* is providing our needs! Indeed, we take a giant step in maturity when we agree with David's words, "Everything we have has come from you" (1Ch 29:14 NLT). You may be writing the check or stirring the soup, but there's more to putting food on the table than that. What about the seed, the soil, and the sun? Who created animals for food and minerals for metal? Long before you knew you needed someone to take care of you— God already had! He's committed to you! He lives with the self-assigned task of providing for His own. *And you've got to admit, so far He's done a pretty good job!*

THE LORD'S PRAYER (5)

Forgive us our debts, as we also have forgiven our debtors.
Matthew 6:12 NAS

*D*oes someone owe you an apology? An explanation? A thank you? A second chance? What are you going to do about it? Hold on to resentment? Talk to others about it? Get even?

Picture this: a big grizzly bear feeding alone on some discarded food. No other creature dares come close. But after a few moments, a skunk walks over and takes his place next to him, and the grizzly doesn't object. Why? Because he knows the high cost of getting even! You'd be smart to learn the same lesson.

Ever notice in western movies that bounty hunters travel alone? Who wants to hang out with a guy who settles scores for a living? Or risk getting on his bad side and catching a stray bullet? No, debt-settling is a lonely occupation.

We describe those who bother us as "a pain in the neck." Yeah, whose neck? Not theirs. *We're* the ones who suffer! If you're out to settle a score you'll never rest. How can you? Your enemy may never pay up. As much as you think you deserve an apology, they may not agree. You may never get a penny's worth of justice, and if you do, will it be enough? What's the answer? "Forgive us our debts as we have forgiven our debtors."

Would you like some peace? Then quit giving others such a hassle. Want to enjoy God's generosity? Then let others enjoy yours. Would you like the assurance that God forgives you? Then you know what to do, right?

THE LORD'S PRAYER (6)

Lead us not into temptation, but deliver us from the evil one.
Matthew 6:13 AMP

*S*atan's power can only be exercised at God's discretion. He's not free to wreak havoc on you at will. Actually, he'd rather you never learn how often God uses him as an instrument to:

(1) Humble us. Even the meekest among us tend to think too highly of ourselves. Paul did. But God protected him from his own pride, using Satan to do it: "To keep me from becoming conceited because of these surpassingly great revelations, there was given me a thorn in my flesh, a messenger of Satan, to torment me" (2Co 12:7 NIV).

(2) Awaken us. When dealing with 2 disciples who'd made shipwreck of their faith and negatively influenced others, Paul wrote: "I have given these men over to . . . Satan, so they will learn not to oppose God" (1Ti 1:20 CEV). Some of us respond to a tap on the shoulder, others need a two-by-four. Whenever God needs a two-by-four, Satan gets the call.

(3) Teach us. Jesus told Peter, "Satan has asked [he needs permission] to test all of you . . . I have prayed that you will not lose your faith!" (Lk 22:31-32 NCV). The Good Shepherd will only permit the attack if, in the long term, the pain is worth the gain. The purpose of the *test* is to provide a *testimony* to God's saving and keeping power in your life. So today you can pray with confidence, "Lead us not into temptation, but deliver us from the evil one."

THE LORD'S PRAYER (7)

For thine is the kingdom, and the power,
and the glory, for ever. Amen.

Matthew 6:13

*J*esus points out 3 things we're *not* built to handle: the *kingdom*, the *power*, and the *glory*. The disciples had no difficulty understanding this. They'd just watched Him calm the worst storm they'd ever been through. In a moment the sea went from a churning torrent to a peaceful pond. Immediate calm! Not even a ripple. And what was their reaction? Listen: "They were in absolute awe, staggered. 'Who is this, anyway?' they asked" (Mk 4:39-40 TM).

They'd never met anyone like Him. The waves were His subjects and the winds were His servants. And that's not all; soon they'd see fish jump into the boat, demons dive into pigs, cripples turn into dancers, and corpses become living, breathing people. Never had they experienced such power, never had they seen such glory.

Face it, we weren't made to run a kingdom; nor are we expected to be all-powerful. And we certainly can't handle the glory. Some of us think we can. We're self-made. Instead of bowing our knees, we just roll up our sleeves and put in another 12-hour day. Now, that may be enough when it comes to making a living, but when we face our own guilt or our own grave, our own power won't do the trick. So, Jesus ends His great prayer with a message we must never forget: "*Thine,* not mine, is the kingdom. *Thine,* not mine, is the power. *Thine,* not mine is the glory." Remember it—and you'll prosper. Forget it —and you don't want to know!

LOOK BEFORE YOU LABEL!

You're looking for someone to blame . . .
look instead for what God can do.

John 9:3 TM

*W*hen the disciples met a man who was blind from birth, they asked Jesus, "Whose sin caused this . . . his own or . . . his parents?" They weren't concerned that the man needed help, or that he'd spent his life in total darkness. No, they immediately started discussing his shortcomings—right in front of him! Why? *Because it's easier to label than to love!* We label things so we'll know what's inside—and we label people for the same reason. We'd rather debate homosexuality than befriend somebody who's gay. We'd rather condemn divorce than help its victims. It's easier to argue against abortion than to support an orphanage, or gripe about social services, than to help the poor.

Jesus said, "In the same way you judge . . . you will be judged" (Mt 7:2 NIV). Think you're not guilty? Oh really? How about when you first meet somebody? Do you think, "Oh you're Baptist:" (translation: must be narrow-minded). "You're an accountant:" (translation: probably boring). "You're unemployed:" (translation: probably a bum). Aren't you glad God doesn't judge *you* by your appearance, or where you grew up, or your job, or the mistakes you've made, or even some of your recent attitudes?

Jesus didn't see this man as a victim of fate, He saw him as an *opportunity* waiting to happen. He told His disciples, "You're . . . ooking for someone to blame . . . Look instead for what God can do" (Jn 9:3 TM). Always remember, when people reject you—God accepts you. When they leave you—He finds you. The work of God is accepting, not judging; caring, not condemning; loving, not labeling. Okay?

A PRAYER FOR "LABELERS"

Everyone who loves is born of God.
1 John 4:7 TM

If you're like the rest of us who fight the urge to "label" others, this prayer's for you:

"Father, remind me that the jerk who cut me off in traffic this evening is a single mom who just worked a 12-hour shift and is rushing home to cook dinner, help with homework, do laundry, and spend a few precious hours with her kids . . . That the pierced, tattooed, bored-looking kid who couldn't get my change right at the coffee shop, is a college student worried about his final exams and not getting his student loans next semester . . . That the scruffy looking bum who begs on the same corner every night (you know—the one who "really ought to get a job"), is a slave to addictions I can't imagine in my worst nightmares . . . Help me to remember that the old couple walking annoyingly slow down the store aisle holding everybody back, is savoring this moment because based on a biopsy report, it may be their last year together.

"Your Word says, 'Everyone who loves is born of God . . . because God is love.' Remind me that the greatest gift is still love, and that it's not enough just to share it with those I hold dear. Open my heart to all your family. Make me slow to judge, and quick to forgive; give me empathy and patience. But above all, Lord, help me not to label and judge others based only on their appearance. In Jesus' name—Amen."

WHAT IT MEANS TO SURRENDER

Surrender yourself to the Lord.

Psalm 37:7 GWT

*S*urrendering to God isn't passive resignation, fatalism, or an excuse for laziness. And it's not accepting the status quo. Actually, it may mean the opposite: sacrificing yourself, in order to change what needs to be changed. God only calls surrendered people to do battle on His behalf. So surrendering is not for cowards or doormats.

Surrendering is best demonstrated by obedience. It's saying, "Yes Lord" to whatever He asks of you. To say, *"No, Lord"* is a contradiction. How can you call Jesus "Lord," then refuse to obey Him?

After a night of failed fishing, Peter demonstrated real surrender when Jesus told him to try again. "Master, we've worked hard all night and haven't caught anything. But because you say so, I will let down the nets" (Lk 5:5 NIV). Surrendered people obey God even when it doesn't make sense—and the rewards are awesome!

Abraham followed God without knowing *where* it would take him. Hannah waited on God's timing without knowing *when.* Mary expected a miracle without knowing *how.* Joseph trusted God's purpose without knowing *why* circumstances happened the way they did. Each of these people were fully surrendered to God. "When will I know I'm fully surrendered?" you ask. When you can rely on Him to work things out instead of trying to manipulate others, force your own agenda, or control the situation. You simply let go and let God. You don't have to be in charge.

THE BENEFITS OF SURRENDER

So give yourselves completely to God.
James 4:7 NCV

$\mathcal{T}$here are 3 great benefits of surrender. First, you experience *peace*. "If you agree with him, you will have peace at last, and things will go well for you" (Job 22:21 NLT). Second, you experience *freedom*. "Offer yourselves to the ways of God and the freedom never quits" (Ro 6:17 TM). Third, you experience *power*. Stubborn temptations and overwhelming problems are defeated by Christ, the moment you surrender!

As Joshua approached the walls of Jericho he encountered God, fell down in worship, surrendered his plans and cried, "What saith my Lord unto his servant?" (Jos 5:14). That surrender led to a spectacular victory. Here's a paradox: victory comes through surrender! Surrender doesn't weaken you, it strengthens you! Surrendered to God, you don't have to fear or surrender to anything else. William Booth, founder of The Salvation Army, said: "The greatness of a man's power, is in the measure of his surrender."

Eventually everybody surrenders to *something!* If not to God, you'll surrender to the opinions or expectations of others, to money, to resentment, to fear, or to your own lusts or ego. You're free to choose whatever you surrender to, but you're not free from the consequences of that choice. E. Stanley Jones said, "If you don't surrender to Christ, you surrender to chaos."

The supreme example of surrender—is Jesus. The night before His crucifixion, He surrendered Himself to God's plan saying, "I want Your will, not mine." *And He's your example!*

A CONTRACT WITH GOD!

Offer yourselves to the ways of God.
Romans 6:17 TM

*S*urrender isn't just the *best* way to live—it's the *only* way! Nothing else works. All other approaches lead to frustration, disappointment, and self-destruction. The Bible calls surrender, "your reasonable service" (Ro 12:1). Your wisest moments will be those when you say "yes" to God.

Sometimes it takes years, but eventually you discover that the greatest hindrance to God's blessing—is you! You cannot fulfill God's purposes for your life while focusing exclusively on your own plans. If God's going to do His deepest work in you, it'll begin with surrender. So give it all to God: your past regrets, your present problems, your future ambitions, your fears, dreams, weaknesses, habits, hurts, and hang-ups. Put Jesus in the driver's seat—and take your hands off the wheel. Don't be afraid; nothing under His control can ever be out of control. Mastered by Christ, you can handle anything.

One of the greatest Christian leaders of the 20th Century is Bill Bright, founder of *Campus Crusade*. Through the *Four Spiritual Laws* tract, and the *Jesus* film (seen by over 4 billion), over 150 million people have been won to Christ. When asked why God used him so much, Bill replied: "When I was a young man I made a contract with God. I literally wrote it out and signed my name at the bottom. It said, 'From this day forward I am a slave of Jesus Christ.'" Think maybe *you* need a contract with God, too?

PLEASING GOD (1)

Figure out what will please Christ . . . then do it.
Ephesians 5:10 TM

*N*oah was a pleasure to the Lord" (Ge 6:8 TLB).
Wanna please God? Do what Noah did:

(1) He trusted God completely. Listen: "By faith, Noah
built a ship in the middle of dry land. He was warned about
something he couldn't see, and acted on what he was told . . .
As a result, Noah became intimate with God" (Heb 11:7 TM).
Noah had never seen rain. He lived hundreds of miles from the
nearest ocean. Even if he could learn to build a ship, how would
he get it to water? And how about rounding up all those
animals? For 120 years he was a laughing stock. Yet he trusted
God—and outlived every critic!

(2) He obeyed God wholeheartedly. Listen: "Noah did
everything exactly as God had commanded him" (Ge 6:22
NLT). Obedience doesn't say, "I'll pray about it." Delayed
obedience is disobedience! God doesn't owe you an
explanation. Understanding can wait, obedience can't! Instant
obedience will teach you more about God, than a lifetime of
Bible discussions. In fact, you'll never understand some
commands until you first obey them.

Sometimes we try partial obedience: "I'll attend church,
but I won't tithe. I'll read my Bible, but I won't forgive the one
who hurt me." Get real—partial obedience is disobedience!
James says, "A person is justified by what he does and not by
faith alone" (Jas 2:24 NIV). Why is obedience so important to
God? Because His Word says: "If you love me, you will obey
my commandments" (Jn 14:15 TEV). *Anything else is just—
infatuation.*

PLEASING GOD (2)

He delights in every detail of their lives.
Psalm 37:23 NLT

*A*fter the flood God told Noah, "Be fruitful and increase in number and fill the earth . . . everything that lives and moves will be food for you. Just as I gave you the green plants, I now give you everything" (Ge 9:1-3 NIV). God told Noah, "It's time to get on with your life! Do the things I designed you to do. Make love. Have children. Plant crops. Eat meals. Excel in business. Be the best you can be."

Do you think the *only* time God's pleased with you is when you're doing "spiritual stuff" like reading the Bible, attending church, praying, or sharing your faith? No, God enjoys every detail of your life, whether you are working, playing, resting or eating. He doesn't miss a trick: "He delights in every detail of their lives."

Every human activity except sin can be done for God's pleasure—if you do it with an attitude of gratitude! You can wash dishes, service a machine, sell cars, write a computer program, grow a crop, or raise a family for the glory of God. Like a proud parent, God enjoys watching us use the talents and abilities He's given us.

In *Chariots of Fire,* Eric Lidell says, "I believe God made me for a purpose, but I also believe He made me fast, and when I run, I feel His pleasure." There are no unspiritual abilities, just misused ones. So start using yours for God's pleasure.

KNOWING GOD'S WILL

It felt like a fire burning in us when Jesus talked to us.
Luke 24:32 NCV

Are you struggling to find God's will? If so, take another look at the two confused disciples on the road to Emmaus. They thought they'd seen the death of Jesus and His movement, so, deeply discouraged, they packed their bags and headed home. Suddenly, Jesus appeared to them. How does Jesus reveal His will to us? You might be surprised at the simplicity of the process.

(1) Through other believers. Their first mistake was to disregard the words of their fellow disciples. Listen: "Today some women among us amazed us. Early this morning they went to the tomb, but they did not find his body there. They came and told us . . . Jesus was alive" (Lk 24:22-23 NCV). God's plan hasn't changed. He still speaks to believers through other believers. That's why you need to be in church regularly.

(2) Through the Scriptures. Listen: "Then starting with what Moses and all the prophets had said about him, Jesus began to explain everything that had been written about himself in the Scriptures" (Lk 24:27 NCV). Their second mistake was disregarding the Word of God and listening to their fears. Hello! Your answer is at your fingertips—check your Bible. God still speaks through His Word!

(3) Through a burning heart. Listen: "They said to each other, 'It felt like a fire burning in us when Jesus talked to us.'" (Lk 24:32 NCV). God reveals His will to us by setting our hearts on fire. What ignites you? Forgotten orphans? Untouched nations? The inner city? Singles? Whatever it is— heed the fire within you!

WHERE DO OUR PRAYERS GO?

So Mary and Martha sent someone to tell Jesus,
"Lord, the one you love is sick."
John 11:3 NCV

*S*omeone went to Jesus on behalf of Lazarus, and because they went, Jesus responded. The healing wouldn't unfold for several days, but the timer was set when the appeal was made. Ever wonder where your prayers go when they leave your lips? Listen: "There was *silence* in heaven . . . and . . . Another angel came and stood at the altar, holding a golden pan . . . with the prayers of all God's . . . people. The angel put this offering . . . before the throne. The smoke . . . went up . . . to God with the prayers of God's people" (Rev 8:1-4 NCV). Why was there silence in heaven? Because someone was praying! Heaven pauses to hear the prayers of—someone like you. Listen: *"The prayers of all God's . . . people . . . went up . . . to God." Awesome! Your words don't stop until they reach the heart of God!*

But notice, the friend who went to Jesus on behalf of Lazarus said, "Lord, the one *You* love is sick." He didn't base his appeal on the imperfect love of the one in need, but on the perfect love of the Savior. He didn't say, "The one who loves You is sick." No, he said, "The one *You* love is sick." That's different!

The power of prayer doesn't depend on the virtue of the one who prays, but on the unchanging love of the One who hears. Aren't you glad? You may be deeply flawed; you may not understand the mystery of prayer, but this much is clear: *action begins in heaven, when someone on earth prays.*

THE TWO SIDES OF FORGIVENESS

Be kind and compassionate to one another,
forgiving each other.
Ephesians 4:32 NIV

*H*enri Nouwen writes, "We've all been wounded. Who wounds us? Those we love and those who love us. When we feel rejected, abandoned, abused, manipulated or violated, it's usually by people close to us: our parents, our friends, our marriage partners, our children, our teachers, our pastors. This is what makes forgiveness so difficult. It's our *hearts* that are wounded! We cry out, 'You, who I expected to be there for me, have failed me.' How can I ever forgive you for that?'" Though forgiveness may seem impossible, nothing is impossible with God! The God who lives within us will *give* us the grace to go beyond our wounded selves and say, "In the name of Christ, I forgive you."

But remember, there are two sides to forgiveness: giving and receiving. Although at first sight giving seems harder, often we aren't able to offer forgiveness—because we haven't fully *received* it ourselves! Only as people who've tasted the joy of forgiveness, can we find the inner motivation to give it.

Why is *receiving* forgiveness so difficult? Because it's hard to acknowledge, "Without your forgiveness, I'm still affected by what happened between us. I need you to help set me free and make me whole again." That requires not only a confession that we've been hurt, but also the humility to admit our dependency on the very one who hurt us. Yet, only when we're able to *receive* forgiveness, can we truly *extend* it to others!

BETWEEN TWO FIRES

As . . . Peter was standing by the fire.

John 18:25 NLT

*E*arlier Peter defends Jesus by cutting off the high priest's ear; now he's denying Him. Ever had that happen? Under pressure your backbone turns to jelly and you falter. Now what do you do? *(a) Dismiss* it and say, "Everybody slips, it's no big deal." *(b) Deny* it and say, "Fall? Are you kidding? Not me!" *(c) Distort* it and say, "Don't blame me; it's society's fault!" But there's another option—*deal with it honestly!*

When Frederick the Great visited Potsdam Prison, every prisoner claimed to be innocent. Only one said, "I'm guilty; I deserve my punishment." When the emperor heard this he told the warden, "Quickly, release him before he corrupts all these other innocent men!" Listen: "Nothing . . . can hide from . . . the God to whom we must explain all that we have done" (He 4:13 NLT). Confession isn't just telling God what you've done; He already knows that. It's agreeing that it's wrong and asking forgiveness. God can't heal what you won't reveal, or cleanse what you won't confess.

That day Peter stood before two fires: first, the fire of *denial;* second, the fire of *discovery.* The first fire was made by men; the second fire was made by the Master. At the first, Peter denied Jesus; at the second, he acknowledged Him as Lord. But in between were two life-changing experiences: Peter's tears and Jesus' cross. When your tears of remorse mingle with God's forgiveness, the result is always losing your guilt and finding new joy!

October 1

WHERE'S YOUR CONFIDENCE?

Blessed is the man who trusts in the Lord,
whose confidence is in him.
Jeremiah 17:7 NIV

Listen: "Then [Delilah] called, 'Samson, the
Philistines are upon you!' He awoke from his sleep and thought,
'I'll go out as before and shake myself free.' But he did not know
that the Lord had left him. Then the Philistines seized him" (Jdg
16:20-21 NIV). A champion who once depended on God for his
every move, now says "I'll just do what I've done before."

Jesus said, "Without me ye can do nothing" (Jn 15:5).
Now we _know_ that Scripture; we even _quote_ it. Yet we keep
going out without bending our knee or committing our way
unto the Lord, acting like it all depends on us, and falling flat
on our faces. Dear God, will we _ever_ learn?

Listen: "Cursed is the one who trusts in man, who depends
on flesh for his strength and whose heart turns away from the
Lord. He will be like a bush in the wastelands; he will not see
prosperity when it comes . . . But blessed is the man who trusts
in the Lord, and whose confidence is in him. He will be like a
tree planted by the water that sends out its roots by the stream.
It does not fear when heat comes; its leaves are always green. It
has no worries in a year of drought and never fails to bear fruit"
(Jer 17:5-8 NIV).

Most of our internal agony, our struggling and frustration
come from _misplaced confidence._ Before you go a step further
today, pause and ask yourself, "Where have I placed my
confidence?"

YOU'LL SENSE IT FIRST IN YOUR SPIRIT

I hear a mighty rainstorm coming!

1 Kings 18:41 NLT

Are you going through a dry spell? Are you busy encouraging others while your own life seems to be falling apart? Maybe your business is floundering, or you're facing some unexpected health concerns or family problems. That's what happened to Elijah; this man who earlier called down fire from heaven, suddenly found himself in the middle of a full-blown famine. So what did he do? Listen: "Elijah . . . got down . . . with his face between his knees" (1Ki 18:42 TLB). Elijah chose to: (a) shut out his surroundings for a while; (b) focus only on what God was saying; (c) keep praying. And when he did, the Bible says he heard "a mighty rainstorm coming!" What Elijah sensed *inside,* was completely contrary to what was happening *outside.* His spirit *sensed* an "abundance of rain"—before a single drop fell.

God speaks in your spirit, not your flesh; what He says *there,* is more real than anything that's happening around you! But be warned, what you sense in your spirit may go against what you have in the bank, or what's happening on the job, or what's taking place at home, or what's happening in your body. Elijah had to discount all the "no rain" reports he kept getting. So will you. When you know God's promised you a certain thing, you must tune out all the negativity around you, reject your doubts, and keep believing God!

MAKE SURE YOU'RE LOOKING
IN THE RIGHT DIRECTION

Go and look out toward the sea.

1 Kings 18:43 NLT

*A*s he prayed for rain, Elijah sensed something in his spirit that he wasn't seeing with his natural eyes. When he told his servant, "Go and look out toward the sea," the same negative report kept coming back, "I don't see anything." But Elijah kept believing. Finally the seventh time his servant told him he saw, "A little cloud . . . rising from the sea" (1Ki 18:44 NLT). When you're a praying person, God will often show you the direction your answer is going to come from. But first you'll have to:

(1) Stop being influenced by others who don't share your vision. The Bible asks, "Can two walk together, except they be agreed?" (Amos 3:3). When his servant didn't share his vision, Elijah sent him away. Why? Because allowing yourself to be influenced by those who aren't in sync with you spiritually can cost you dearly.

(2) Disregard conflicting voices. Elijah put his head down and tuned out every voice except God's. And you must too! Learn to tune out the voices of confusion and doubt, until you hear only what God has promised: like . . . the restoration of your family, your business, your emotions, your health or your ministry.

(3) Get into birthing mode. Elijah went into "labor" by travailing in prayer. Today, what you're feeling inside is *real;* there's another ministry, a fresh visitation of God's spirit, a new joy. There's a storm in your spirit—but if you don't push, it won't rain. On the other hand when you do, God will send a blessing that'll overwhelm you.

IT'S A LITTLE CLOUD—BUT IT'S LOADED!

I saw a little cloud.
1 Kings 18:44 NLT

*W*hen there was no sign of rain anywhere, Elijah instructed his servant to keep looking. Finally, the servant who kept reporting that nothing was happening saw something, and had to admit that things were changing. It was just a little cloud —but it was loaded!

God loves to use things we think are insignificant. He used: (1) a brown-bag lunch to feed 5,000; (2) a slingshot to bring down a giant; (3) a handful of clay to restore a man's eyesight. He can use a little job . . . a little money . . . a little favor . . . to bless you. Little clouds are indicators of what's coming; they're the *conduits* God has chosen to use. When God promises you abundance, He doesn't need anything big to make it happen. The change that eventually impacts multitudes, usually starts with one individual. Whether it's a Noah or a Paul or a Mother Teresa or a Billy Graham, God only needs one person who believes Him, who dares to be different.

When God pours out the rain of His blessing you'll: (1) see that your problems are just opportunities for God to "show himself strong on your behalf" (See 2Ch 16:9); (2) discover that His "strength is made perfect in [your] weakness" (See 2Co 12:9); (3) be able to thank Him for your enemies, because when you reach *that* level of maturity, He's promised to prepare a feast for you right in front of them (See Ps 23:5). In fact, when the opposition is at its *worst,* is when God puts on His apron and starts cooking up a miracle for you!

NEVER AGAIN!

I will see the rainbow . . . and remember my . . . promise.
Genesis 9:16 TLB

*I*n Genesis, when Noah preached about rain, it was a symbol of *judgment.* But after the flood God said, "Never again will [I] . . . destroy all life . . . I will see the rainbow . . . and remember my eternal promise to every living being" (Ge 9:15-17 TLB). From that point on, rain became a symbol of *blessing.*

Maybe you've been to hell and back and you're afraid it's going to happen again. Don't be! Just keep walking with the God who promised: *"Never again!"*

When God turns the thing that should have destroyed you into a blessing, you'll be able to look back and say, "The suffering you permitted was good . . . it taught me to pay closer attention to your principles" (See Ps 119:71). Without it you'd never have discovered: (a) that isolation creates determination and makes you lay hold of God; (b) the power of your own prayers; (c) what God can accomplish in the face of adversity; (d) that when He heard you crying in the night, your tears were so precious that He collected them in a bottle (see Ps 56:8); (e) that the Angel of the Lord protected you when the enemy wanted to take you out (see Ps 34:7); (f) that God didn't need your friends to support you, in order to bless you; (g) that He alone brought you through, because He saw the rainbow and remembered His promise!

HOW CAN I CHANGE?

Be transformed (changed) by the [entire] renewal of your mind.
Romans 12:2 AMP

 $\mathscr{A}$ re you wrestling with a certain problem thinking, "If I could just get beyond this, everything would be okay." Sorry to disappoint you, but when you've conquered this particular problem, God will reveal something else that needs to be dealt with. Relax, you're *always* going to be working on something!

Change doesn't come through human effort without God, frustration, self-rejection, guilt, or the white knuckling works of the flesh. No, change comes as a result of having your *mind renewed daily* by the Word of God. As you agree with God, believing that what He says is true, change automatically begins. You start to *think* differently, then *talk* differently, and finally *act* differently. Be patient with yourself: it's a process that develops in stages.

Would you think there was something wrong with your child because they couldn't walk perfectly the first few tries? No, you're delighted each time they take another step. When they fall you pick them up, comfort them, bandage them if necessary, encourage them to try again, and keep working with them. Do you think God does less for His children?

God's not angry with you because you haven't "arrived," He's pleased that you're pressing on, trying to stay on the path. It's God's job to "cause [you] to . . . be governed by the Holy Spirit" (2Co 3:8 AMP). If you could do it by yourself you wouldn't need God! So instead of driving yourself harder and harder, start leaning on God more and more!

TAKE BACK YOUR LIFE (1)

Having gifts . . . that differ . . . let us use them.
Romans 12:6 AMP

*S*ometimes life is like a maze; it's easy to get lost. Pressure is coming at us from every direction to keep others happy. We spend a ton of energy studying the important people in our lives, trying to decide what they want from us, and in the process we lose ourselves. Sound familiar?

Today ask yourself, "What am I living for? Why am I doing the things I do? What has God gifted and called me to do?" Those who succeed at being themselves don't allow others to control them because they're led by God.

Don't get mad because people place demands on you. It's your life—take charge of it! The pressures you're feeling may not be coming from others at all, they may be coming from your own fears and insecurities. Sure there are times when we all do things we'd rather not do. We do them because we love others, and in so doing we're being led by God's Spirit. But that's different from being controlled by our own insecurities, or the endless demands of others.

When you try to become everything to everybody, you get lost in the process! When you live for their approval, you risk forfeiting God's! It's time you started praying, "Lord, what wilt thou have me to do?" (Acts 9:6). Once He reveals it to you, commit yourself to it fully, regardless of who does or doesn't agree. *Don't reach the finish line only to discover you ran on somebody else's track.*

TAKE BACK YOUR LIFE (2)

Having gifts . . . that differ . . . let us use them.
Romans 12:6 AMP

*G*od created you to be *different* from others, not the same. Each of us plays a unique role. When we struggle to be like someone else, we lose ourselves in the process. God wants us to fit into His plan, not feel pressured to fit into somebody else's. It's alright to be different; different is okay!

Find out what you're good at, throw yourself into it wholeheartedly and you'll discover your highest level of joy! When you try to do what somebody else is good at, you generally fail. Why? Because you're not *assigned* to do what they're doing; or at least, not in *the way* they're doing it. But that doesn't mean you're not good at anything!

Here's an important key: focus on your potential, not your limitations! We all have limitations and we must accept them. That's not bad, it's just a fact. Actually, it's wonderful to be different without feeling like something's *wrong* with you. Secure people know that God loves them as they are and has a plan for them, so they're not threatened by the abilities or accomplishments of others. Actually, they *enjoy* what other people can do, because they enjoy what they *themselves* do. Paul writes, "Let us not become . . . competitive . . . envying . . . jealous of one another" (Gal 5:26 AMP).

In the end, what matters most is being able to say, "I have brought You glory on earth by completing the work You gave me to do" (Jn 17:4 NIV). *Anytime you can say that—you're a winner!*

FOCUSED LIVING!

Let's keep focused.
Philippians 3:15 TM

$\mathcal{T}$here are 4 great benefits to focused living:

(1) It simplifies life! When you don't know your purpose, you try to do too much—and that causes stress, fatigue and conflict. You've only enough time and energy to do God's will. Not getting everything done may be an indicator that you're doing more than God intended you to do. Focused living leads to a simpler lifestyle and a saner schedule. Listen: "You, Lord, give perfect peace to those who keep their purpose firm" (Isa 26:3 TEV).

(2) You become effective by being selective! If you want your life to have impact, focus it! Don't confuse activity with productivity. Defused light has limited impact, but when it's focused like a laser it can cut through steel.

(3) It motivates you! Nothing energizes, like clear purpose. It's meaningless work, not overwork, that wears us down. George Bernard Shaw wrote: "This is the true joy of life: being used up for a purpose recognized by yourself as a mighty one; being a force of nature instead of a selfish little clot of ailments and grievances, complaining that the world will not devote itself to making you happy."

(4) It prepares you for eternity! People who spend their lives trying to create a lasting legacy on earth, fail to realize that —all achievements are eventually surpassed, all records broken, all reputations fade, and all tributes forgotten. Ultimately what matters most isn't what others say about you, but what God says. So live with that in view!

GUIDELINES FOR BLENDED FAMILIES (1)

I'm doing the very best I can . . . at home, where it counts.
Psalm 101:2 TM

*I*f you succeed everywhere else but fail at home, your success will be hollow indeed. Dr. Gayle Peterson offers some helpful insights for strengthening blended families:

(1) Take time to resolve your problems and build intimacy. The key to a strong family is the love, care, and respect you show one another as a couple. Never forget, your kids take their cue from you.

(2) Remember, as stepparents you had a choice—your kids didn't. They didn't ask to be in this situation. So be understanding. Work to strengthen their sense of security during this difficult transition.

(3) Don't expect instant love. Be realistic about the "work" involved in blending 2 families. There's no such thing as instant intimacy. It takes time to develop strong bonds and stabilize a family, so be patient!

(4) Allow time to grieve past losses. Jesus said, "Those . . . who grieve . . . will find comfort" (Mt 5:4 CEV). At the time of their parent's second marriage, many children have already lived in 3 different family units: (a) their biological family; (b) their single-parent family; (c) their new blended family. Plus, if your own biological children aren't living with you, you may experience a personal sense of loss. Failure to grieve can result in anger and alienation, so deal with the past before taking on the future!

GUIDELINES FOR BLENDED FAMILIES (2)

I'm doing the very best I can . . . at home, where it counts.
Psalm 101:2 TM

*A*lmost half of all two-parent households are now blended families. If you're in one, here are some things you need to consider:

(1) Every child is unique. Small children accept step-parents more easily than teenagers. Don't assume your authority will carry the same weight with older kids. You may need to approach them more as a friend, while toddlers need nurture and security.

(2) Create new family systems. Each family has its own system; "In our house we always . . ." It's what makes family members feel like part of an intimate group. Things like attending church together, sharing daily devotions, playing games, or just enjoying a good laugh, all help to establish that important sense of bonding and belonging.

(3) Don't deny kids access to their other biological parent. Remember, "God blesses those . . . who make peace" (Mt 5:9 CEV), so don't demean your "ex" before your kids, and don't use them as "messengers." Research confirms that kids who spend time with both parents adjust better. It also decreases the possibility of them getting caught in the crossfire and wounded!

(4) Always work in the children's best interests. There'll be events where you'll have to interact with your "ex," so get used to it—for the kids' sake! They need your love and understanding, especially when feelings are riding high and everybody's adjusting. Respect what's gone before, and don't try to enforce *your idealized interpretation* of what a family should be. Whether you've come by it biologically or through marriage, parenting requires maturity—lots of it!

FAITH ON TRIAL

Don't be surprised at . . . fiery trials.
1 Peter 4:12 NLT

*W*e live in a "here and now" generation; we're not programmed to delay gratification. And this has spilled over into the church. Instead of us setting the pattern for the world, now they're setting the pattern for us.

It's *wrong* to manipulate Scripture and distort truth just to inspire or excite people. Get this—God's not Santa Claus or your bellhop! It's not His job to give you everything you want, exactly when you want it! Sure, God promised to bless us abundantly, but when you major only on "getting," by implication, you question the faith of those who may not have as much as you, and that's a mistake!

All the naming, claiming, and declaring of God's Word doesn't mean you'll escape adversity. Who told you that anyway? Not God! His Word says, "Don't be surprised at . . . fiery trials . . . as if something strange were happening." We're into microwaving, but God's into marinating! Nobody escapes His courtroom. Maturing takes place in the furnace of affliction; you'll never *know* how strong your faith is until you've been there. Besides, when you get to heaven and stand beside all those heroes who sacrificed their lives for their faith, how will you feel when all you can claim is that somebody said a harsh word to you, or that you were overlooked for a position on the church board? Hebrews, Chapter 11, celebrates men and women whose faith was tried by fire, and despite their human frailties, God saluted every one of them. Like Job they each said, "Though he slay me, yet will I trust in him" (Job 13:15). Can you say that?

YOUR ADVOCATE IN HEAVEN

The Spirit pleads for us.

Romans 8:27 NLT

If your faith's on trial today, rejoice, you've got a great lawyer—Jesus! And His Word to you is: "Don't worry about how to answer the charges . . . I will give you the right words and such wisdom that none of your opponents will be able to reply!" (Lk 21:14-15 NLT). Could it be that you're asking God to move mountains He won't move just yet, because He wants to give you grace to endure instead of a strategy for escape? He wants to demonstrate His strength through your weakness (See 2 Co 12:9).

Are you asking, "Lord, how much longer do I have to go through this?" Remember, when God doesn't deliver you immediately, He'll be your thermostat in the furnace. If He hadn't *already* been regulating the heat, you'd have burned up long ago, right? Each time you reached breaking point and thought you couldn't take it another day, God put a hold on the enemy and said, "Cool it! Give him a little grace today."

Paul said, "We don't even *know* what we should pray for . . . But the Holy Spirit prays for us . . . And the Father . . . knows . . . what the Spirit is saying . . . for the Spirit pleads for us" (Ro 8:26-27 NLT). You keep coming through because you've got an Advocate in heaven, pleading your case. Your "Lawyer" was on the job during all those sleepless nights and depressing days. You're only here today because of Him. And you can trust Him to keep on defending you! When this trial's over, you're going to come out like gold! *That's a promise!* (See Job 23:10).

DARE TO BELIEVE THE BEST

Love never fails.
1 Corinthians 13:8 CEV

*P*rofessor Howard Hendricks writes: "By the 5th grade I felt insecure, unloved and angry at life. My teacher, Miss Simon, apparently thought I was blind to the problem because she regularly reminded me, 'Hendricks, you're the worst child in this school.' So I proceeded to live up to her opinion of me. Upon entering the 6th grade, my new teacher, Miss Noe, glanced over to where I was sitting, defiantly, just waiting to go into action. Smiling she said, 'Hendricks, I've heard a lot about you but I don't believe a word of it!'

"That was a turning point in my life. For the first time, somebody saw potential in me! Miss Noe put me on special assignments. She invited me to stay after school and work with her. As a result, I couldn't let her down. Once I got so involved in my homework, I stayed up until 1:30 am. My father came down the hall and said, 'Son, are you sick?' I replied, 'No, I'm doing my homework.' He rubbed his eyes and shook his head in disbelief; he'd never heard me say anything like that before. *What made the difference?* Somebody was willing to believe in me, while challenging me with higher expectations. That was risky, because there was no guarantee I'd honor her trust."

Everybody likes the end product of mentoring, especially when it yields a peak-performer. But how many of us are willing to risk dealing with the person on the front end? *Those who are, demonstrate the kind of love that—never fails!*

WANNA KNOW THE SECRET?

Be kind to each other.
Ephesians 4:32 NLT

*T*he secret to closeness in marriage isn't necessarily sparkling conversation, or shared interests, or even incredible sex. As good as those are, the secret of intimacy is—plain, old-fashioned kindness! You know, the stuff learned in kindergarten, like thoughtfulness, courtesy, and caring. Think your relation-ship needs a tune-up? Then listen up:

(1) Never underestimate the power of touch. Seems like a "no-brainer!" Right? You'd be surprised; we can go days or weeks without touching each other, yet a hug works wonders. God designed us so that when we touch one another in caring ways, our bodies produce oxytocin, which calms us and helps us to bond physically and chemically. Pretty clever, eh?

(2) Forget the grandiose gestures. When you routinely build little kindnesses into your marriage they become a source of strength for later, like money in the bank. So think "personal" and "sweet," like helping to clean up, making the coffee, walking the dog, or taking out the trash!

(3) Remember your manners. Just because you're married doesn't mean common courtesy should go by the wayside. Paul says, "Be kind to each other." That means listening without interrupting, and practicing the basics like saying, "please," "thank you," and "I'm sorry." This stuff's not rocket science— but it really works!

(4) Compliments are key. Remember, whenever you think something nice about your mate—tell them! We live in a cold competitive world and hearing we're loved, smart, attractive, and fun, from someone whose opinion we really value, means everything.

DARE TO BE YOURSELF!

Every one of us shall give account of himself to God.
Romans 14:12

*B*oldness *is required if you're ever to be led by God!* Why? Because He may direct you to do things that others don't understand or agree with. Insecure people tend to feel safer doing what others do. They're fearful of breaking the mold or standing alone. Anytime you step outside the boundaries of what others think is wise or proper, you risk rejection. But you mustn't allow that to keep you from fulfilling your God-given purpose.

Confronting criticism becomes a little easier when you remember that ultimately "every one of us shall give an account of himself to God." Sure it hurts to be criticized, but if you're to succeed at anything you must have the same attitude Paul had. Listen: "I am not the least concerned with the fact that you are deciding what is right and what is wrong with me . . . Neither you nor anyone else can put me down unless I first put myself down (and I'm not doing that) . . . though I don't know of anything against me, my ignorance doesn't mean that I am correct in my appraisal, because the final evaluation is in God's hands" (1Co 4:3-4 Ben Campbell-Johnston para).

Secure people can handle being the *only* ones doing something. They can also allow others that same choice, because they know we have been called to accept one another —not *analyze* and *categorize* one another! Please don't grow old and feel like somewhere along the way you lost yourself, and never succeeded at being who God called you to be.

FINDING YOUR PLACE AT THE TABLE

Lazarus and his sisters invited Jesus to dinner.
John 12:2 TM

*A*fter Jesus raised Lazarus from the dead, we read that, "Lazarus and his sisters invited Jesus to dinner." Martha served, Mary anointed Jesus' feet, and Lazarus talked to the guests. Notice: there's room at God's table for *all* kinds of people. Let's look closer:

Martha: Marthas are generally in the background with their sleeves rolled up, making sure everybody's fed and watered. Because they rarely seek the spotlight, often we don't appreciate them—until they're missing! The "downside" to Marthas is, they're inclined to make the mission more important than the Master. They need to remember that worship is also service.

Mary: Marys can forget there are bills to be paid and meals to be cooked. They're sometimes so heavenly minded that they're no earthly use. They need to realize that service is worship too. But we need Marys. They bring passion to our worship, and you can always count on them to intercede before God on behalf of others.

Lazarus: Listen: "They flocked to see . . . the man Jesus had raised from the dead . . . because of him . . . many . . . believed in Jesus" (Jn 12:9-11 NLT). Lazarus had a testimony so amazing that those who heard it became instant converts. He reminds us that we each have a story to share about God's grace and mercy. When was the last time you shared yours?

So today if you're a Martha, God sees your labor of *love.* If you're a Mary, He delights in your *worship.* And if you're a Lazarus, He promises to honor your *testimony.* There's room at the table for all of us!

TAKING YOUR CUE FROM MARY

Jesus' mother said to him, "They have no more wine."
John 2:3 NCV

*I*n Bible times offering wine to your guests at a wedding was a sign of respect, so running out would be considered a social disaster. But notice how Mary handled it; instead of trying to fix the blame she decided it was better to fix the problem. John Dewey said, "A problem well stated is a problem half solved," so before Mary did anything else, she talked to Jesus. Smart move! Jesus told the servants to fill the jars with water and give some to the headwaiter. When he tasted it, the Bible says, "the water had become wine" (Jn 2:9 NCV). But note, it happened *after* they'd obeyed Jesus, not before.

At a particularly tense church-board meeting, when one board member suggested they pray about the problems, another responded, "Has it really come to *that?*"

There are basically two reasons we make prayer our last resort instead of our first: (1) We like to think we're mature enough to solve our own problems. (2) We feel insignificant and think, "It's okay for Mary to ask Jesus; she's His mother, but He's got bigger problems to solve than mine." No, your problems are important to Him! He delights in you (Ps 18:19). He rejoices over you as a bridegroom rejoices over his bride (Is 62:5). You're never too big or too small to ask your Father for help. *Just take your cue from Mary: (a) identify the problem; (b) bring it to Jesus; (c) do what He says and you'll love the results!*

CARRYING YOUR FATHER'S NAME

Take care of . . . business . . . then people . . . will respect you.
1 Thessalonians 4:11–12 NCV

*A*t the christening for their newborn son, a young wife told the pastor, "My husband wants to name him after his dad and I want to name him after mine." The pastor said, "What's your dad's name?" "Joseph," she replied. "What's your husband's father's name?" he asked. "Joseph," she said again. "Then what's the problem?" The husband replied, "Well, her dad's a criminal and mine's a respected Christian. How will people know which one he's named after?" "That's easy," the pastor said, *"Call him Joseph and see which one he turns out like. That way everybody will know whose name he carries."*

St. Francis once took a young monk with him to preach in town. But when they arrived they just chatted with vendors and talked to people on the street. Returning home, the novice asked St. Francis why they hadn't preached. St Francis replied, "People listened; they observed our attitude and behavior—*that* was our message."

Listen: "Take care of . . . business . . . do your . . . work then people who are not believers will respect you." That means: (a) insuring that your walk matches your talk; (b) truly caring about others; (c) not cheating on your spouse, or your income taxes; (d) paying your bills on time; (e) not short-changing your employer. Peter writes: "Put on the apron of humility, to serve one another" (1Pe 5:5 TEV). Remember, it's one thing to *call* yourself a Christian—it's another, when those who know you *agree!*

STAYING SANE IN A CHANGING WORLD (1)

Under pressure . . . your faith . . . shows its true colors.
James 1:3 TM

*S*omebody said that the reason lightning never strikes twice in the same place, is because the same place isn't there the second time! Because we live in a constantly changing, stress-filled world, we need to learn to recognize:

(1) When to "give up." We're surrounded by escape artists trying to avoid the stress that accompanies change. But there is no escape—change is inevitable. So stop regarding it as the enemy and instead make it your ally. Only when you decide to ride the horse in the direction it's going, will you get to where you need to be!

(2) When to "wise up." When we're hit with sudden change, our "fight or flight" instincts aren't very effective at handling it. But there's a solution: by entrusting your life fully into God's care and asking for His wisdom, "He takes us firmly by the hand and leads us into . . . change" (Ro 2:4 TM).

(3) When to "toughen up." Somebody said, "If it wasn't for stress I'd have no energy at all!" Stop and take inventory! Are you making it harder on yourself than it needs to be? Is your self-talk faith, or fear? Are you convincing yourself that you can't handle the changes? Are you ready to give up without even *trying?* Listen: "Under [the pressure of change], your faith-life is forced into the open and shows its true colors. So don't try to get out of anything prematurely. Let it do its work so you become mature and well-developed" (Jas 1:4-5 TM).

STAYING SANE IN A CHANGING WORLD (2)

We are pressed on every side . . . but . . .
we get up again and keep going.
2 Corinthians 4:8–9 NLT

*M*ax Gunther says, "If you're losing a tug-of-war with a tiger, give him the rope before he gets to your arm. You can always buy a new rope!" Resistance to change just creates ulcers, sleeplessness and stress. So here are some attitudes you may need to adjust:

(1) Thinking like a victim. Stop expecting others to reduce your stress levels, and get behind the wheel of your own life. Remember, you "can do everything with the help of Christ" (Ph 4:13 NLT). Did you hear that? Everything!

(2) Deciding not to change. Instead of banging your head against the wall of hard reality, invest your efforts into changing what you can—like your attitude and your approach! It takes more energy to hang on to old habits and beliefs than it does to embrace new ones.

(3) Trying to play the new game by the old rules. When a car that's stuck in second gear keeps trying to do 100 mph, guess what happens—meltdown! If you don't want to burn out, learn to change gears. Figure out how the game has changed. Learn to play by the new rules, otherwise you'll keep losing.

(4) Trying to control the uncontrollable. When the music changes it's time to learn some new steps, otherwise you'll finish up sitting on the sidelines. You don't have to like change, but you do have to accept it, adapt to it, pray for grace, and get on with your life!

STAYING SANE IN A CHANGING WORLD (3)

We don't know why things happen as they do,
but we don't give up.
2 Corinthians 4:8 TLB

Change and stress are both inevitable, but here are some steps you can take to help you cope with them better:

(1) Choose your battles. Do you: (a) instinctively give in to fear and oppose change, even when it might benefit you? (b) think no issue is too small to be ignored? (c) keep throwing yourself across the tracks, hoping to stop the freight train of reality? Waging war on too many fronts results in battle-fatigue, so only choose battles big enough to matter.

(2) Work at becoming more adaptable. What's your most common response to change? Dragging your feet? Assuming a "have to" attitude? Doing only what's necessary? Once you stop caring, life loses its sparkle and, ironically, you become even more stressed. Become resilient! Paul said, "I have learned (and you don't learn it overnight), in whatsoever state I am, therewith to be content" (Php 4:11).

(3) Welcome new experiences. If you're moving forward your surroundings should be constantly changing. Clinging to the familiar just buys you comfort today at tomorrow's expense. Don't do it! Plunge in and take the bull by the horns!

(4) Learn to live with uncertainty. Always struggling to "stabilize" in a constantly-changing world is like sweeping water uphill—as soon as you stop, you lose it. Learn to live with uncertainty; "wing it" a little more, instead of struggling to make sure that life always happens on your terms.

STAYING SANE IN A CHANGING WORLD (4)

We've been thrown down, but we haven't broken.

2 Corinthians 4:8 TM

*R*obert Orben says, "Sometimes I feel like the whole world's against me, but I know that's not true—some of the smaller countries are neutral!" We all want to live stress-free without having to work at it, but it can't be done. Here are 15 things you can do to make your life better:

(1) Take time each day to pray and read God's Word, it'll transform your outlook! (2) Take a vacation. If you look like your passport photo you probably need one! (3) Cut back on caffeine; what goes up must come down! (4) Eat right—a balanced diet isn't having a cookie in each hand! (5) Exercise 3–5 times a week for 30 minutes; it's nature's "magic bullet" for stress. (6) Develop better time-management habits. (7) Make room in your life for fun. (8) Get 8 hours sleep when possible. (9) Maintain your sense of humor. "A cheerful disposition is good for your health; gloom and doom leave you bone-tired" (Pr 17:22 TM). (10) Start counting your blessings. David said, "I am overcome with joy because of your unfailing love" (Ps 31:7 NLT). (11) When you talk to yourself, say nice things. (12) Simplify your life by eliminating "clutter." If you haven't used it for two years, you probably don't need it. (13) Develop a sense of purpose by setting personal goals. (14) Forgive; grudges are too heavy to carry: "If you refuse to forgive others, your Father will not forgive [you]" (Mt 6:15 NLT). (15) Read the end of the book—we win!

STAYING SANE IN A CHANGING WORLD (5)

I'm awake all night—not a wink of sleep;
I can't even say what's bothering me.
Psalm 77:4 TM

*W*hen you can't sleep—it's time to stop counting sheep and start talking to the Shepherd! Here are some Biblical stress-relievers to live by:

(1) Let go of what no longer works. Paul says: "Let us strip off every weight that . . . hinders our progress" (Heb 12:1 NLT). The trouble is, we hate giving up what we do well. So, we focus on doing things right and end up failing to do the right things. Then we wonder why we don't succeed. There are limits to what you can carry. Letting go of what doesn't work, frees you up to focus on what does.

(2) Don't let change paralyze you. In new situations our first inclination is to slow down, play it safe, and buy ourselves some time. And sometimes that's wise. But most times we just fall further behind. Being overly cautious makes you freeze, like a deer caught in the headlights. The Bible says that God, "Gives power to the faint, and strengthens the powerless" (Is 40:29 NRS). So trust Him and move forward, instead of giving in to the impulse to "just do nothing."

(3) Approach the future with confidence. Recent events have everybody on edge, but as a child of God you can say, "I can lie down and sleep soundly because You, Lord, will keep me safe" (Ps 4:8 CEV). The truth is, you can't build a decent argument for giving in to fear; the only way to prepare for tomorrow—*is by adjusting and living fully today!*

DO IT GOD'S WAY!

I can do all things through Christ which strengtheneth me.

Philippians 4:13

*T*his much-quoted verse doesn't mean you can do *whatever* you want, or even do what *somebody else* does. No, Paul is saying you can do anything God assigns you to do, for with the assignment comes the ability. This verse actually teaches you to stay *within* the boundaries of what God's called you to do and not try to undertake things that are not part of His will for you. That's not negativism; it's godly wisdom!

God wants you looking to *Him* for answers, not others. That doesn't mean you can't learn from others, it just means the plan that will lead you to success—must come from God alone! He has a unique plan for you. Please accept that, otherwise you'll live in constant frustration!

John said: "A man must be content to receive the gift which is given him from heaven" (Jn 3:27 AMP). Read the previous verses; some of John the Baptist's disciples were getting concerned that Jesus was baptizing too, and the crowds were leaving John and flocking to Jesus. Had John not been secure in his own identity and calling he may have become fearful, jealous, and competitive. But not John! No, he manifested a *different* attitude, one we all need to take to heart. Listen: "I can only do what I have been divinely authorized and empowered to do . . . I must be content with that gift and calling" (See Jn 3:27-29). *The same goes for you too!*

ARE YOU HOSPITABLE?

Be hospitable . . . do it ungrudgingly . . .
without complaining . . . as representing Him.
1 Peter 4:9 AMP

A family who had guests over for dinner one evening, asked their 5-year-old to say grace. Puzzled, the child asked, "What should I say?" Her mom replied, "Just say what I always say." So, bowing her head the little girl prayed, "Dear God, why did I invite these people to dinner anyway?"

Let's be honest, hospitality's hard work! It involves sacrifice! Nevertheless, you're to "Do it ungrudgingly (cordially and graciously) . . . without complaining . . . as representing Him." Representing who? God! That changes things, doesn't it? Paul writes: "[Make a habit . . . of] . . . hospitality" (Ro 12:13 NAS). Peter writes: "[Be hospitable . . . with brotherly affection for . . . unknown guests . . . foreigners, the poor, and all others]" (1Pe 4:9 AMP). *Had any unknown guests, foreigners, or poor folk over to dinner lately?*

A man conducting a church survey recently wrote to advice columnist, Dear Abby, saying, "Of the 195 churches I visited, I was spoken to in only one by someone other than an "official greeter"—and that was to ask me to move my feet!" It's easy to extend hospitality to people you know, but Jesus said, "If all you do is love the loveable . . . Anybody can do that" (Mt 5:46 TM). So, how about those you don't know? Those who don't fit your social circle? Sure, you can find excuses . . . you're too busy, you don't want to get involved, you're uncomfortable around strangers. But God says you represent *Him;* that means: (a) sacrificing your personal agenda; (b) giving of your time and money; (c) going out on a limb for people you don't know—or even like; (d) seeing others through God's eyes. So, are you hospitable?

DOING TIME IN THE PEN

Son, you are always with me,
and everything that I have is yours.
Luke 15:31 NIV

$\mathscr{T}$he prodigal son broke his dad's heart by leaving home, squandering his inheritance and living with pigs. Later, when he came back asking to live in the barn and work as a farmhand, he found that his father had left the porch light on and kept him a place at the table. In fact, he was so glad to see him that he threw a party!

But big brother wasn't about to celebrate little brother's return. Listen to him: "I have served . . . obeyed your commands. But you never gave me . . . a feast . . . your other son who wasted . . . money on prostitutes, comes home, and you kill the fat calf" (Lk15:28-30 NCV). It's the kind of thing you hear in church from those who lift themselves up by putting other people down.

Both sons did time in the pen. One in the pen of rebellion, the other in the pen of resentment. One *came* home to a welcome, the other *stayed* home and wallowed in self-pity.

When you're jealous you miss the party! Bitterness incarcerates you along with all those other "victims" of betrayal, abuse, the system, who've chained themselves to the walls of their prison. Put away your hurt before it turns to hate. You're God's child and *nothing* can ever change that! Go to the feast. There's a seat reserved for you. Listen: your Father is saying, "Child you are always with me and all I have is yours." *So, don't let your lousy attitude rob you of what God has in store for you today!*

ABBA

[We] have received the spirit of adoption . . .
by which we cry out "Abba! Father."

Romans 8:15 NASB

$\mathcal{P}$aul writes, "[We] have received the spirit of adoption . . . by which we cry out 'Abba! Father'" (Ro 8:15 NASB). Adoptive parents understand these words. They know what it means to have an emptiness in their hearts, to hunt, set out on a mission, take responsibility for a child with a spotted past and a dubious future. And that's what God did for you! Knowing full well the trouble you'd be and the price He'd pay, He sought you, found you, paid an awesome price, signed the papers, gave you His name, took you home and gave you the right to call Him "Abba," which literally means, "My daddy." Don't you love it?

Adoption isn't something you earn. It's a gift you receive. Can you imagine prospective parents saying, "We'd like to adopt little Johnnie, but first we want to know does he have a house, money for tuition, a ride to school in the morning and clothes to wear every day? No agency would stand for such talk. They'd say: "Wait a minute, you don't adopt little Johnnie because of what he *has,* you adopt him because of what he *needs.* He needs a home."

Paul didn't say we've *earned* the spirit of adoption. He said we've *received* it. Why's that important? Because if we can't earn it by our stellar efforts, we can't lose it through our poor performance. How reassuring! *Why does any parent want a child? To love and to share their life with—and that's how God feels about you today!*

MORE THAN LOOKS (1)

What matters is not your . . . hair . . . jewelry . . . clothes.
. . . Cultivate inner beauty.
1 Peter 3:3 TM

*F*ashion designers are concerned with the *total look* of the models they send down the runway. They must have perfect accessories such as the right hairstyle and make-up. And it's the same with God: He created you as a whole person with specific features, personality traits and emotional responses. He designed you to be a vibrant, thinking, feeling, fully functioning human being with your own unique attractiveness.

And He endowed you with more than just *physical* appearance. He also gave you talents and spiritual gifts—inner qualities He wants you to develop and display for His glory. You see, who you are on the *inside* should determine how you see yourself on the *outside*. When your "looks" determine your sense of worth, a few extra pounds or a bad-hair day can wipe you out! Refuse to live that way!

The Bible says, "What matters is not your . . . hair . . . jewelry . . . clothes . . . but your inner disposition. Cultivate inner beauty, the . . . kind that God delights in" (1Pe 3:3-4 TM). When your self worth comes from God instead of men, you can wear a $5 outfit from the thrift shop or a $500 one from an upscale boutique. You're fine either way, because you recognize that your outer appearance doesn't define who you are.

Inner beauty can't be bought, taken off a rack, applied like make-up or put on like a new suit. It's "an inside job" that always finds a creative and appropriate expression on the outside. *So, look at yourself today in God's mirror and try to see what He values most—your inner beauty.*

MORE THAN LOOKS (2)

Be strengthened . . . by His Spirit in the inner man.
Ephesians 3:16

A celebrity counselor recently told his television audience: "A lady flew across the nation to tell me how her husband had left her for another woman. The woman who came to see me was young, vibrant and beautiful. But suddenly she pulled out a photograph and said, 'Just look at her! He left me for *that!*' Sadly I thought, 'Ma'am, *what* you've been conditioned by society to think of as being all-important, really isn't. Outer appearance isn't the biggest issue at all.'"

Advertisers spend billions to get us to decorate a *shell* that's in a losing battle with Mother Nature and Father Time; all to create what we *think* will attract others. What we create may momentarily turn a head or two, but it has little or no ability to capture and hold a heart or mind. We think that by enrolling at the latest weight-loss center, using the right toothpaste, being seen in the right places with the right people, we'll end up enjoying the right kind of life. And when it doesn't work, we get depressed and wonder what went wrong.

Sure it's important to always look your best, but when you become obsessed with your "looks" you become shallow and superficial. And others quickly lose interest because they discover that although the box you came in is beautifully wrapped—it's empty! The real source of attractiveness is "His Spirit in the inner man." *That's* what ultimately wins hearts and attracts the right people to you, for the right purpose, at the right time.

GUARDING YOUR ATTITUDE

Martha, you are worried . . . but only one thing is necessary.
Luke 10:41–42 CEV

*E*rma Bombeck writes: "I'm good at worrying. I worry about making introductions and going blank when I get to my mother, or what the dog thinks when he sees me coming out of the shower, or that one of my kids will marry an Eskimo and set me adrift on an iceberg when I'm no longer able to feed myself!"

Martha was so worried that she even tried to tell *Jesus* what to do! Listen: "My sister has left me to do the work . . . Tell her to help me." (Lk 10:40 NIV). Worry makes you forget who's servant and who's Lord. Note 3 things:

(1) Martha was busy serving, but she wasn't enjoying it! Doubtless, she wanted to please Jesus; it's just that she allowed the work of the Lord to become more important to her than the Lord of the work. Has that happened to you?

(2) Satan didn't take Martha out of the kitchen, he just stole her purpose for being there! He doesn't turn you against church, he just makes you focus on yourself. He doesn't take away your ministry, he just disillusions you by saying you're overworked, underpaid and unappreciated.

(3) God values your attitude more than your service! Listen: "Do everything without complaining" (Ph 2:14 NIV). A bad attitude spoils the gift you bring to the altar. Jesus said, "Martha . . . only one thing is necessary. Mary has chosen it." And what was it? Mary worshipped at Jesus' feet! He always prefers the quiet devotion of a sincere heart, to the noisy attitude of a complainer. *Is there a message here for you?*

RAISE YOUR EXPECTATIONS!

I'll tell you . . . things . . .
you could never figure out on your own.
Jeremiah 33:3 TM

*W*hen hard times come, we've the tendency to *lower* our expectations and end up settling for less than God wants us to have! When the Bible asks, "Is anything too hard for the Lord?" (Ge 18:14 NKJV), it's easy to say, "No, Lord." But it's what we do *next* that proves whether or not we actually believe Him. John says, "If ye know these things, happy are ye if ye do them" (Jn 13:17). If you don't *act* on what God tells you, can you *really* say you believe Him? One of our problems is that we get attached to methods that worked for us in the past and keep going back to them. By always looking to a certain book or tape or person for the answer, we seriously limit what God can do for us. He's much greater than any human source. And He's never predictable!

Today if you'll let Him, God will "tell you . . . things . . . you could never figure out on your own" (Jer 33:3 TM). What an offer! When He decided that Moses would lead the greatest migration in the Old Testament, Moses never questioned *God's* ability, he just questioned whether God could do it through *him.* And what was God's answer? "Go, and I will be with thy mouth and teach thee what thou shalt say" (Ex 4:12). Now *there's* a promise you can live by!

God's not enhanced by your strengths nor limited by your weaknesses; there's *more* He wants to do through you than what you've experienced thus far. Just *ask* Him—then respond in faith to whatever He tells you.

IT'S THAT SIMPLE!

What does God want us to do? . . .
Believe in the one he has sent.
John 6:28–29 NLT

*D*id you hear about the old man taking his first flight? After he got off the plane somebody asked him what he thought of it. "Okay," he replied, "but I never did put my whole weight on it." And we do the same when we refuse to put our whole weight on the finished work of Calvary.

Satan's sneaky. Instead of leading you away from God's grace, he makes you *question* it or try to *earn* it. When the disciples asked Jesus, "What does God want us to do?" He didn't say work harder, pray longer, give more. No, He said, "Believe in the one he has sent." When the Philippian jailer asked, "What must I do to be saved?" Paul answered, "Believe on the Lord Jesus Christ, and thou shalt be saved" (Acts 16:30-31). Salvation is about believing—not behaving!

Does that mean God doesn't require good works? No, He requires both. The problem is you don't have enough of *either* to qualify. Listen: "We should be holy and without blame" (Eph 1:4). Without blame? Wow! The only way you'll pull that off, is if God credits some of *His* righteousness to your account. And He does! Charles Wesley wrote: "Clothed in *his* righteousness alone, faultless to stand before thy throne. On Christ the solid rock I stand, all other ground is sinking sand."

"So how can I get to heaven?" you ask. Abandon your own efforts and trust in Christ alone. That way you can stand before God in *His* righteousness, not *yours!*

GROW UP!

God wants us to grow up . . . like Christ in everything.
Ephesians 4:15 TM

*T*oo many of us grow old without ever growing up! We're stuck in spiritual infancy. Why? Because we never *intended* to grow! Spiritual growth isn't automatic. You must want to grow, decide to grow, make an effort to grow, and persist in growing.

Growth always begins with a decision. Jesus calls us and we respond: Listen: "Come, be my disciple . . . So Matthew got up and followed him" (Mt 9:9 NLT). Matthew didn't understand all the implications of his decision, he simply decided to follow Jesus. That's all you need to get started—a decision! Nothing shapes your life more than the commitments you make; they develop you or destroy you, but either way they define you. Tell us what you're committed to today, and we'll tell you what you'll become 20 years from now!

It's at the point of commitment that most of us miss God's best. Because we're afraid to commit to anything we: (a) drift through life aimlessly; (b) make half-hearted commitments to too many things and end up living in frustration and mediocrity; (c) make a commitment to the wrong things such as becoming wealthy or famous, and end up with regrets. *Every* choice you make has consequences, so choose wisely! Christ-likeness is the result of making Christ-like choices, then depending on Him to help you fulfill those choices. Listen: "God accurately reproduces his character in you" (Eph 4:24 TM). "Like father, like son," God wants you to bear His likeness. *That's* what growing up is all about!

A-STEP-AT-A-TIME!

Don't try to get out of anything prematurely. Let it do its work.
James 1:4 TM

*T*ry to recognize the *seasons* in your spiritual life. Sometimes you'll have a short intense burst of growth (spring time), followed by a longer period of stabilizing and testing (fall and winter).

"But what about these problems I'd like God to remove?" you ask. It's okay to pray for a *miracle,* but don't be disappointed if the answer comes through a *gradual change!* Over time, a slow steady stream of water will erode the hardest rock and turn giant boulders into pebbles.

You may feel frustrated with the pace of your progress, but God's never in a hurry. He took 80 years to prepare Moses, including 40 in the wilderness. For 14,600 days Moses probably wondered, "Is it time yet?" But God kept saying "Not yet." Contrary to many popular book titles, there are no "easy steps to maturity." When God wants to make a mushroom He does it overnight. When He wants to make a giant oak He takes 100 years.

With God a delay is not a denial. Remember how far you've come, not just how far you have to go. Sure, you're not where you *want* to be, but neither are you where you *used* to be. Years ago people wore a popular button with the letters PBPGINFWMY—it stood for "Please be patient, God is not finished with me yet." *And God isn't finished with you either, so just keep moving forward, a-step-at-a-time!*

MAINTAIN YOUR CONFIDENCE IN GOD!

I am sufficient in Christ's sufficiency.
Philippians 4:13 AMP

*J*ust because we're *destined* to do something doesn't mean it'll automatically happen. No, in order to succeed at *anything,* you must maintain your confidence in God! David writes, "My times are in thy hands" (Ps 31:15). What times? Times when you feel like quitting. Times when you wonder, "Did God really call me to do this?" Times when you ask, "Will I ever get through this?" Times when God will have to correct you. Times when you'll have to rise above your circumstances and say, "I am sufficient in Christ's sufficiency!"

Listen: "David encouraged himself in the Lord" (1Sa 30:6). Don't wait for others to come along and encourage you. Learn to do it for yourself! David had no one to believe in him, so he believed in himself. If you don't believe in yourself you don't believe in God, for God can only do through you, what you *believe* Him to do.

"I wish I had your confidence," you say. No, confidence is something you decide to have. You learn about God—about His love, His ways, His power—then you *decide* to believe Him. When you do, you've got confidence; it's that simple.

So, be confident about your ability in Christ. Believe you hear from God and that He's leading you. Expect people to like you and you'll discover that more of them do. Be bold in the Lord. See yourself as a winner because of Him. Rise up today and declare, "I am sufficient in Christ's sufficiency" (Php 4:13 AMP).

THE PRISON OF WANT

The Lord is my shepherd; I shall not want.
Psalm 23:1

*W*hat's the *one* thing that separates you from joy? Fill in the blank: "I'll be happy when _____." Now, with that thought clearly in mind, answer this: if you never get it could you be happy? If not, you're living in the prison of want. Think: if you've a shepherd, you've *grace* for every trial, *direction* for every turn, an *anchor* for every storm. You've everything you need, right? And who can take it from you? Recheck your position. Are you not privileged to be part of the greatest kingdom of all—God's? Paul writes, "I have learned . . . to live when I am poor, and I know how to live when I have plenty. I have learned the secret of being happy at *any* time in *everything* that happens" (Php 4:11-12 NCV).

So had the leper in Tabago. A short-term missionary met her on a mission trip. On his final day when he was leading worship in the leper colony, he asked if anybody had a favorite song. A woman with no ears, no nose, no lips and the most disfigured face he'd ever seen, raised her fingerless hand and asked, "Could we sing, *Count Your Many Blessings?*" The missionary started the song but couldn't finish it. Somebody later commented, "I suppose you'll never be able to sing that song again?" "No," he answered, *"I'll sing it again—just never the same way."*

The truth is, when you can say, "The Lord is my shepherd; I shall not want," you're covered—you've got *everything* you need!

FOCUS ON YOUR CORE COMPETENCIES

This one thing I do.
Philippians 3:13

*H*oward Hendricks says, "As a young leader, my biggest mistake was allowing my time to be eaten up with things *outside* my core competencies. I wanted to set the pace for others, to demonstrate that nothing was beneath me, so I devoted an inordinate amount of time to things I wasn't good at — things I'd never be good at. At the same time I invested little energy into developing my strengths. I worked hard but not smart. Finally I realized that my true value lay within the context of my giftedness — not the number of hours I worked. There were some balls I'd no business juggling. When I finally got the courage to let them fall to the floor, I began to excel in juggling the 2 or 3 balls I was created to keep in the air in the first place. And the amazing thing is, people came long and picked up the other balls. What I couldn't relinquish, were the opportunities they'd been waiting for. What drained me fueled them."

Of the 2 or 3 things that define success for you, which of them are in line with your core competencies? *That* is where you must focus your energies! *That* is where you'll excel. Within *that* narrowed context you'll make the greatest contribution. And best of all, you'll *enjoy* what you do! "But I can't afford to focus all my energies on 1 or 2 things." Maybe not yet, but that should be your *goal.* It's something you should be working toward if you ever hope to maximize your potential.

IS THE CROWD STOPPING YOU?

When she heard about Jesus,
she came up behind him in the crowd.
Mark 5:27 NIV

*W*e don't know her name, but we know she'd been bleeding for 12 years; suffered under many doctors; spent all she had and grew worse. What Western culture discreetly refers to as a female condition, had devastated this Jewish woman's life. *Sexually,* she couldn't touch her husband. *Maternally,* she couldn't have children. *Domestically,* whatever she touched was considered unclean. *Spiritually,* she couldn't enter the temple. Now physically exhausted and socially ostracized she thinks, "If I can just touch Jesus I'll be made whole."

But first she had to get through the crowd that stood between her and Him. And so will you! To those who tell you the day of miracles is past, you'll have to say: "There is no *day* of miracles, there's only a *God* of miracles and He never changes." To those who tell you, "There are too many hypocrites in the church," you'll have to say, "I'm not looking to Christians, I'm looking to Christ. Others may fail me, but He never will." The crowd has its reasons, but not one of them is worth missing Jesus for.

When this woman finally got to Jesus, two things happened: (1) He made her whole. Her faith summoned His immediate response—and yours will too! (2) She's the only woman He ever called "daughter" (vs. 34). Imagine how she must have felt! She probably couldn't remember when she'd last heard a kind word! *Today Jesus is within range of your prayers and your faith. So reach out, touch Him and be made whole!*

ACCOMPLISH MORE EACH DAY

Conduct yourself wisely . . . making the most of . . . time.
Colossians 4:5 NRSV

*C*harles Schwab once offered to pay Ivy Lee, a management consultant, any reasonable amount if he could just show him how to accomplish *more* each day. Lee gave him the following formula: "Sit down every night and list in order of priority, your 6 most important tasks for the next day. Then spend that day working down the list until it's completed. At the end of that day destroy the list and make a new one for the following day. Don't worry if you only finish one or two jobs. *Just do first things first!* If this method doesn't work, nothing will, because without a system you don't even know what's important. Try it, then pay me whatever you think it's worth." A month later Schwab sent him a $25,000 check saying it was the best advice he'd ever received! *That system will work for you too!*

The term "time management" is misleading because you can't really delay, hasten, save or manage time. You can only manage *yourself* by establishing the right priorities. That's why the Bible says "Conduct yourselves wisely . . . making the most of . . . time." C. S. Lewis said, "Put first things first and you get second things thrown in. But put second things first and you lose both."

Today ask God to show you *His* priorities for your life, then set your personal goals and agenda accordingly. Go ahead, try it! There's no feeling like knowing you're in God's will, doing the right thing at the right time!

SEEING OURSELVES AS GOD SEES US!

Woe is me! For I am undone . . .
for mine eyes have seen . . . the Lord of hosts.
Isaiah 6:5

*A*fter a successful crusade someone asked Billy Graham, "Is this revival?" "No," he replied. "When revival comes we'll see two things we haven't seen yet: (1) A fresh sense of God's holiness. (2) A heightened awareness of our own sin and carnality!"

Isaiah was probably happy enough with his level of commitment. After all, he was a prophet. Then he "saw the Lord high and lifted up" (Isa 6:1). In that instant, Isaiah became aware of all the "junk" he'd allowed to accumulate in his life. Listen to him: "Woe is me! For I am undone . . . for mine eyes have seen . . . the Lord of hosts."

A real encounter with God always brings: (a) a greater awareness of our shortcomings; (b) an acknowledgement of our own inadequacy; (c) a new humility and hunger for more of God.

The wear and tear of life dulls the sharp edge of our spiritual sensibilities. And gauging our holiness by that of those around us, just lulls us into thinking we're living a consecrated life when we're not. We can fall so far below God's standards that when somebody's actually living by them, they make us uncomfortable.

Today God wants to bring us to a new place of intimacy with Him, to produce in us the character and attractiveness of Christ. When that happens others will notice the difference, because we'll have *influence* and *impact* like we never had before!

STOP COMPARING YOURSELF!

We will not compare ourselves . . . each of us is an original.
Galatians 5:26 TM

*A*re you so busy analyzing your vices that you don't have time to appreciate your virtues? Are you so caught up in scrutinizing *others,* that you don't value what God's given *you?* God never intended you to compare yourself with anybody. Listen: "We will not compare ourselves with each other as if one of us were better and another worse. We have far more interesting things to do with our lives. Each of us is an original."

By making comparisons: (a) you imply that God made a mistake by making you as you are; (b) you allow others to define your idea of attractiveness; (c) you give them control of your self-esteem. That's too much power to give anybody! Paul says, "Since we find ourselves fashioned . . . excellently . . . and marvelously . . . let's just go ahead and be what we were made to be" (Ro 12:3-5 TM). Focus on the talents and abilities God's given you, and stop coveting what you don't have. Base your self-esteem on the fact that God made you exactly, precisely, intricately, wondrously and uniquely who you are. You're without comparison, a genuine "one of!"

What you are is God's gift to you; what you do with yourself is your gift back to Him. Until you stop comparing yourself to others you'll never be able to give birth to the unique gifts He's placed within you. So, thank God today for making you who you *are,* and begin believing that He's transforming you day by day into who He wants you to *become.*

"I'M PRAYING FOR YOU!"

I will intercede with the Lord for you.
1 Samuel 7:5 NIV

*W*hen somebody says, "I'm praying for you," do you respond with a polite "Thank you," then promptly forget it? Don't! There is no greater expression of love than that!

You may be reading this, unaware of the fact that you wouldn't be around to read it, had not somebody prayed for you! Jesus told Peter, "Satan hath desired to have you . . . but I have prayed for thee that thy faith fail not: and when thou art converted, strengthen thy brethren" (Lk 22:31-32). Did God answer that prayer? Absolutely! In spite of his shameful denial of Christ, Peter ended up leading one of the greatest spiritual awakenings in history, and two books of the Bible are named after him.

There's no distance in prayer! Through prayer you can project yourself into *any* situation at *any* time claiming the promise, "Whatever you ask for in prayer, believe that you have received it, and it will be yours" (Mk 11:24 NIV).

When the Philistines were about to annihilate Israel, Samuel said, "I will intercede with the Lord for you." As a result, "The Lord thundered . . . against the Philistines" (1Sa 7:10 NIV). Maybe that's where the old timers got their expression "prayin' up a storm!"

God comes by invitation. Your prayers are His entry point into the situation. Anytime you ask in the name of Jesus, the Holy Spirit is *authorized* to go to work accomplishing things on your behalf that *cannot* be accomplished any other way. Remember that, next time someone says, "I'm praying for you."

ARE YOU BATTLING INSECURITY?

May you be . . . founded securely on love.
Ephesians 3:17 AMP

*I*f so, reflect on these 10 Scriptural truths about yourself: (1) I know God loves me and that He has a great plan for my life. (2) Yes, I've faults, but God's working on me, changing me day by day; while He does, I can still enjoy my life. (3) I realize I'll always have issues to deal with, so I won't be discouraged when God convicts me of areas that still need improvement. (4) Everybody has weaknesses, so I'm not a failure because I'm not perfect. (5) I want people to like me, but my sense of worth isn't dependent on them. No, Jesus has already proven my worth by dying for me. (6) I refuse to be controlled or manipulated by others. Even if they reject me I'll survive, for Jesus has promised never to leave me nor forsake me. (7) No matter how often I fail I won't give up, because God is with me, to strengthen and sustain me. (8) I like myself. I don't like everything I do and I want to change, but I refuse to reject myself because God loves and accepts me as I am. (9) In myself I may be nothing, but in Christ I'm everything I need to be. (10) I matter to God. My life makes a difference. Regardless of the challenge, "I can do all things through Christ which strengtheneth me" (Php 4:13).

As you reflect daily on these principles, you'll be amazed at how *differently* you begin to feel about yourself!

FACING THE FIRE (1)

Praise be to the God of Shadrach, Meshach, and Abednego.
Daniel 3:28 NIV

*I*t's easier to "risk it all" when there's little to risk. Success always raises the stakes. The higher you climb, the more the Nebuchadnezzars of this world will claim to have control over what you lose and what you keep. Their threats will sound real and the consequences of ignoring them, intimidating. That's what happened to Shadrach, Meshach and Abednego. Their commitment to God landed them in a fiery furnace. It also brought them out and promoted them to a higher level of blessing. There's a lesson here for you.

For something to be an authentic test of character, it must be a situation in which the outcome is entirely out of your hands. You simply make the choice to do what's right before God, then leave the consequences in His hands. It's a trial by fire, but it's a fire of refinement, and on the other side of it you'll be better and stronger.

Each time you make the right decision, choosing to embrace rather than escape the consequences, you enter a new level of freedom. You're: (1) free from the threats of those who claim to have control over the outcomes of your life; (2) free to say "no" to those who'd abuse their authority by attempting to manipulate you; (3) free to serve your all-powerful King and to say no to all the other would-be kings who are just blowing hot air!

In that moment of decision, you not only gain insight into *who* you are, but more importantly—*whose* you are!

FACING THE FIRE (2)

Our God whom we serve is able to deliver us.
Daniel 3:17

*S*hadrach, Meshach and Abednego were set for life. They'd nothing to gain by challenging the king. So why did they? Because he ordered them to violate their convictions by bowing before his pagan image. No doubt they could've said, "Better a live dog than a dead lion. If we stay alive, we can do some good for God and others." That line would have sold most of us, but not them. Why?

Because they understood that Nebuchadnezzar wasn't the reason for their success! He may have been the instrument God used to bless them, but he wasn't the source. Their blessings came from God—and they understood that you can't abandon the principles of God and still maintain the blessings of God. Why grieve or disobey the One who controls everything, to get along with somebody who only *thinks* he controls everything?

There'll always be those in your life who think they're big enough to control your future. But you know better, don't you? "Our God . . . is able to deliver us . . . out of thine hand, O king" (Dan 3:17). God controls our outcome! He's also bigger than those who *think* they control our outcome. By refusing to bow, when bowing seemed their only option, these 3 slave boys radically influenced a pagan king and turned the hearts of an entire nation to Jehovah. Not bad—eh? Now maybe *your* influence won't be that widespread, but one thing you can count on: others are watching who'll be *greatly impacted* by the stand you take!

DO YOU NOTICE PEOPLE?

Whenever you failed to do . . . these things to someone . . .
overlooked or ignored . . . you failed to do it to me.
Matthew 25:45 TM

*D*o you know your neighbors? Or the woman who checks your groceries? Or the kid who serves you at the drive-through? Or your mailman? Haven't a clue? Well, here's what one professor told his students: "I remember in college the teacher gave us a pop quiz. I was a conscientious student and breezed through it—till I came to the last question: "What's the name of the cleaning lady?" Surely this was a joke! I'd seen her many times; she was dark-haired and fiftyish. But how would I know her name? So I handed in my paper leaving that answer blank, and asked if it counted towards my final grade. 'Absolutely,' replied the teacher! 'In life you'll meet many different people. They're all important and deserve your attention, even if you just smile and say hello.' I never forgot that lesson. I've tried to live by it. (Incidentally, the cleaning woman's name was Dorothy!)"

When the disciples asked, "Master, what are you talking about? When did we ever see you hungry . . . thirsty . . . homeless . . . shivering . . . sick or in prison and didn't help?"(Mt 25:44 TM). Jesus answered, "Whenever you failed to do . . . these things to someone . . . overlooked or ignored, that was me—you failed to do it to *me*."

The God who said, "I have called thee by thy name: thou art mine" (Isa 43:1), remembers the names of people *you* think are unimportant. If you want to be like Him, maybe you should take a leaf out of His book!

STOP SECOND-GUESSING GOD!

I don't think the way you think.
The way you work isn't the way I work.

Isaiah 55:8 TM

*H*ave you ever done the will of God, but the results weren't what you expected? If so, you may have second-guessed Him. He says, "I don't think the way you think. The way you work isn't the way I work . . . [my way] surpasses the way you work, and . . . is beyond the way you think." We usually have to re-learn the meaning of those words each time we face a new challenge.

God told Moses, "I'm going to deliver the Israelites from Egypt." Sounds good so far, right? But things didn't turn out the way Moses anticipated because Pharaoh made their lives even *harder.* Instead of becoming a hero, Moses is now despised by his own people. Later when some other things didn't turn out as Moses expected, He got discouraged and complained, "Lord, we did what You told us to do. How come we're having such a hassle?" (See Ex 5:22). Moses didn't understand the results of his obedience, *because God didn't tell him how things would turn out.* Sound familiar?

Generally our frustrations have little to do with what God does or doesn't do, and everything to do with our own mistaken assumptions about how we *think* He should act. When we second-guess God we get into trouble every time. Listen: "You don't really know what I am doing, but later you will understand" (Jn 13:7 CEV). It's only in *looking back* that we see how God led us! So trust Him today, and stop second-guessing Him!

DOES GOD SEEM DISTANT?

The Lord has hidden himself . . . but I trust him.
Isaiah 8:17 TEV

*F*loyd McClung writes: "You wake up one morning and all your 'spiritual feelings' are gone. You pray but nothing happens. You rebuke the devil but it doesn't change anything. You go through spiritual exercises, have your friends pray for you, confess every sin you can imagine, then you go around asking forgiveness of everyone you know. You fast, still nothing. You begin to wonder how long this spiritual gloom will last. It feels like your prayers bounce off the ceiling. In utter desperation you cry out: 'What's the matter with me?' *This is a normal part of the testing and maturing of your friendship with God. We all go through it! It's painful, but absolutely vital to developing your faith.* You see, God is always present, even when you're unaware of Him. His presence is too profound to be measured by intellect or emotion. He's more concerned that you *trust* Him, than that you *feel* Him. Faith, not feelings, is what pleases God."

"So what can I do?" you ask. Focus on God's unchanging love for you! Cling to His promises! During times of spiritual dryness rely on God's Word, not your emotions. Realize that He's taking you to a deeper level of maturity. Any friendship based on emotion is shallow indeed. So don't be troubled by trouble. God's grace is still in full-force. *He's for you, even when you don't feel Him.*

THRIVING IN THE MIDST
OF UNCERTAINTY (1)

Neither know we what to do, but our eyes are upon thee.
2 Chronicles 20:12

Uncertainty is a permanent part of all progress; it never goes away! Furthermore, uncertainty isn't an indication of poor leadership; it just underscores the need for it; it's the environment in which good leadership is most often discovered. As a leader you may *think* you should always know what to do, but in reality there'll be very *few* occasions when you are absolutely certain. Since you'll constantly be called on to make decisions with limited information, your goal should not be to eliminate uncertainty, but to develop the ability to be courageous and clear in the midst of it.

As you rise through the ranks, you'll be called upon to make decisions regarding relationships, money, time, values, opportunities and disputes. Eventually your decisions will show up on the bottom line, and there in the clear light of day your leadership will be judged. And there's something else you need to know; in that realm it takes *longer* to recognize your brilliance or stupidity, because you're forced to lead for long periods of time without the benefit of knowing whether or not you made the right call. And by the time your crop starts coming in, it's too late to change your agricultural procedure. You have to wait until the next planting season.

But don't let that throw you. It's not your job to remove uncertainty, it's your job to inspire clarity, courage, and progress in the midst of it. *When you can do that, you're a leader!*

THRIVING IN THE MIDST
OF UNCERTAINTY (2)

Neither know we what to do, but our eyes are upon thee.
2 Chronicles 20:12

*B*y the time Moses passed the reins of leadership to Joshua, everything had changed. For 40 years Joshua has been taught to navigate and survive in a wilderness, but now it was time to enter the Promised Land. Can't you hear his thoughts: "I know a lot about wandering, but not much about warfare." No wonder God told him, "Be strong and courageous . . . for the Lord your God will be with you wherever you go" (Jos 1:9 NIV). Why would God tell Joshua not to be afraid? Because he must have *been* afraid! Everything about his new situation wreaked of uncertainty. The only thing Joshua knew for sure was that God said, "Go." Listen: "Then Joshua commanded the people, saying, 'Prepare . . . yourselves, for within three days you are to cross this Jordan . . . [and] possess the land" (Jos 1:10-11 NAS).

Can you imagine what the people must have thought? Question: "But Joshua, how are we going to get across the river?" Answer: "I'm not sure, but in 3 days be ready to go." Question: "But Joshua, what are we going to do when we get to the other side?" Answer: "I'll tell you when we arrive. Just be ready to move out in 3 days."

You'll always be uncertain as to many things, especially as you move into new territory. But you can never afford to be unclear or in doubt as to your call, your vision, and your destination. *So where does such confidence come from? God's promise, "I am with you."*

THRIVING IN THE MIDST
OF UNCERTAINTY (3)

Neither know we what to do, but our eyes are upon thee.
2 Chronicles 20:12

*T*o thrive in uncertain territory, you must be able to successfully do these 4 things:

(1) Understand your certainty quotient! Think back to your last big decision that turned out right. How certain were you? 80 percent? 50 percent? If your best decisions are usually made at the 75 percent mark, that is your "certainty quotient." When you reach that point, it's time to stop debating and start moving.

(2) Express your uncertainty with confidence! Never look at successful people and assume that single-handedly and with no hesitation, they fearlessly navigated the currents of uncertainty. No, they just understood that with each step, answers would be given. So instead of pretending to know more than you do, begin to encourage a culture of transparency that fosters the free exchange of ideas. When you don't know, just say, "I don't know, but I'll find out."

(3) Consult with others! King Solomon wrote more about seeking counsel than any other biblical writer. Do kings need counsel? You bet! And only those with the humility to acknowledge it ever prosper.

(4) Measure your success by the scoreboard, not the playbook! Every good coach goes into the game with a plan. But he's willing to change his plan in order to win. Pencil in your plans, but write your vision in ink! Good leaders, like good coaches, are often forced to abandon or amend some of their plans in order to deliver on the vision. *The ones who do, are the ones who reach their destination.*

"TAR BABIES"

They . . . continued praying . . . with . . .
Mary the mother of Jesus, and Jesus' brothers.
Acts 1:12–14 NCV

*I*n the children's story, *Brer Rabbit,* Wiley Fox creates a doll out of tar, and when he can't communicate with it, he gets ticked off and starts hitting it. And do you remember what happened next? They end up glued together! Are some of your relationships like that? You're stuck to somebody you can't communicate with, but can't escape either: an abusive father, an overbearing mother, a jealous controlling mate; everybody has a "Tar Baby" somewhere. They're stuck in a relationship that's more pain than pleasure.

Maybe you've dreamed about the perfect family. Not Jesus. He said, "My true brother and sister . . . are those who do what God wants" (Mk 3:35 NCV). When His earthly family made problems, He didn't try to control them, demand they agree with Him, sulk because they insulted Him, or dedicate his life to trying to please them. Jesus didn't try to control His family at all—so why are you trying to control yours? Give it up! You could be the world's greatest son or daughter, mother or father, husband or wife, and it *still* wouldn't change things. Don't you know that those who anger you control you; that by trying to change others you remain a prisoner to their opinions?

But what became of Jesus' family? The Bible says that in the upper room the disciples continued praying with "Mary the mother of Jesus, and Jesus' brothers." Those who rejected Him yesterday, revere Him today! Jesus gave them time and space to change, and they did. So take heart, your "Tar Baby" could one day become your biggest fan!

AT HOME IN HIS PRESENCE!

Lord, you have been our home since the beginning.
Psalm 90:1 NCV

*A*fter a hard day, it's wonderful to come home to a place you know; a place where you can kick off your shoes, run around in your bathrobe and not worry about what somebody thinks. And God's presence can be equally familiar to you. With time, you can learn where to go for *nourishment,* where to hide for *protection,* where to turn for *guidance.*

God doesn't want to be your Sunday getaway, He wants to be your permanent residence. We think of God as a deity to discuss instead of a place to dwell, but God wants to be much more. He wants to be the One in whom "we live and move and have our being" (Acts 17:28 NIV). When God led the children of Israel through the wilderness He didn't just appear once a day, then abandon them. No, the pillar of fire was present *all* night and the cloud of smoke was present *all* day. Our God never leaves us. He promised, "I am with you always"(Mt 28:20 NIV).

David said, "I'm asking God [Yahweh] for . . . only one thing: to live with him in his house my whole life long" (Ps 27:4 TM). "That's nice" you say, "I'd love to live in God's house too, but I'm stuck in the real world." No, just the opposite; you're only *one decision* away from your Father's presence. You don't need to change your *address*—just your *perception.* Wherever you go today, whatever you face today, remind yourself, "He is with me!"

TIMES CHANGE—GOD DOESN'T

As I was with Moses, so I will be with you.
Joshua 1:5 NKJV

*C*an you imagine trying to fill the shoes Moses wore? God had used him to turn the Nile River into blood, part the Red Sea, destroy the Egyptian army, receive His law on Mount Sinai, and feed over 2,000,000 Israelites each day in the wilderness. How would you like to follow somebody with *that* kind of a resume? But once God told Joshua, "No man shall be able to stand before you . . . as I was with Moses, so I will be with you," he had the confidence he needed to pick up where Moses left off.

If you've read the stories of those God used to accomplish great things and wondered if He *still* works like that today, wonder no more! Times change—God doesn't. The same God who worked through Moses and Paul, Deborah and Esther, will work through *you* too! He can give you victory in the face of defeat, or turn last year's disaster into this year's celebration. The heroes of the Bible all had one thing in common—they were just ordinary folks who took risks in obedience to faith, then trusted an extraordinary God to give them results! And He did!

Paul writes, "We walk by faith, not by sight" (2 Co 5:7). The enemy doesn't mind your *words* of faith as long as they're not followed by *acts* of faith. When God says something to you, it's always for a good reason; He won't command you to do, what He won't empower you to do. So, what's God talking to *you* about?

EXCESSIVE REASONING!

The mind of the flesh [sense and reason] is death . . .
but the mind of the Spirit is life.

Romans 8:6 AMP

$\mathcal{D}$o you have a need to control things? To find a solution for every problem? To have a back-up plan in case God doesn't come through the way you think He should? Have you noticed that the more you try to fix things, the more anxiety you experience? Paul calls this, "The mind of the flesh." *Fixing* is the opposite of *trusting;* usually you can't do both. Now that doesn't mean God wants you to be mindless or helpless; it just means He wants you to live by *faith,* not *head* knowledge! When you learn to trust God and operate in "the mind of the Spirit," you experience peace in spite of the circumstances.

One of the pitfalls of excessive reasoning is that it causes you to become double-minded and stuck. Listen, "A man of two minds is unstable and unreliable and *uncertain about everything"* (Jas 1:8 AMP). Does that describe you?

Instead of always trying to figure things out—learn to be comfortable not knowing, and start trusting the One who does! Make a decision today that every time you feel anxious, you'll stop and pray: "Lord, I'm not going to try and figure this out myself, I'm bringing it to You and I'm waiting for Your answer." When you stop struggling with the *when's, why's,* and *how's,* you'll begin to experience God's peace in a way you never have before. You'll also position yourself for Him to intervene on your behalf. So make a decision today—to let go and let God!

WHY DOES IT TAKE SO LONG?

You have begun . . . becoming like the one who made you.
Colossians 3:10 NCV

$\mathcal{G}$od could instantly transform us, yet He's chosen to develop us slowly. Why? Because:

(1) We're slow learners! Often we have to learn the same lesson 50 times over in order to get it. We think, "Not again. I thought I'd already learned that!" But God knows better. The history of Israel illustrates how quickly we forget and revert to our old patterns. We need repeated exposure.

(2) We've a lot to unlearn! Your problems didn't develop overnight and they won't disappear overnight. There's no pill, prayer or principle that'll instantly undo years of habits. It requires the hard work of removal and replacement.

(3) We're unwilling to humbly face the truth! And our unwillingness keeps us living in denial. Only when we allow the truth to shine into our hearts, can we begin to work on ourselves. That's why we cannot grow without a humble, teachable attitude.

(4) Growth is scary! Though our old ways are self-defeating, we fear letting go of them because, like an old pair of shoes, at least they're comfortable and familiar. Some of us even build our identity around our old ways. We say, "It's just the way I am." Our unconscious worry is, "If I let go of my habit, hurt or hang-up, who will I be?" There's only one way to develop the habits of Christ-like character; you have to practice them—and that takes time! *Listen: "Practice these things, devote your life to them so that everyone can see your progress."*

MORAL AUTHORITY (1)

Don't be so naïve . . . you could fall flat on your face.
1 Corinthians 10:12 TM

*B*efore you set your goals, determine your values! To envision what you can do without first determining what you should *be,* is to set yourself up for a fall. Your accomplishments may make your name known, but your character will determine what people associate with it. Your gifts dictate your potential, your character determines your legacy. "What is character?" you ask. It's the will to do what's *right* even when it's *hard.* It's deciding *ahead of time* what's non-negotiable. Count on it, the day will come when "progress" calls for compromising your convictions. In that moment what hangs in the balance—is your moral authority!

You'll be tempted to believe that once you reach a certain level, these challenges disappear. Wrong! Success doesn't make anything easier. It just raises the stakes. What was once applauded is now simply expected. It's a lot easier to win the title than defend it.

Furthermore, with promotion comes the inclination to see yourself as the final authority on right and wrong. It's not uncommon to find leaders playing by a different set of rules. Everything really does look different at the top. Once intoxicated by success we start to believe that the rules don't apply to us. That can be fatal!

In the final analysis your reputation is how you're known before men but your character is how you're known before God. "But why cling to something that has the potential to slow me down?" *Because what's at stake is—your moral authority!*

MORAL AUTHORITY (2)

Be careful how you think; your life is shaped by your thoughts.
Proverbs 4:23 TEV

*T*he nameplate on your office door may prompt people to lend you their hands, but only your moral authority will inspire them to give you their hearts. Moral authority is established when it becomes clear to all that progress, financial reward and recognition are not your gods; that you value something more, something you refuse to sacrifice on the altar of profit or popularity. With moral authority comes *influence.* You can manage people without moral authority but you can't influence them. Wake up! Talking one way and living another "wounds" you, and depending on time and circumstance, you may or may not recover from it.

You can tell yourself that how you conduct your private life is nobody's business, but if there's a perceived difference between what you demand of others and what you do yourself, it'll erode people's respect for you. While your *position* may make you secure, your *influence* and *moral authority* will always remain fragile. At any given time you're only one decision, one word, one reaction away from destroying what took years to build.

"Why is it important to know this?" you ask. Because the fastest route from where you are today to where you'd like to be tomorrow, isn't always the most honorable one. Leading, and being the person you want to be, don't always line up. It's in those moments, however, that you discover a great deal about yourself—*you find out what you value most!*

AN ATTITUDE OF GRATITUDE!

Worship God if you want the best;
worship opens doors to all his goodness.
Psalm 34:9 TM

*F*our-year-old Martha hugged a doll in each of her little arms. Looking up at her mother she asked, "Mom, how come I keep loving them but they never love me back?" When we go out of our way to do something nice for someone, it's disheartening not to get back a response. On the other hand when they respond with delight and appreciation, it justifies our efforts and makes us want to do even *more* for them. Jesus promised, "the Father will give you whatever you ask for in my name" (Jn 15:16 NIV). But like any giver, God looks for an attitude of gratitude.

King David knew he wasn't worth two-cents without God. He struggled with all kinds of moral and family issues. But he had one thing going for him; he never stopped praising God. He said, "I bless God every chance I get." Then he added, "Worship God if you want the best; worship opens doors to all his goodness" (Ps 34:1&9 TM). *Note: It's our praises, not our petitions, that open the doors to God's goodness!* God likes to get thanked before He gets involved. David knew he'd still be shoveling sheep dung and sleeping under the stars, had God not brought him to the palace and blessed him beyond anything he deserved or imagined. That's why he never stopped praising God!

So, don't take your blessings for granted. When you drink from the stream, remember the source—and be grateful!

AN ETERNAL PERSPECTIVE

Rejoice . . . your reward is great in heaven.

Luke 6:23

*J*esus said, "Blessed are you when men hate you . . . exclude you . . . and reject your name as evil . . . Rejoice in that day and leap for joy" (Lk 6:22-23 NIV). Now, Jesus didn't mean, "If you're persecuted on my behalf you'll be so happy you'll dance an Irish jig." No, read on:

"Your reward is great in heaven." Those 6 words reveal *why* you can rejoice in the worst of circumstances. You see, there's a direct connection between something you do for God on earth, and something "great" He's going to do for you in heaven. Jesus isn't asking you to enjoy misery on His behalf. That's masochism. He's saying that your rewards in heaven for certain actions on earth will be so wonderful, that simply *knowing* they're coming, can transform how you live now. Yes, even create spontaneous outbursts of joy!

Listen to these 3 verses: "He will *reward* every man according to his works" (Mt 16:27). "You will have *treasure* in heaven" (Mt 19:21 NIV). "You will be . . . *repaid* at the resurrection" (Lk 14:14 NIV). Wow! God's keeping track of what you do for Him every day. You have more to gain by serving the Lord than you ever imagined. Yes, He'll bless and reward you in this life, but nothing by comparison to what awaits you in eternity. Simple decisions such as how you spend your time, your money and your energy, suddenly become opportunities of great promise.

Once you understand this, you begin to live with an unshakable certainty that *everything* you do today—matters forever. *And that truth can change your life for the better!*

DARE TO DREAM!

Know where you are headed,
and you will stay on solid ground.
Proverbs 4:26 CEV

*E*very great accomplishment began as a dream in somebody's heart. All things are created twice: first in your mind, then in your life. Dreamers allow their minds to wander outside the boundaries of what *is,* creating a mental picture of what *could be.* They're not always the most talented or the best educated—just the ones who refuse to put brackets on their thinking or to limit themselves by what others have done, or failed to do. And that requires courage—lots of it!

On the heels of every dream there's a demon of doubt. No sooner is our dream conceived than our minds are suddenly filled with all the reasons why it *won't* work. And certain folks around us will be quick to confirm those fears! In spite of that we must forge ahead and dream; otherwise, we'll spend our lives fulfilling the dreams of others.

Andy Stanley writes: "I keep a little card on my desk that reads: *'Dream no small dreams, for they stir not the hearts of men.'* More than once that simple statement has kept me from retreating from my dreams. I know from experience that it's impossible to lead without a dream. When leaders are no longer willing to dream, it's only a short time before followers are unwilling to follow. So dream! Dream big. Dream often. Somewhere in those random ideas that flood your mind, is one that will capture your heart and imagination. *And that seemingly random idea, may very well evolve into a vision for your life."*

IDENTIFY YOUR OPPORTUNITIES

The Lord . . . will deliver me from the hand of this Philistine.
1 Samuel 17:37 NIV

*D*avid didn't show up that day with the intention of becoming a hero, he was just delivering bread to his brothers. But when he saw Goliath, he seized an opportunity that other warriors only dream about. Today's opportunities will catch you by surprise—if you're not alert and ready, you'll miss them.

What others saw in David had actually been there all along. If you're truly a leader, you *already* possess the talent necessary to lead. But your *courage* is what will establish you as a leader before others. The leaders we revere most, walk on to the pages of history through timely displays of courage: courage on the battlefield or in the boardroom, courage to defend the defenseless, or simply to attempt what nobody else thought possible.

"But I don't have the money," you say. Don't worry; capital follows courage. *What* always precedes *how.* Don't be intimidated by the numbers, God isn't moved by spreadsheets and market conditions. He responds to *faith!* Don't let *how* intimidate you. It's because *how* is so challenging, that it provides you with great opportunity. If the pathway to success were well lit, it would already be crowded. If *how* wasn't a problem, somebody else would have already figured it out.

All progress begins with one question: *"What* needs to be done?"* And somebody needs to be asking that question—why not you? To those who have the courage to ask that question and the faith to hang on until they *discover* or *create* the answer, belongs the future.

PREPARE NOW!

Wherefore let him that thinketh he standeth
take heed lest he fall.
1 Corinthians 10:12

Greater success always leads to greater temptation! And your response to that temptation will depend entirely upon the condition of your soul at the time. Nobody plans to fail, but ignoring your spiritual condition guarantees failure. "So what can I do?" you ask. Begin preparing—now! You can wait until the night before your real estate final to prepare, but there's no cramming for a test of character. It comes up like a pop-quiz, and you're either ready or you're not.

Refuse to make the journey alone! Letting others in on what you want to be, reinforces your perimeter of protection. Becoming accountable is a powerful incentive to check any behavior that might take you out of bounds. And on those inevitable occasions when you do drift across the line, the fact that someone else knows and will "call you on it" is a compelling motivator to take responsibility for your actions and correct them quickly.

Constantly ask yourself: "What small thing in my life right now has the potential to become destructive? And who knows about it other than me?" It's better to expose your struggles to a handful of people who really care about you, than run the risk of being publicly exposed before those who couldn't care less. You owe it to yourself to identify and conquer those baby dragons that have the potential to grow up and wound not only you, but also those who put their trust in you.

REEDS AND WICKS

A bruised reed he will not break,
and a smoldering wick he will not snuff out.
Matthew 12:20 NIV

What do all these people have in common: (1) A woman cowering before an angry mob that's threatening to stone her? (2) A paralyzed man on a stretcher begging his friends not to give up as they stare at a house overflowing with people? (3) A blind man crying out to a rabbi? They're all "bruised reeds" and "smoldering wicks" that God refused to give up on!

What's more fragile than a bruised reed? Kids playing beside the River Jordan made music pipes out of them. As they were hollowed out and holes bored in them, they were often bruised and discarded. Perhaps you once stood tall and strong, nourished and rooted in the river bed. But now you're hidden in the rushes, bruised by hurtful words, a mate's betrayal, your own failure, or harsh religion. What's closer to extinction than a smoldering wick? When the oil in primitive lamps was gone and the wick burned low, it was extinguished, thrown away as worthless and replaced. Did you once glow with faith, lighting the path for others until the icy winds of criticism, unforgiveness and judgmentalism left you one snuff away from darkness?

The world *thinks* it knows what to do with you—break you off and snuff you out! But not Jesus; "A bruised reed he will not break, and a smoldering wick he will not snuff out." No matter how far gone you may feel, you're not beyond the reach of God's grace. So, come to Him today and let Him make you whole again!

BE SURE TO ENJOY YOUR KIDS!

God all-powerful was my closest friend,
and all my children were near by.
Job 29:4–5 CEV

*I*n her book, *Forever Erma,* Erma Bombeck writes, "When my children were young I made them pick up their rooms, make their own snacks and put the laundry in the utility room. "Now when they come home I put all the rules aside. I'm like a concierge looking for a big tip. I follow them around asking, 'Are you hungry? Can I get you something? Do you have any laundry? Do you need some money?'

"I eat when they want to eat, cook their favorite foods just before they tell me they're going out with their friends, then watch helplessly as they eat their way through a pound of baked ham at 3:00 in the afternoon.

"On their visit my life changes. I have no care. My washer is set on extra-large load and has 2 socks and a t-shirt in it. The phone rings constantly and it's never for me.

"At the end of their visit we set aside a day, pack a lunch and head for the airport. It isn't until I return home that I sense how orderly my life has become. I enjoy the quiet. The TV tuner is rescued from the clothes hamper and returned to its proper place on the coffee table. The empty milk and juice cartons are removed from the refrigerator, the wet towels are put in the washer, the bathroom is returned to health standards. It is my world again—*so why am I crying?"*

SPIRITUAL LANDMARKS

Thus far hath the Lord helped us.
1 Samuel 7:12

$\mathscr{I}$t's a good idea to establish some spiritual land-marks, reminding us of the times God intervened on our behalf. Without them we quickly forget, lose our bearings, or claim credit for things we'd nothing to do with.

When God miraculously opened the Jordan River for the Israelites to pass over, He knew something they didn't—that soon they'd come up against Jericho, their biggest battle. That's when they'd need *reminders* and a *reference point.* So He told them to collect 12 stones from the Jordan and build a memorial. This would act as a reminder of His past faithfulness. God was saying, "When you can't cope with the future, check with the past. My goodness will stand inventory." Samuel did the same after Israel defeated the Philistines. He took a stone and named it Ebenezer saying, *"Thus far* hath the Lord helped us" (1Sa 7:12).

Think of some of the spiritual landmarks in your life "thus far." Like the day you met Jesus; or specific instances when He guided you; or doors He opened that you thought were per-manently shut; or scrapes He brought you through. Go ahead, establish some spiritual landmarks by keeping a record of these events! They're important, because whenever you're struggling, they'll remind you of how God has cared for you. They'll help you to see His past goodness, even when you weren't aware of it. They'll give you a sense of gratitude for yesterday's blessings, and the confidence to face whatever tomorrow brings!

MAKING WITHDRAWALS!

Be strong in the Lord.
Ephesians 6:10

*G*enerally speaking, God calls us to step out and do things we don't feel qualified to do. Why? So that we'll learn to lean more on Him. "Does that mean I won't make mistakes?" No, it means you probably *will*. But instead of being discouraged you'll accept them as part of the learning curve and go on to greater things! Often we look at a task and think, "There's no way I can do this." Hey, you're looking through the wrong end of the telescope! You're looking at *yourself* instead of *God!*

When God called Joshua to take the place of Moses, He promised him: "As I was with Moses, so I will be with thee" (Jos 1:5). Now if God promises to be with you (and He does), that's all you need! His strength is best shown through your weakness (see 2Co 12:9). Whatever ingredients are lacking in the natural realm, you can withdraw from your account in the spiritual realm. Listen: "Be strong in the Lord [be empowered through your union with Him]; draw your strength from Him [that strength which His boundless might provides]" (Eph 6:10 AMP). What kind of might? "Boundless might!" Where do you draw it from? The ultimate source—God!

Christ empowers and equips you as you fellowship with Him, so stop selling yourself short! Armed with His might you have *more* capabilities than you think, and you're able to do a lot *more* than you've done in the past. So today, put your confidence in God and stop doubting yourself!

THE COURAGE TO GO FIRST

I am with you; that is all you need.
2 Corinthians 12:9 TLB

We all know what needs to be changed. Many of us come home from work every night frustrated because of it. We don't lack insight, we just lack the courage to *do* something about it!

But real leaders are different; they'd rather risk criticism and experience failure on the way to success, than remain silent and die on the sidelines. That's what gives others courage to follow them! Most folks have a dream they long to fulfill— they just need somebody to take the first step to show them the way. *You* can be that somebody!

Without courage we simply accumulate a collection of good ideas and regrets. Most of our missed opportunities would *not* have been missed, had we only been willing to push through our fear and embrace what could be. All of us feel fear, but here's the difference: eventually a true leader's need for progress overwhelms his reluctance to take a risk. He can live more easily with the prospects of having tried and failed, than not having tried at all. He knows that failure is an inevitable part of success. He also realizes that failure looks and feels completely *different* in the rearview mirror, than it does when it is staring at you through the windshield. The truth is, while the average person fears *stepping out* into a new opportunity, the true leader fears *missing out* on it.

ONLY YOU!

I know you by name and you have found favor with me.
Exodus 33:12 NIV

*W*hen actors and actresses audition for a part, the director conducts what are known as "call-backs." At that point the performer either gets the part or it goes to somebody else. You know you've "got it made," when the director offers you the part *without* even auditioning for it.

Well, God doesn't need to do auditions and call-backs. That's because He's *already* designed a role just for you. Nobody else could possibly fill it or meet the requirements. You're a "designer original" with a PhD in being yourself! Even if others were to study you endlessly, they still couldn't be you.

When God says, "I know you by name and you have found favor with me," it means He's already chosen you for a particular role. *So be careful about responding to any other call except the one that comes from Him, because good ideas aren't necessarily God ideas!*

Since God designed you with all the built-in qualifications you'll ever need, you don't have to compromise your convictions, work angles, drop names or do special favors. The part is yours because you were born for it! That also means you need never be jealous of or intimidated by anybody else, no matter how talented, popular or successful they are. In God's eyes there are no other contenders. You're it! You're the only one who can fill the slot, because He created it with you in mind. *Isn't that a nice, secure feeling?*

WHEN YOUR MOMENT COMES

If you're content to . . . be yourself, your life will count.
Matthew 23:12 TM

*W*hen the moment comes for you to stride confidently into the spotlight and fulfill your God-given role, try to remember that there's no room for self-importance and pretense. This moment calls for: (a) stripping away all the lesser roles you've acted out and settled for; (b) discovering who you are and what you're *really* all about; (c) depending totally on God to help you give the most authentic performance of your life.

Remember Rosa Parks, the black woman who refused to surrender her seat and move to the back of the bus? There was more at stake here than just a ride home from work. By simply being herself, Rosa Parks suddenly moved to center stage. She wasn't playing games. She was the real thing and God shone a light on her soul that day that made history. That's how it works: when *His* light shines on *your* efforts, little becomes much.

Now since *God's* the only one who knows when your time will come, you must be prepared. "How do I do that?" you ask. Listen: "Be content with who you are . . . don't put on airs. God's . . . hand is on you. He'll promote you at the right time" (1Pe 5:6-7 TM). Allow the Holy Spirit to be your agent and advance man. Don't get ahead of Him. Just be faithful, then when the time's right, He'll shine His spotlight on the *next* stage, and assign you an even *bigger* role!

PREPARING FOR THE SPOTLIGHT

Except the Lord build the house, they labor in vain that build it.
Psalm 127:1 NJKV

*I*n God's kingdom, center stage isn't for people who think they've "got it all together" and deserve public recognition. Nor is it limited to those in leadership and public ministry. No, it's a call to action to you, *whoever* and *wherever* you are today. When you trust God's timing, He grooms you for bigger and better parts. But there are some things you must (and must not) do:

(1) Don't try to make it on your own: Because popular wisdom says, "Fake it till you make it," you'll be tempted to debut in your own strength. Don't do it! If you do, you'll get in the way of a much greater production. Remember, "Except the Lord build the house, they labor in vain that build it" (Ps 127:1). Trust God, and when your moment comes, He'll give you your cue.

(2) Leave the shadows: Are you ready to transform "acting" into an authentic performance that reveals the real you? Fear of rejection is powerful. It takes courage to be yourself. But you gain strength from the struggle and power from the pain when you're willing to risk moving from the shadows into the light.

(3) Confront your inner critic: We're all subject to that little voice which says, "You'll never be smart enough, loving enough, pretty enough, good enough to stand in the spotlight." Confront your inner critic with God's Word! And always remember, when God raises you up, nobody can put you down!

So, if you're afraid to step out today, listen: "I am with you; that is all you need" (2Co 12:9 TLB).

MERCY

His compassions never fail . . . They are new every morning.
Lamentations 3:22–23 NIV

*E*ach day when you wake up, be like the lady who said, "It's a good thing God's mercy is new every morning, because I used up all of yesterday's supply!" Webster's Dictionary defines mercy as "tenderness of heart that disposes a person to overlook injuries or to treat an offender better than he deserves." *That's* a picture of God's mercy toward you!

David was a man who loved God very much, yet lust overcame him causing him to commit adultery, then have the woman's husband killed. The reason David talked about God's mercy is because he needed so much of it! Only a person who's gut-level honest in their evaluation of themselves can say, "Oh give thanks to the Lord, for He is good; for His mercy and loving-kindness endure forever" (Ps 107:1 AMP).

If you think you're solely responsible for your success, think again. Paul, the greatest of the Apostles, wrote: "I know that in me (that is, in my flesh) dwelleth no good thing" (Ro 7:18). It's impossible to be merciful until we've thoroughly come to terms with our own need for mercy—and learned to receive it from the Lord. The truth is, if any of us were "perfect," nobody could stand us, because we'd expect the same of others. Every time we have a memory lapse concerning our own faults, we end up being hard to live with. At such times God reminds us again of our flawed condition. He allows us to get into just enough trouble to need His mercy, to keep us humble, and therefore useable.

HOW'S YOUR HEART?

Guard your heart.
Proverbs 4:23 NIV

We think of the heart as the center of our emotions. But it's more; it's the origin of our desires, imaginations, motives and intentions. That's why God says, "Above all . . . guard your heart . . . it is the well-spring of life."

Just as low-grade fuel makes your car perform badly, Jesus says, "The things that come . . . from the heart . . . make a man 'unclean' . . . evil thoughts, murder, sexual immorality, theft, false testimony, slander" (Mt 15:18-19 NIV). And again He said, "A . . . person produces good deeds from a good heart, and . . . evil deeds from an evil heart. Whatever is in your heart determines what you say" (Lk 6:45 NLT).

So, how's *your* heart today? Do you get upset easily? Do you constantly compare and resent? When you hear gossip, do you silence it or spread it? What kind of thoughts do you entertain? Your answer depends on the state of your heart. Jesus said that those whose hearts are pure, will *see* God in everything and act accordingly (See Mt 5:8 NLT).

Only by going directly to the source and cleaning out the pipeline, can you get a pure product. We reverse things by trying to clean up the outside first. But it doesn't work! If a tree produced bad fruit you wouldn't just treat the fruit, would you? No, you'd treat the root! Likewise, it's not enough just to try and change your bad habits; you must go to the heart of the problem—which is the problem of the heart! David realized this, so he prayed, "Create in me a clean heart, O God" (Ps 51:10 NLT). Think maybe you should pray that too?

"CONNECT FOR CHRIST!"

By all possible means . . . save some.
1 Corinthians 9:22 NIV

*W*hat would you think of someone who had a cure for cancer or Alzheimer's, but refused to share it? Well, we're guilty of worse when we refuse to "connect for Christ" with those outside our social, cultural, ethnic, generational or religious circle. You don't have to like everybody. (Hello! Is everything about *you* likeable?). But you do have to give them the cure. If you don't they'll die and be lost. "What can I do?" you ask.

(1) Pray for a desire! Jesus said, "When the Holy Spirit comes on you . . . you will be my witnesses" (Acts 1:8 NRSV). When God's Spirit lives in you, you'll see others through His eyes and seize every opportunity to share His love with them.

(2) Get over your fear! Don't be intimidated by words like Generation X, Muslim, atheist, intellectual, addict, etc. Everybody needs the same cure. Bury your ego. If they reject you, you'll only lose face; if they reject Jesus they'll lose out eternally.

(3) Loosen up! Blessed are the flexible for they won't get bent out of shape. Paul says, "I have become all things to all men so that by all possible means I might save some." Be willing to be stretched, including rethinking the way you share your faith. If your message isn't getting through, check the messenger, then the delivery system.

(4) Break out of your Christian bubble! To reach people you've got to go into their sometimes-not-so-nice environment. Jesus said, "You are salt" (Mt 5:13 NKJV). So shake yourself up and start spreading around what you've got. Come on, go out today and tell somebody about Jesus!

WHEN YOUR REQUEST IS WRONG

You don't know what you're asking.
Matthew 20:22 NIV

One day James and John came to Jesus asking for the best seats in His kingdom. It wasn't just a good view they were after, they wanted the top spot. Jesus said, "You don't know what you're asking!" Later, when the folk in a certain village refused to welcome Jesus, His disciples asked: "Lord, do you want us to call fire down and destroy them?" (Lk 9:54 NIV). Again Jesus rebuked them. Now, if Jesus' closest disciples could be so misguided in their requests, so can we. Fortunately God loves us too much to always say yes. Aren't you glad? Would you trust a God who'd do otherwise?

Perhaps the most famous wrong request is, "Lord, please change ___(?) _____." Anytime two of us have to get along together, one of us is likely to pray that way. But it's self-serving. A more genuine prayer would be, "Lord, I don't want to face my own shortcomings or work on the relationship, or have to mature, so I'm asking you to change ___(?)___." If that's your request, don't be surprised when God says no.

If you've been praying and getting nowhere—your request may be the problem! Maybe it's a cop-out on your part. Maybe it's destructive in ways you don't understand. Maybe it's self-serving, shortsighted and too small; God may have something better in mind. Whatever the reason, when your request is wrong, He turns it down. And as you become more mature, you'll look back on some of your old prayer requests and thank God that He loved you enough to say "no."

December 16

THE TIME TO RESPOND IS—NOW!

Lord, let me first go and bury my father.
Matthew 8:21 NKJV

$\mathcal{I}$n Bible times, Jewish people were expected to do the honorable thing by caring for their elderly parents until they died. So when a group of would-be disciples pledged their allegiance to Jesus, one man's family obligations immediately began to compete with God's call on his life. When He said, "Lord, let me first go and bury my father" Jesus replied, "Follow Me, and let the dead bury their own dead" (Mt 8:22 NKJV). Was Jesus being insensitive or uncaring? No, He knew the man's family situation and no doubt had a plan to take care of it.

Usually our dilemma isn't deciding whether or not to do God's will—but _when_ to do it! It's easy in theory to commit to following Christ and doing whatever He asks of you. But _timing_ is everything! When God tells you to do something, it's usually a call to respond immediately. Jesus said, "Those who want to be my disciples _must . . ._ follow me . . . and . . . the Father will honor them" (Jn 12:26 NLT). God-given opportunities generally come with a limited shelf life; they can be lost if you don't respond when He speaks. When Jesus called His disciples, the Bible says that "immediately" they left their nets and followed Him. Didn't they have responsibilities? Sure, but none more important than this! So, if God interrupts your schedule today and tells you to pray for somebody, or call and encourage them, or help them financially, stop whatever you're doing and get in sync. When He speaks, the time to respond is—now!

PRAYER BARRIERS (1)

You do not have because you do not ask.

James 4:2 NIV

*W*hen our prayers are not answered, we want to know what's wrong with God. It's easier to blame Him than look in the mirror and say, "Maybe I'm the problem." For the next few days let's look at some common prayer barriers.

Barrier #1—prayerlessness. Be honest; how often do you decide to pray about something, add it to your prayer list, say you'll pray about it, and *almost* do? You think about it from time to time, but you hardly pray about it at all. Why isn't God answering? Because you haven't prayed yet! Some of us live by the motto "Why pray when you can worry? Why pray when you can work yourself to death trying to get it? Why pray when you can go without?" Get this: when we work, *we* work; when we pray, *God* works!

Barrier #2—unconfessed sin. Listen: "Your sins have hidden his face from you so that he will not hear" (Is 59:2 NIV). God expects you to maintain your personal integrity, to show thoughtfulness and love toward others, and to put Him first in your life. Listen: "What does the Lord require of you? To act justly and to love mercy and to walk humbly with your God" (Mic 6:8 NIV). Those aren't suggestions—they're requirements! If you don't meet them, don't expect God to answer your prayers; you're wasting your breath unless it's a prayer of confession. First seek His forgiveness, then He'll listen when you pour out your heart to Him.

PRAYER BARRIERS (2)

First, go and be reconciled to your brother; then come.
Matthew 5:24 NKJV

*B*arrier #3—*unresolved conflict.* Listen to these Scriptures: "If you are offering your gift at the altar and there remember that your brother has something against you, leave your gift . . . go and be reconciled . . . then come and offer your gift" (Mt 5:23-24 NIV). Listen again: "Husbands . . . be considerate as you live with your wives, and treat them with respect . . . so that nothing will hinder your prayers" (1Pe 3:7 NIV). Most of us underestimate how committed God is to building and maintaining loving relationships. There's no point praying if you're engaged in constant conflict. John writes: "Anyone who claims to be in the light but hates his brother is still in the darkness" (1Jn 2:9 NIV). God will only listen when you come out into the light, deal with the thing that drove you and the other person apart, and attempt to mend the relationship.

Of course it isn't always possible to make amends. Paul writes, "If it is possible, as far as it depends on you, live at peace with everyone" (Ro 12:18 NIV). But sometimes the other person would rather keep the issue alive than accept your apology. If this happens, look deep into your heart. Have you sincerely tried to mend fences, or are you still holding something back? Do you really want restoration, or would you rather "place blame" and let things fester? If your attempts have been wholehearted and honest, God won't let a broken relationship stand in the way of your prayers. But if your attempts have been half-hearted and self-serving, try again—this time for real.

PRAYER BARRIERS (3)

You ask but you do not receive,
because you ask with wrong motives.
James 4:3 NIV

B̶arrier #4—selfishness. To take a closer look at our praying, is to come face to face with selfishness. There's such confusion over wants and needs, rights and favors, justice and grace, creature comforts and conformity to Christ. It's impossible to grow spiritually without trials. To pray, "give me an easy, happy, problem-free life," is a prayer God cannot answer because if He did, you'd be destroyed.

Barrier #5—uncaring attitudes. The Israelites wondered why God was not answering their prayers. Here's what He told them: "Stop oppressing those who work for you and treat them fairly . . . share your food with the hungry . . . Clothe those who are cold and don't hide from relatives who need your help. If you do these things . . . the Lord will answer" (Is 58:6-9 TLB). God's committed to developing a people who will reflect His character—and His character always expresses compassion for others. Have you seen the cartoon picturing hundreds of people lined up as far back as the eye can see? Each is thinking the same thing: *What can I do, I'm just one person?* As just one person you may not be able to change the world. You can, however, look for small ways to show you care. Perhaps your church works with a food pantry or prison ministry. Maybe your skills could make a small difference in the evils of unemployment, illiteracy, child abuse, alcoholism or suicide. As long as your ear is open to the hurting, God will keep His ear open to you.

USE YOUR FAITH!

To be carnally minded is death,
but to be spiritually minded is life.

Romans 8:6

$\mathcal{S}$ome of us are so intent on proving God's existence that we miss the whole concept of faith. God can't be proven or explained. In the final analysis, He's known only by faith—and faith defies understanding. If salvation was based on I.Q., most of us wouldn't stand a chance. But God designed it so that, "the most stupid cannot miss the way" (Is 35:8 TLB), and children can "enter the kingdom of heaven" (Mt. 18:3).

Our hardest struggles usually come from wanting explanations and proof. That's why Paul says, "To be carnally minded is death, but to be spiritually minded is life." God's looking for people who simply take Him at His Word. When He finds them, He uses them greatly and rewards them richly.

In the Old Testament He found a man named Abraham and called him His friend (2Ch 20:7). Was that because Abraham was perfect? Hardly; not once, but twice he lied saying his wife was his sister. And when God told him to leave his relatives behind, he decided to bring along his nephew and father-in-law! But one thing Abraham had going for him was, "God considered him righteous on account of his faith" (Ge 15:6 TLB). Faith gives you a credit line with God!

Hebrews, Chapter 11 chronicles a list of people who received blessings through faith. Just like money in the natural world, faith is the exchange that's used in God's kingdom. It defies reason, transcends feeling, and gets results every time. So, today start using your faith!

A STRANGE REASON TO REJOICE!

Don't be afraid . . . all that is secret will be made public.
Matthew 10:26 NLT

*H*ow would you like to have all your private thoughts and sins exposed? The Bible says it'll happen. Listen: "Each of us must . . . account . . . for what we do" (Ro 14:12 CEV). "Everything is . . . bare before . . . him to whom we must give account" (Heb 4:13 NIV). "He knows all hidden things . . . darkness is no obstacle to him" (Dan 2:22 TLB). "You must give an account on judgment day for every idle word you speak" (Mt 12:36 TLB). " He will bring . . . secrets to light and . . . reveal . . . private motives" (1 Co 4:5 NLT).

So when Jesus says, "All that is secret will be made public," it sounds more like cause for panic than reassurance, doesn't it? So why is it a reason for rejoicing? The answer's found in Romans 2:16. Listen: "God will judge men's secrets through Jesus Christ" (NIV). Did you get that? Highlight those last 3 words: "through Jesus Christ" then heave a big sigh of relief! Jesus is the filter through which God sees and judges you. Listen: "Those . . . in Christ are not judged guilty" (Ro 8:1 NCV). "Faith in him sets us in the clear" (Ro 3:25 TM). "Everyone who believes . . . is freed from . . . guilt and declared right with God" (Acts 13:39 NLT). "I will forgive their wrongdoings, and . . . never again remember their sins" (He 8:12 NLT). "Your . . . sinful self has died . . . your new life is . . . with Christ in God" (Col 3:3 NCV).

Today when God looks at you—He sees only the One who surrounds you! Your weaknesses still need to be dealt with, but they don't disqualify you. Because you're "in Christ" your victory is secure! You can rejoice!

IT WAS ALWAYS PART OF THE PLAN!

*This happened, so that what the prophets wrote
would come true.*
Matthew 26:56 CEV

$\mathcal{H}$ow can we be sure that Jesus' death wasn't just
the passing of another man? Well, for starters, it fulfilled 29
different prophecies. Discussing the odds of that happening,
mathematician Peter Stoner draws this analogy: "Cover the state
of Texas two feet deep in silver dollars, then on one place a
mark. Now, what's the probability that a person could, on their
first attempt, select the marked dollar?" *That's* the likelihood of
just 8 prophecies being fulfilled in one lifetime—and Jesus
fulfilled 29 in one day! Here are some of them:

(1) "He was wounded for our transgressions . . . bruised for
our iniquities; the chastisement for our peace was upon Him,
and by His stripes we are healed" (Is 53:5 NKJV). (2) "They
pierced My hands and . . . feet" (Ps 22:16 NKJV). (3) "They
divide My garments . . . and . . . cast lots" (Ps 22:18 NKJV). (4)
"In that day . . . that I will make the sun go down at noon, and
. . . darken the earth in . . . daylight" (Amos 8:9 NKJV).

Jesus wasn't the victim of circumstances—He was the
arranger of them! He orchestrated every event, including Judas'
betrayal, the high priest's hypocrisy and Peter's denial. Why?
"So that what the prophets wrote would come true." Wow! You
can trust what He says!

And He can change your situation. His Word says He's
"able to do immeasurably more than we ask or imagine" (Eph
3:20 NIV). Did you get that? "Immeasurably more." What
seems impossible to us, is all in a day's work for Him. So come
to Him today!

SPEND MORE TIME WITH GOD!

They that wait upon the Lord shall renew their strength.
Isaiah 40:31

*M*ost folks today seem to have a cell phone growing out of their ear. They've learned to drive in the fast lane, listen to music, talk on the telephone and do business— all at the same time. Nobody wants to wait! Yet, when it comes to our spiritual lives, waiting quietly in God's presence brings rewards that nothing else will. Here are a few of them:

Strength. Listen: "Those who [spend time with] God get fresh strength. They . . . soar like eagles, they run and don't get tired; they walk and don't lag behind" (Is 40:31 TM). Do you feel drained today? "Wait on the Lord . . . and He shall strengthen your heart" (Ps 27: 14 NKJV).

Vindication. Are you upset because you've been misunderstood? Or because your critics seem to be prospering? Listen: "Do not fret . . . evildoers shall be cut off; But those who wait on the Lord . . . shall inherit the earth" (Ps 37:8-9 NKJV). Cheer up, the last chapter hasn't been written. When it is, we win!

Deliverance. Do you feel trapped by circumstances? Listen: "I waited for God . . . He lifted me out of the ditch" (Ps 40:1-2 TM). Relax. Start trusting God more. He'll bring you through!

Growth. Do you long to become more mature? Listen: "Let [patience] do its work" (Jas1:4 AMP). Patience really works! It eliminates *worry* because God's bigger than your problem. It eliminates *works* because your job is to simply obey and leave the rest in God's hands. It eliminates *wanting* because your wants become less important than His will. So start spending more time with God!

THE CHRISTMAS STAR

When they saw the star, they rejoiced.
Matthew 2:10 NKJV

*E*ver wonder why educated men would drop every-thing to follow a star for hundreds of miles? You're not alone: there's been a lot of speculation about the star. Think what it represents:

(1) Hope. Listen: "God loved us, and through His grace He gave us . . . hope . . . that continues forever" (2Th 2:16 NCV). Hope for all eternity, what a gift! This star didn't merely lead the wise men to the fulfillment of their expectations, it points each of us to the only hope of salvation—Jesus!

(2) Joy. The Bible says, "When they saw the star, they rejoiced with . . . great joy." Why? Because Jesus is the source of transcendent joy; the kind that lifts us above our circum-stances and makes others think, "Whatever you've got, I need!"

(3) Guidance. The star united shepherds and philosophers, rich and poor, intellectual and illiterate—around Jesus—heaven's answer to earth's dilemma. Notice, after the wise men worshipped Him and laid their treasures at His feet, the Bible says, "They departed into their own country another way" (Mt 2:12). Understand this: it's impossible to meet Jesus and go home the same way! "If any man be in Christ, he is a new creature; old things are passed away; behold, all things are become new" (2Co 5:17). So when somebody asks you, "What did you get for Christmas?" just smile and say: (a) hope that gets brighter each day; (b) joy that's greater than any threat or circumstance; (c) guidance for every step of the way.

ARE YOU LOOKING?

Unto them that look for Him shall He appear.
Hebrews 9:28

*I*t's hard to imagine humbler circumstances than those surrounding the birth of Jesus. Max Lucado paints this picture: "The stable stinks, the ground is hard, the hay scarce. Cobwebs cling to the ceiling and a mouse scurries across the floor. Mary looks into the face of her son. Her Lord. His Majesty. At this point the human being who best understands who God is and what He's doing, is a teenage girl in a smelly stable. She remembers the angel's words, 'His Kingdom will never end.' Majesty in the midst of the mundane. Holiness in the filth of manure and sweat. Divinity entering the world on the floor of a stable.

"This baby had once overlooked the universe. His robes of eternity were exchanged for the rags keeping Him warm. His golden throne room abandoned in favor of a dirty sheep pen. Worshipping angels replaced with shepherds. Meanwhile the city hums, unaware that God has visited their planet. The innkeeper would never believe he'd just sent God into the cold. And people would scoff at anyone who told them the Messiah lay in the arms of a teenager on the outskirts of their village. They were all too busy to consider the possibility.

"But those who missed His Majesty's arrival that night missed it not because of evil acts or malice. *No, they missed it because they weren't looking for Him!*" Little has changed in 2,000 years, has it? The Bible says, "Unto them that look for him shall he appear the second time without sin unto salvation." This Christmas—look for Him!

IT'S AN "INSIDE JOB!"

Christ in you, the hope of glory.
Colossians 1:27 NIV

𝒯he Virgin birth isn't just part of the Christmas story. *It illustrates how close God wants to get to us!* In a sense, God's asking you the same question He asked Mary, "Are you willing to let me in?"

Notice, Jesus told the disciples, "I am in you" (Jn 14:20 NCV). Paul prayed, "That Christ may dwell in your hearts"(Eph. 3:17 NIV). John said, "Those who obey . . . live in him, and he in them" (1Jn 3:24 NIV). Again Paul wrote, "Christ in you, the hope of glory." Then he added, "It is no longer I who live, but Christ lives in me" (Gal 2:20 NKJV). Jesus promised, "If any one . . . opens the door, I will come in" (Rev. 3:20 NIV). Are you getting the idea? All He asks is an invitation and an open heart.

In the Old Testament God was *with* Adam and Eve in the Garden. He was *with* Abraham and called him His friend. But modern-day Mary, He's *in* you. And He'll keep growing in you until He comes out in what you say, how you live and the decisions you make.

Struggling with bitterness? Worry? Unforgiveness? Bad habits? Not Jesus! And since *He's* living in you, you have full access to His awesome power! That's why Paul talks about, "striving according to *His* power, which mightily works within me" (Col 1:29 NASB). Today God's looking for trust, not talent. When the Angel appeared to Mary she said, "May it be done [in me] . . . according to *your* word" (Lk 1:38 NASB). Make that your prayer this Christmas!

SIX TYPES OF PRAYER (1)

Pray . . . with all [manner of] prayer.
Ephesians 6:18 AMP

$\mathcal{L}$et's examine 6 different types of prayer:

(1) The prayer of agreement! Listen: "If two of you . . . agree about anything you ask for, it will be done for you by my Father" (Mt 18:19 NIV). When you're up against something too big to handle alone, find a prayer partner and come into agreement with them. This isn't for people who generally live in strife then decide to agree because they're desperate. God honors the prayers of those who pay the price to live together in harmony.

(2) The prayer of petition! Be confident in asking God to meet your needs. Jesus said, "What things soever ye desire, when ye pray, believe that ye receive them, and ye shall have them" (Mk 11:24). If we'd stop trying to impress God we'd be a lot better off. Length, loudness or eloquence isn't the issue; it's the sincerity of our heart, our confidence before God, and the knowledge that it's according to His will—that gets results!

(3) The prayer of thanksgiving! When our petitions outweigh our praises it says something about our character. Self-centered people ask but rarely appreciate. God won't release us into the fullness of all He's planned for us until we become thankful for what we've *already* received. Petition avails much, praise avails much more! Listen: "In everything, by prayer and petition, with thanksgiving, present your requests to God" (Php 4:6 NIV). Powerful living comes through thanksgiving. We can "pray without ceasing" by being thankful all day long, praising God for His favor, mercy, loving kindness, grace, longsuffering and goodness.

SIX TYPES OF PRAYER (2)

Long before daylight, he got up and . . . prayed.
Mark 1:35 AMP

*L*et's continue looking at the 6 different types of prayer.

(4) The prayer of intercession. Listen: "I looked for a man . . . who would . . . stand before me in the gap on behalf of the land" (Ez 22:30 NIV). To intercede means: "to stand in the gap" for someone else. If there's a breach in that person's relationship with God due to a particular sin, you have the privilege of placing yourself in that breach and praying for them. "The gap" is the distance between what is—and what can be.

(5) The prayer of commitment. Listen: "Casting the whole of your care [all your anxieties, all your worries, all your concerns, once and for all] on Him" (1Pe 5:7 AMP). As long as you keep trying to control events your stress levels will just keep mounting. But when you learn to hand things over to God, you'll wonder why you spent even a single day worrying.

(6) The prayer of consecration. On the Damascus Road, Paul prayed: "Lord, what wilt thou have me to do?" (Acts 9:6). That's like signing your name to a blank check. It's saying, "Here I am, do with me as you please. I hope I like what You choose, but even if I don't I'll do it anyway; Your will be done, not mine." Now you're deciding to voluntarily follow God, rather than struggling to get Him to follow you. As a result, God will do the work that needs to be done *in* us, so that He can do the work that He desires to do *through* us.

WHERE'S YOUR CONFIDENCE?

Blessed is the man who trusts in the Lord,
whose confidence is in him.
Jeremiah 17:7 NIV

*T*o succeed at whatever God wants you to do, you must learn to be confident—not self-confident, but confident in Christ. Listen to Paul: "I am self-sufficient in Christ's sufficiency" (Php 4:13 AMP). Jesus said, "Without me, you can do nothing" (Jn 15:5). It seems to take forever to learn this truth. Most of our struggling and frustration comes from misplaced confidence. Paul says, "put no confidence in the flesh" (Php 3:3 NIV). Now, he's not saying we aren't supposed to trust anyone. No, he's saying if we give *others* or *ourselves* the trust that belongs to God alone, we won't succeed. He won't let us!

To succeed at anything we must have confidence, but first and foremost it must be confidence in God. We must believe that He wants us to succeed. We may fail on our way to success, but if we trust God He'll take our mistakes and cause them to work for our good and His glory (Ro 8:28).

Sometimes our confidence is shaken when trials come, especially if they're lengthy. When this happens we must learn to do what David did: "David encouraged and strengthened himself in the Lord" (1Sa 30:6 AMP). When David had no one else to believe in him, he believed in himself. He also believed in God's ability through him. One lady writes: "The Lord told me that if I didn't believe in myself, I really didn't believe in Him. He said, 'I am *in* you, but I can only do *through* you, what you believe Me for.'"

DISCOURAGED? GO TO CHURCH!

Not forsaking the assembling of ourselves together,
as the manner of some is.
Hebrews 10:25

*W*hy do we stay away from church when we get discouraged? (a) We're embarrassed because our faith isn't working as well as we think it should. (b) We're ashamed because we're still struggling with certain problems. (c) We're depressed because it looks like everyone else is succeeding but us.

Don't let discouragement keep you away from your spiritual family! You need their love and support, to hear them say, "We made it, and by God's grace you can too!" Listen: "Not forsaking the assembling of ourselves together, as the manner of some is." This word "forsaking" is taken from three Greek words which could be translated "out," "down," and "behind." They describe someone who feels left out, spiritually and emotionally down, and far behind everyone else. The moment you feel like that Satan whispers, "Just stay home from church today, you don't need to go down there with all those good people."

Understand this: if Satan can isolate you from other believers at the very time when you need them most, he can rob you of God's blessing! Sure you can stay home, read your Bible, turn on Christian radio and television, but surrounded by your spiritual family you'll get answers, experience joy, and receive encouragement you can't find anywhere else. Church is the *last* place the devil wants you to go when you're feeling low. He knows if you go, you'll be touched by the presence of the Lord and be able to crawl out of the hole he's put you in.

QUESTIONS FOR THE NEW YEAR!

God said . . . "Be fruitful and multiply."
Genesis 1:28

$\mathcal{I}$t's miserable trying to play a part for which you're ill suited. It's like walking in shoes that don't fit. So this coming year ask yourself: What am I good at? What do I enjoy doing most? What accomplishments make me feel best? List 5 moments in your life when you were acutely aware of this sensation. Does this reveal anything about your purpose? If money was not a consideration what would you want to do to fill your days? How does this compare with where you are now? What one small step can you take right now—one phone call made, one letter written, one e-mail sent—to move you toward your true calling? What have you learned about your purpose through failures? Are some areas clearly not a part of your calling at this point? Who do you admire for the way they've applied their talents? How are you like them? What can you learn from them? How would you describe your vision for your life this year? Five years from now? Ten? Who are the people in your life who really "get" who you are? Have you asked them what they think your purpose might be? Have they given indications of how they think you should use your talents? If you could write your own obituary, what would you want it to say? What would you like to be remembered for?

While we never *arrive* at our final destination in this life, we can get on the right path, with the right tools, making the right choices along our way!

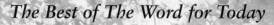
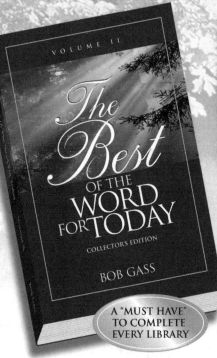